# *The*
# COACHING
# ORGANIZATION

# JAMES M. HUNT
*Babson College*

# JOSEPH R. WEINTRAUB
*Babson College*

# *The*
# COACHING
# ORGANIZATION

## *A Strategy for Developing Leaders*

**SAGE** Publications
Thousand Oaks ▪ London ▪ New Delhi

*For information:*

Sage Publications, Inc.
2455 Teller Road
Thousand Oaks, California 91320
E-mail: order@sagepub.com

Sage Publications Ltd.
1 Oliver's Yard
55 City Road
London EC1Y 1SP
United Kingdom

Sage Publications India Pvt. Ltd.
B-42, Panchsheel Enclave
Post Box 4109
New Delhi 110 017  India

Printed in the United States of America.

*Library of Congress Cataloging-in-Publication Data*

Hunt, James  M. (James Michael)
The coaching organization : a strategy for developing
leaders / James M. Hunt, Joseph R. Weintraub.
    p. cm.
Includes bibliographical references and index.
ISBN 1-4129-0575-3 (cloth) — ISBN 1-4129-0576-1 (pbk.)
    1. Employees—Coaching of. 2. Executive coaching. 3. Organizational
learning. 4. Career development. I. Weintraub, Joseph R. II. Title.
HF5549.5.C53H86 2007
658.3′124—dc22                                                2006002943

This book is printed on acid-free paper.

06   07   08   09   10   10   9   8   7   6   5   4   3   2   1

| | |
|---|---|
| *Acquiring Editor:* | Al Bruckner |
| *Editorial Assistant:* | MaryAnn Vail |
| *Project Editor:* | Astrid Virding |
| *Copyeditor:* | Carla Freeman |
| *Typesetter:* | C&M Digitals (P) Ltd. |
| *Indexer:* | Kathy Paparchontis |
| *Cover Designer:* | Janet Foulger |

# Contents

Preface ........................................................................... xi

Acknowledgments .......................................................... xv

1. **The Coaching Organization?** ..................................... 1
   Should Leaders Develop an Internal Coaching
      Capability in Their Organizations? ......................... 3
   An Organizational-Level View of Coaching ............... 6
      Case 1.1 Learning From an Executive
         Coaching Intervention ..................................... 10
   The Coaching Organization ...................................... 11
      Box 1.1 *The Zone of Execution* ............................. 11
   An Organizational Coaching Capability ..................... 15
      Coaching Managers ............................................. 16
      External Expert or Executive Coaches ................... 17
      Internal Expert Coaches ...................................... 20
      Peer Coaching ................................................... 21
   A Coaching Capability "Infrastructure" ..................... 22
      Organizational Assessment 1.1 The
         Coaching Value Proposition ............................. 23
      Box 1.2 *The Coaching Value Chain in*
         *Your Organization—Sample* ............................ 24

2. **An Overview of Developmental Coaching** ................... 27
   The Goals of Developmental Coaching ....................... 28
      Case 2.1 The "Anti-Coach" .................................. 30
      Case 2.2 Everything Is Changing ........................... 31
      Case 2.3 One Too Many Résumés ........................... 32
   Developmental Coaching and Other Forms of
      Coaching and Counseling .................................... 33
   Formal and Informal Coaching ................................. 35
   The Core Elements of Developmental Coaching ........... 37

Box 2.1 *Core Elements of Developmental Coaching*    38
A Goal-Directed, Willing, Effective Coachee    39
A Developmental Coach    39
Box 2.2 *The Dreyfus Model of Skill Acquisition*    40
A Coaching-Friendly Context    42
A Learning Opportunity    43
A Coaching Relationship    44
The Coaching Dialogue    44
Feedback    45
An Opportunity to Keep Learning    46
Summary    47

3.   **The Coaching Organization Assessment**    49
Organizational Assessment 3.1 The Coaching
Organization Assessment    51
Box 3.1 *The Coaching Organization Assessment*
*Exercise*    51
The Cultural Context    57
There Is an Adequate Level of Trust    57
Employees Are Viewed as Ends Rather Than
as Means to an End    58
Relationships Are Valued    59
Learning Is Valued    59
Those Facing Challenges Should Seek Out Guidance    60
Organization-Specific Knowledge Is Valued    61
Management Is Valued    62
Performance and Performance Management
Are Valued    62
Diversity Is Valued    63
Innovation Is Valued    64
Total Quality Management and Continuous
Improvement Are Valued    64
The Business Context    64
The Business Strategy Requires Learning    65
The Human Resource Management Context    67
Talent Is Critical to the Organization's Success    67
Human Resource Management Practices    68
Supporting Strategic Human Resource Development
Practices    71
Organizational Experiences With Coaching    73
The Coaching-Friendly Organization    77

Overview of Biotech                                                 78
*Box 3.2 The Coaching Organization
   Assessment at BioTech*                                           80
A Coaching Initiative At BioTech?                                   81

4.   **A Strategic Approach to Coaching**                          85
     The Need for a Coaching Strategy                               86
         *Box 4.1 Coaching Initiative Outcomes That Promote a
            Sustainable Organizational Capability*                  88
     Outcomes That Support a Growing Coaching Capability            88
         Case 4.1 Was That Really Coaching?                         89
         Case 4.2 I Couldn't Believe What I Was
            Able to Accomplish!                                     90
     A Comprehensive Assessment of a Coaching Initiative            95
         *Box 4.2 Alternative Coaching Initiative Outcomes*         95

5.   **Driving Strategic Transformation Through
     Executive Coaching at Whirlpool**                             99
     Coaching and Leadership Development Challenges                 101
     Leading the Whirlpool Enterprise: The Leadership Model         102
         *Box 5.1 The Whirlpool Leadership Model*                   103
         *Box 5.2 LWE External Coaching Support
            Program Flow*                                           107
     The Context for Coaching at Whirlpool                          107
     The Management of Coaching in LWE                              108
     Coaching Practices in LWE                                      110
     The Experience of Coaching in LWE                              111
     Lessons Learned at Whirlpool                                   116

6.   **Building and Leading a Coaching Capacity**                  119
     The Need for Leadership                                        120
     The Organizational Evolution of a Coaching Capability          120
     Why on Faith Alone?                                            126
         *Box 6.1 Athletic Coaching Versus Psychotherapy*           128
     The Rise and Role of the Coaching Practice Manager             130
         *Box 6.2 The Tasks of the Coaching Practice Manager*       130
         Case 6.1 The Management of Executive
            Coaching at Omgeo                                       132
     Managing the Coaching Capability                               137
         Before Coaching                                            137
         Educating and Aligning Key Stakeholders                    138
         Qualifying Coaches                                         139

Orienting Coaches     141
Assessing the Need for Expert Coaches in
    Individual Cases     141
Matching Coaches and Coachees     142
Supporting Ongoing Coaching     143
Coordinating Coaching and Related Employee
    or Leadership Development Activities     143
Measuring Results     144
Closing Thoughts on the Management of the
    Coaching Capability     144

7.   **The Internal Coaching Capability**     **145**
What We Mean by "Expert" Internal Coaches     146
Why Expert Internal Coaching?     147
Case 7.1 Sam the Coach     150
Case 7.2 The Management Effectiveness
    Business Partner     151
Critical Issues in Building an Effective Internal
    Coaching Capability     154
The Purpose of the Internal Coaching Program     154
Selection of Internal Coaches     156
Box 7.1 *International Coach Federation Competencies*     158
Box 7.2 *NASA Competencies for Internal Coaches*     159
Guidelines for an Internal Coaching Practice     160
The Ongoing Development of Internal Coaches     161
The Results: Do Well-Run Internal Coaching
    Programs Yield Different Outcomes?     163

8.   **The ELP Internal Coaching Program at Wachovia Corporation**     **165**
The Wachovia Executive Leadership Program     166
The Decision to Build an Internal Coaching Capability     167
Program Design Elements     168
Box 8.1 *The Wachovia Executive Leadership Model*     168
The Internal Coaches     170
Training and Support for the Internal Coaching Cadre     172
Box 8.2 *ELP Coach Development Process*     172
Box 8.3 *Phases of the 360-Degree Debrief*
    *Coaching at Wachovia*     174
Ongoing Support and Development of ELP Coaches     174
Comments on Being an Internal Coach From HR     175
Evaluation of the Program     176

9.  Building a Coaching Manager Capability                    179
        Can Managers Coach Developmentally?                   180
        The Major Differences                                 181
            The Coaching Contract                             181
            The Coaching-Friendly Context                     182
            Assessment                                        182
            The Ongoing Coaching Process                      183
            Accountability for Results                        184
            Expert Coaching Versus the Coaching
                Manager: An Assessment                        184
        The Competencies of the Coaching Manager              185
            Self-Awareness                                    185
            Promotes Learning                                 185
            Communications                                    185
            Accessibility                                     185
            Listening                                         186
            Creates a Trusting Environment                    186
            The Perfect Manager?                              186
        The Organizational Context and the Management
            of Role Conflicts                                 186
        Organizational Readiness                              188

10. The Coaching Manager in Nursing                           189
        Children's Hospital Boston
            and the Department of Nursing                     189
        A More Realistic View of Nursing Leadership           190
        Building Leadership Through Coaching: The
            Coaching Initiative                               192
            *Box 10.1 Coaching-Skills-Building Curriculum*    193
        Nurses' Evaluation of the Coaching-Skills-Training
            Components                                        194
        Customizing the Coaching-Skills Training              195
            Hiring the Right People                           195
            Defining Success                                  196
            Establishing a Coaching-Friendly Context          196
            Working With a Coachable Coachee                  197
            Maintaining a Coaching Mind-Set                   197
            Stopping the Action and Starting
                a Coaching Dialogue                           197
            Observing Effectively and Providing Balanced
                Feedback                                      199

|  | Defining Next Steps and Following Up | 199 |
|  | Follow-Up, Post–Skills Training | 199 |
|  | Some Additional Lessons | 200 |
|  | Developmental Coaching Must Leverage the Work | 201 |
|  | Developmental Coaching Shouldn't Create More Work | 201 |
|  | Developmental Coaching Ultimately Involves a New Way of Relating to Old Problems | 201 |
|  | Developmental Coaching Can Represent a Means of Reaching Groups of Previously Ignored but Talented Individuals | 202 |
|  | Developmental Coaching Skills Can Be Useful in Dealing With a Variety of Relationship Challenges | 202 |
|  | Conclusion | 203 |

**11. Peer Coaching at Citizen's Financial Group (CFG)** — 205

The Advanced Leadership Development Program at Citizens — 206
The Value Proposition for a Successful Peer Feedback System — 210
*Box 11.1 Peer Coaching at Millennium Pharmaceuticals* — 210
The Formula for a Successful Peer Coaching Program — 212
Peer Coaching as a Follow-Up Strategy to Executive Education — 213
*Box 11.2 Phases of Peer Coaching in Executive Education Programs* — 214
Feedback Is Not Always Easy, Even From a Peer — 214

Concluding Remarks: The Frontiers of the Coaching Organization — 215

References — 217

Appendix A: The Competencies of the Expert Executive Coach — 223

Appendix B: The Coaching Manager Self-Assessment — 233

Index — 239

About the Authors — 247

About the Contributors — 249

# Preface

In our previous book, *The Coaching Manager: Developing Top Talent in Business,* we explored developmental coaching, how thoughtful managers can and do help their direct reports learn on the job. We have been gratified by the interest shown in our effort to put forth real-world "best practices." Some managers really do coach their people! We found them and tried to tell their story. However, it was a story of individuals, not of organizations.

Over the past decade, we have noted two major trends under the rubric of "coaching" within organizations. First, the business press would suggest that it is a fad: "Everyone has to have a coach." Fads don't do well in business over the long haul.

Second, we have noted a growing number of serious organizations and leaders within some organizations making a concerted effort to use various forms of coaching in a strategic way. These organizations are doing their best to really create value from their efforts, value for the individuals involved and value for their organizations. As with the perhaps not-so-rare "coaching manager," we felt that it was critically important to tell the story of "coaching organizations." If the individuals who are trying to use coaching in a systematic and strategic fashion don't carry the day, then trend Number 1, coaching as a fad, will win out.

We believe in developmental coaching, but we also believe that organizational leaders and their financial advisors are more likely to share that belief if and only if it helps their organizations achieve success. We wanted to find out if this does happen and, if so, how. We close this book with a comment much like the one we make now: There is not enough research on coaching in organizational contexts to give us the answer we need. So we had to start somewhere, with organizations and organizational leaders who were trying to use coaching to help their organizations. Can we prove that they have been successful in this effort? No, not yet. We challenge scholars and practitioners who are serious about linking people and strategy to help us move ahead on that front. For now, we present a number of best-practice cases and what we have learned from them.

*Most importantly, this is a book for human resource professionals, organizational effectiveness professionals, leadership development practitioners, and organizational leaders who are interested in building an organizational coaching capability, a systematic approach to using developmental coaching to help achieve business results.* We have gone to the field and talked with a great many people who are involved in the effort to create coaching organizations and asked for their experiences and their ideas. We present both here, to the best of our abilities, and with the help of a number of case coauthors. It is our hope that others who are charged with leadership development in their firms will find ideas here that will help them organize an approach to coaching, rather than dealing with coaching-related issues on an ad hoc or reactive basis.

Just to give two examples of the latter,

- A human resource (HR) professional calls because he has been tasked by the CEO to "bring in a coach" to help a derailing executive. The HR person has no idea what the key issues are but does his best to find a qualified coach. Unfortunately, he is about to unleash a chain of events that may result in his firm becoming "coaching-unfriendly." And he may expose his firm to a variety of risks in the process.

- A training and development professional wants to provide coaching-skills training for his supervisors. He brings in an off-the-shelf coaching-skills-training program, albeit a well-constructed one. Supervisors are forced to go to the program. The idea of coaching makes sense to them. But when they return to work, they don't have a clue regarding how to apply what they have learned. Their own bosses, by the way, think that the whole idea is silly.

The reactive approach to coaching is event oriented and typically disconnected from where the business is going. As such, it is likely to fail. Failure brings with it some significant consequences, not the least of which is that organizational members are unlikely to spend much more time thinking about how they can best help their people grow. This has some very serious consequences for businesses, health care institutions, and not-for-profits that exist in a rapidly changing environment. In the absence of on-the-job learning, most organizations cannot be expected to mount an effective response to the challenges they face. They will be left with the "sink-or-swim" approach to employee development, an approach largely rejected now by industrial leaders (thank-you, Jack Welch). It just does not work.

Coaching (all varieties of developmental coaching), offers organizations a real opportunity to provide cost-effective learning experiences for individuals that build directly on their work. This statement reflects our bias, but we really do believe that the strategic use of developmental coaching leads to a win-win situation. It is good for employees and good for their firms. However, developmental coaching conversations have to be properly conducted to be effective. Coaching initiatives or interventions at the organizational level likewise need to be properly constructed. We hope this book will help. Here is our plan.

Chapters 1 through 4 represent a deep dive into the background of a strategic use of developmental coaching in an organizational context. We lay out the challenge and the basic options in Chapter 1 by exploring the rationale for an organizational view of coaching, and we offer a quick overview of the options for creating a coaching organization. These options, which will structure our presentation in the second half of the book, including engaging managers in a developmental coaching culture for their direct reports, the use of expert coaching provided either by external consultants or internal coaches employed by their organizations, and an exciting "naturalistic" development in the organizational coaching world, peer coaching. The use of each of these has pros and cons, requires decision making, and must be managed so as to grow the coaching capability. Each coaching activity should leave the organization, not just the individuals involved, in better shape for the next coaching engagement.

Chapter 2 describes developmental coaching in some detail. This will be a review for the well informed. For those who don't have a good understanding of developmental coaching, as opposed to other forms of coaching, this is a "must read."

Chapter 3 presents an organizational assessment that the reader can use to help consider his or her organization's readiness for a coaching initiative and what kind of coaching initiative would make the most sense under their unique circumstances. Coaching initiatives have to link to an organization's business needs or strategy and culture. Every coaching initiative should be custom tailored.

In Chapter 4, we summarize a strategic view of coaching and the kinds of changes one might hope to see from the exercise of a strategic perspective. Ultimately, these developments all move toward greater use of developmental coaching tools by managers and the creation of a more learning-oriented organizational culture.

This brings us to Chapter 5 and the Whirlpool Corporation story. We have been thoroughly impressed by Whirlpool's deployment of most of the tools and ideas we discuss in this book. Their approach to coaching is strategic and comprehensive. It has senior management support and involvement. It is seen as essential to their business success. We present only one example of how they have used coaching to support their business needs. Coaching is not a fad at Whirlpool.

In Chapter 6, we discuss the management of coaching. If an organization is to build a coaching capability, someone has to be responsible for it. It may not be a full-time job, but some ONE has to own it (something we learned in MBA school). We describe in some depth what ownership of that task means and offers for the World Bank, and give an in-depth example from Omgeo LLC of Summer Turner, who runs their coaching initiative.

In Chapter 7, we begin a more in-depth exploration of various options for coaching initiatives. Expert coaching provided by internal coaches is a growing and thoughtful trend. We explore the role and qualifications of the internal coach, as well as some of the challenges associated with the role. In Chapter 8, we present an example of a well-constructed internal coaching program at Wachovia Corporation. Again, we note that there is careful attention given to the management of coaching, linking it with business strategy, and ongoing attention given to the quality of its outputs.

Similarly, in Chapter 9, we describe the challenges of creating a cadre of "coaching managers"; and in Chapter 10, we present a description of a major coaching initiative at Children's Hospital Boston. Here, we see the role of cultural and organizational readiness. Similarly, in Chapter 11, we describe peer coaching as deployed at Citizens Financial Group. In both cases, we see the power of senior-management support.

Throughout, we invite you to put on your own "leadership hat" and consider what you and your colleagues can do to make the best use of coaching in your organizations. Move through the book and make notes. Look for ideas that might work in your context. This field is still in its infancy, so we encourage you to join us in the process of learning how we can make the most out of helping those we work with learn from experience.

# Acknowledgments

We would like to start by thanking Al Bruckner and MaryAnn Vail from Sage Publishing for their patience with us. This has been a long process, in large measure because we hoped to offer a number of real-life examples. We hope that your patience has been rewarded!

This book represents a continued exploration of the role that developmental coaching plays in organizations. As such, we cannot move forward without thanking those who made it possible for us to start this journey: Babson College and the Babson College Alumni Association. Babson is an amazing and wonderful community. Every year, 800 or so of our alumni and advanced-MBA students join us to provide a developmental coaching experience for our undergraduates through the Coaching for Leadership and Teamwork Program (http://www.Babson.edu/Coach). We cannot thank everyone associated with the coaching program enough for allowing us to participate in this community. In particular, since our last book, the Alumni Association has continued to assert positive leadership in guiding the Babson College coaching program and encouraging us to expand our reach beyond the borders of the campus. We would like to particularly thank in that regard Amy Weil, Dan Riley, Patrick McGonagle, Steve Gaklis, Lisa Rose, and Doug Adams. We also want to thank Kristen Shulman, manager of the coaching program, for her support and for being such a great colleague. Bob Bonnevie, also a faculty member of the Coaching for Leadership and Teamwork Program, also deserves our thanks for his support and friendship.

We would like to formally thank Charles C. Barton for his support of our ongoing efforts through the generous grant of two term chairs. We receive tremendous support at Babson from Dean Patti Greene and the Undergraduate Program Academic Services Group. Patti has stepped up to help us in numerous ways, and her support and validation for this effort have been invaluable. We would also like to thank everyone on her team, including Rob Major, Richard Mandel, and their colleagues.

Our work has expanded far beyond the borders of the campus and has involved us in some exciting relationships with individuals, many of who are named in this book. We want to thank in particular Lew Stern, Judy Otto, Susan Ennis, Bill Hodgetts, Bob Goodman, and Dick Mansfield from The Executive Coaching Forum, from whom we have learned so much about executive coaching and whose dedication to the creation of appropriate standards of practice has been so important to the field. Catherine Fitzgerald, one of the top executive coaches in the United States, has been an inspiration throughout, and we thank her for her behind-the-scenes support. Derek Steinbrenner, from Cambria Consulting, has been a good friend and support throughout.

We also wish to offer a special thanks to those individuals who gave of their time and energy to contribute to the book through opening their doors and providing us case study material and, in some instances, serving as coauthors to their cases. In that regard, we would like thank Patty Hickey, Susan Shaw, Herminia Shermont, and Eilene Sporing from Children's Hospital Boston; Summer Turner from Omgeo LLC; Steve Leichtman; Nina Mickelson from the World Bank; Colleen Gentry from Wachovia Corporation; Christine Williams from NASA; Joe Frodsham from Tenet Healthcare; Nancy Snyder from Whirlpool; Fabio Sala from Millennium Pharmaceuticals; Paul Carroll from Citizens Financial Group; and Ellen Kumata from Cambria Consulting, for their active participation in this effort to put forth a robust view of what coaching could be.

Last, but certainly not least, we would like to thank our families, Chris and Molly Hunt, and Carol, Sarah, and Sylvia Weintraub, for their help and love. Chris read every word of this book, numerous times! We could not have done this without you!

# 1

# The Coaching Organization?

*One of the more obvious lessons of history is that there is no such thing as a self-made man or a self-made woman. We are, all of us, the result of many people who have influenced us through the years, those who guided and encouraged us—a parent, a teacher—those who reprimanded, or scolded, or corrected, or gave the advice that set us on a different course.*

—McCullough (2004, p. 1)

Senior managers and human resource/organizational effectiveness professionals say something like the following in nearly every organization we visit:

• The career development of our people is just not being addressed by their managers or by anyone else. We have to do something.

• Our people complain that they just don't get enough feedback, and they don't know where they stand. We tell our managers to coach their direct reports, but it just doesn't happen.

• We're going to have a lot of people retiring over the next few years, and I just don't know how we're going to replace them. We've got good people in the pipeline, but they don't have the *right* knowledge, and what they need to learn can't be taught in the classroom.

- We're a very flat organization now, and that's not going to change. Our people are confused about advancement. They don't know what "getting ahead" means anymore, and no one is talking about it.

- We've used external coaches, and some of them have been great, but we're not sure where to go from here. The CEO is saying, "I want our managers to coach, we're not going to keep paying for high-priced executive coaches at this level much longer." But we don't know how to make that happen. Do they have time? We've tried training them, and we really felt that the results were mixed.

- I have to sleep at night, and the only way that's going to happen is if I know that we've got the right people on the night shift making sure that the work is getting done—leading, not waiting for me to tell them what to do. We don't have enough of these people now, and we're just going to need more.

These comments are representative of the worries of leaders who are trying to describe a problem that to them seems intangible, even mysterious. How do we pay attention to the developmental needs of a large number of employees, at all levels? Everyone knows that managers should coach, but for the most part, they don't. Executive coaching, coaching by external experts, is now widely accepted, but for a variety of reasons, it isn't a comprehensive solution for most organizations. Some organizations are now using internal expert coaches, with good results. People remain confused about the different kinds of coaching. They are confused about who should be coaching and to what ends. They aren't always sure what the word *coaching* means. Perhaps most importantly, they aren't always sure how all this relates to their business or organizational goals. For over a decade, we have worked with individual managers and organizations on this problem in a wide variety of contexts.

Early on in this effort, it was the more progressive or cutting-edge business firms, not-for-profits, and hospitals that raised such questions. Much has changed during the past decade, however. Despite a very soft economy, talent has become more important than ever. We are truly in a *knowledge economy*, which means that people, and their ability to think, spot problems and opportunities, and lead others toward change, are more important than ever. Even during the recent economic downturn, the concept of human capital, the view of people as an asset rather than a cost, has continued to take hold in the business world. In health care, for example, the situation is even more pressing. Health care has always been in the knowledge business and is facing an intensifying labor shortage in most professional disciplines.

Demographic trends exacerbate these challenges in all segments of society. In the coming years, the carriers of a great deal of the knowledge that made developed economies so powerful will retire. This knowledge has to be transferred, somehow, to the next generation. Much of this knowledge, particularly the knowledge required of leaders, innovators, and those with special expertise, is not written down.

Coaching, that is, providing relationship-based, on-the-job learning, is an effective means of developing a more capable workforce at all levels and creating a very competitive organizational culture, one that can successfully compete for human capital and achieve business results. Coaching is also a very important means by which knowledge can be transferred from one generation of employees to the next. One would imagine, then, that coaching and related forms of relationship-based learning will become a business imperative in the coming years. Experience to date, however, suggests that addressing this imperative will be more difficult than one might imagine. Fundamental assumptions about the role of coaching, feedback, and teaching in the modern organization need to be reexamined.

## Should Leaders Develop an Internal Coaching Capability in Their Organizations?

Many business leaders and managers have assumed that learning takes place in the classroom. The job of "teaching" belongs to someone else. The professional comes to work to do his or her job, not to learn that job. Learning, though important to some, has a lower priority. Teaching others perhaps has a lower priority still. Understandably, many often believe that through an effective hiring process, they select and "onboard" individuals who are motivated, ready, and able to do their jobs. The reality, of course, is quite different. Given the pace of change, driven by competitive pressures, globalization, the need to improve quality, and the introduction of new technologies, all organizational actors are nearly always learning, or least they'd better be. The classroom makes it possible for a worker to compete, to get his or her foot in the door, but that's only the beginning. The average knowledge worker and certainly the average leader at any level needs to be able to put concepts into action in their challenging and often idiosyncratic contexts. This requires on-the-job learning.

The only question for organizational leaders is this: Do you want to guide the learning process or not? Of note, there is the option of leaving it up to chance. It is a characteristic of human beings that they will seek out opportunities to learn and, when they get a chance, engage others in that process.

However, unguided learning may be slow and inefficient and ultimately lead the learner to the wrong conclusions. (If you've ever tried to straighten out a recalcitrant golf swing on your own, you can relate to the problem.) The learning process can be enhanced through various interventions. Once that fact becomes clear, it should likewise become obvious that if learning is important in your organization, learning effectiveness can become a source of competitive advantage. The choice, then, of guiding learning rather than leaving it to chance seems obvious. The next question is this: How should your organization go about doing so?

When workers are asked about the experiences from which they learned the most, they usually talk about on-the-job learning experiences in which they faced a challenge and in which other individuals played a very important part. Particularly for adults, learning through facing important challenges is a most potent stimulus for personal development. Challenge by itself is insufficient, however. Research at the Center for Creative Leadership has demonstrated conclusively that for experiences to result in personal development, challenge must be accompanied by assessment and support (Van Velsor & McCauley, 2004).

*Assessment* here refers to, in particular, an assessment of the effectiveness of one's efforts. The individual facing a challenge will likely need to try a variety of new actions or learn to make sense of the situation in a different way. Is the new behavior constructive in addressing the challenge? Does the new understanding of the situation help? These become critically important questions when one is in the process of learning. Unfortunately, answers to such questions in the form of feedback that helps the individual assess the effectiveness of his or her actions or understandings are often lacking just when they are needed most.

Imagine, for example, an individual engineer leading a team for the first time. She called a meeting, presented her agenda, passed around some donuts, and suggested that the group get to work. Several hours later, the first team meeting was coming to a close, and those sitting around the table seemed to the team leader to hold a variety of attitudes about what had transpired. Some were excited, but some were very skeptical. One individual seemed downright angry, or at least the team leader *thought* he was angry (he didn't really say). Had she done something wrong? Was it the donuts? Had she included some people for the project who really shouldn't have been there? Or was she sensing an inevitable reaction to change on the part of some team members? Her interpretation of what had transpired in the meeting could have a significant impact on what she and others on the team would do next.

In a recent seminar on team leadership, this particular team leader was encouraged to do a "process check" at the end of each meeting, to ask the group for feedback on how they, and she, were doing. Luckily, she remembered to ask the group for some feedback in the last few minutes of the meeting and found out that things weren't quite as bleak as she had thought. The one individual who seemed so angry was, in reality, just demonstrating the body language he normally does when he's confused. He was still interested in working on the project team. Relieved, the team leader said good-bye to the team members after they reviewed their assignments and planned the next session. The feedback she received for the team was invaluable, in that it gave her at least some idea of where the various team members stood. However, she still didn't get much information about her own performance in the meeting. She needed a clearer sense of how she should manage the team in general, and she needed to figure out what to do next.

If she's lucky, the team leader is working in an organization that has a coaching capability of some sort. If she's fortunate enough to work for a coaching manager or if she's lucky enough to have a mentor, she might spend a few minutes talking with that individual about the meeting that just transpired. In that conversation, she would probably review her own perception of what happened in the meeting. She would try to describe what she did and how team members reacted. Her coach or mentor might ask her some questions with the intent of clarifying what happened and at the same time encourage the new team leader to deepen her own thinking. The coach or mentor then might offer some feedback; perhaps she should have given the members of the team a bit more time to get to know one another (they actually come from different plants), and she will probably need to further refine management's vision for the project so that the team members can get a clearer sense of the task they face. The two then might discuss next steps and agree to talk again after the next meeting. This process might be informal if the team leader is talking with a manager who has the ability to coach others or a mentor, or it might be formal if she is working with a designated coach from the firm's organizational development department or an externally sourced executive coach.

We hope the reader can see the difference between sending the team leader ahead on her own, to sink or to swim, and helping her learn more about the challenges she is facing and develop a more informed response. Yes, she's been to courses on team dynamics and project management, but when actually running a project and a team for the first time, translating classroom-based concepts into action is extremely difficult. Each situation is at least to a degree unique. If she sticks with roles that involve team leadership and project management, in time, she'll become an expert. She'll get to know her own strengths and weaknesses as a project leader. She'll get a feel for the rhythm and life cycle of teams and projects. She will become a better communicator.

In the absence of coaching, the team leader might survive in her role as team leader, though the road might be more stressful and her performance, though adequate, might not be stellar. Alternatively, she might not survive in that role. The team might not be successful. The project might not reach its goals: another strategic initiative that failed at the execution stage. This is what leaders, not just human resource and organizational development leaders, but business, not-for-profit, government, and hospital leaders need to consider when pondering the question of whether or not they should build a coaching capacity within their organizations. Organizational capability expands when people learn from challenges they face, on the job, through the mechanisms of coaching within supportive, learning-oriented relationships.

## An Organizational-Level View of Coaching

We'll describe what we call *developmental coaching* in greater detail in Chapter 2. For now, though, coaching can simply be viewed as an activity taking place within a relationship that promotes learning from experience in one or both of the partners in that relationship. Despite the difficulties organizational leaders face in building a coaching capability, the situation is not entirely bleak. Over the past decade or so, the concepts of coaching and mentoring have begun to have a significant impact on the workplace. Some call coaching a fad, but we doubt that is the case. Although coaching in any of its varied forms is underresearched to date, the research that has been done clearly indicates that coaching benefits both individuals and their employing organizations. The benefits we outlined for our team leader and her organization are quite real.

Individuals who have been the recipients of effective coaching report that it is satisfying, helpful, and often leads to better performance (Buckingham & Coffman, 1999; Goleman, Boyatzis, & McKee, 2002; Hall, Otazo, & Hollenbeck, 1999; Hunt, 2004). They further report that they have changed and that they are not only more skillful but also more confident, more certain of their direction, more self-aware, and more able to understand the perspectives of others (Hunt, 2004). Coaching-related activities are also clearly associated with improved business results as measured by variables such as profitability and customer satisfaction (Buckingham & Coffman, 1999). Our own work has also shown that coaches reap the benefits of learning from their time spent in coaching others.

Once he or she is solid on the value of guided on-the-job learning, the organization leader who wants to build a coaching capability has some basic issues to address. First, the leader will either have to train the existing staff in coaching or import coaching skills through the use of external consultants. The skills of coaching will then be available to a group of employees. Coaching is seen as a skill—a tool, if you will—that can be added to the toolkit and used as needed.

While this is one very valid way of looking at the building of a coaching capability, we've found this view of coaching to be somewhat limited. To view coaching as a skill to be deployed both underestimates its value and underestimates what it means to put that skill into action. Such a view implies that the only benefit of coaching is the building of employee skills or employee development. In our experience, a coaching capability can create value that goes well beyond the development of more skilled employees and leaders.

We initially explored the field of coaching in an effort to understand the behavior of managers who are known as being effective coaches to their direct reports. Coaching by managers is one of the leadership behaviors most desired by subordinates, but unfortunately least practiced (Lombardo & Eichinger, 2001). Through interviews with a large number of such managers, we were able to articulate the "real-world tactics" employed by such individuals. That effort resulted in the book *The Coaching Manager: Developing Top Talent in Business* (Hunt & Weintraub, 2002a). That work, however, also accompanied an ongoing action research practice, in which we further explored the means by which that rare species of manager, the "coaching manager," emerged from the large majority of managers who are not willing and/or able to coach people who work for them. In the process, we learned more about the value proposition of coaching.

One important benefit of the widespread deployment of coaching by managers, for instance, is a not-so-subtle shift in their leadership styles. In an early paper, we described how the act of coaching itself requires not just the learning of a skill but also considerable personal growth on the part of the manager (Hunt & Weintraub, 2004). They must learn to view their roles and relationships in a very different way. Coaching requires that managers lead rather than control. The impact of such a change in leadership style on the organization can be considerable. Coaching managers have to increase the overall level of real communication and trust in their units. Learning requires both.

We found in our earlier research that one of the most significant challenges that managers face, if they realistically hope to become coaching managers, is creating what we have called a "coaching-friendly context."

The coaching-friendly context can be viewed as a subculture within an organization that directly supports coaching-facilitated learning. In a coaching-friendly context, employees feel more able to talk frankly with others about their development, challenges, and mistakes. In such an environment, employees' natural interest in learning and self-improvement comes to the fore, and the responsibility for driving learning is shared between the manager and his or her direct reports. Coaching is not limited to the performance appraisal. Informal, though extremely valuable, coaching takes place on a routine basis. Under these circumstances, people are more comfortable with taking the risks associated with stretch assignments. Failures, within reason, aren't punished, and support for facing challenges is widespread. What does such a coaching culture look like in practice? Here are the perspectives of two different managers from Southwest Airlines:

> If there's a delay, supervisors find out why it happened. We get ideas on how to do it better next time. If you've got that kind of relationship, then they're [the employees] not going to be afraid. Say there was a ten-minute delay because freight was excessive. If we're screaming, we don't know why it was late. (Gittell, 2003, p. 74)

> We work real hard to remove that barrier so that agents can come in and talk to a supervisor or manager. There's an open-door policy so when employees have a problem, they know we can work on it together. It's a totally different environment here. We sit and listen. When that person walks away, he'll have self-esteem. (Gittell, 2003, p. 74)

These are examples of conversations that we would describe as developmental. Note that the employee learns something about how to address a problem, a work-related challenge. At the same time, the organization learns more about those same problems and how to resolve them more effectively. At its best, in a coaching-friendly context, the work drives the learning for employees, and the coaching serves as a link between the two: work and employee. Employee and manager must have honest and open conversations about the problems they face. We suggest that when an organizational leader begins to think about building a coaching capability, he or she think carefully about the potential benefits of viewing the goal as not just that of building skills (which may not be used, as we see below) but also of changing the organization's culture.

We realize that culture change is not easily accomplished. Whatever changes are made have to really work; they have to help the organization accomplish its goals. We'll address this challenge in a later chapter, but for now, consider the question of how an individual manager can create a coaching-friendly context. We have found that managers use a variety of leadership interventions. They take care to hire people into their groups who are interested in and seek out learning. They orient new employees to their management styles, which might appear to newcomers to be quite unusual (because most people haven't worked for coaching managers). Very importantly, they "walk the talk" when it comes to dealing with the inevitable mistakes that are made during the learning process. They hold their tempers and manage stress effectively. They ask for coaching themselves, from their direct reports. They seek out feedback. They are available, within reason, for coaching discussions. Importantly, they also make sure that they spend their "coaching capital" on good and great employees, not just on those with performance problems. This has the impact of "destigmatizing" the coaching conversation. We'll come back to this important observation repeatedly.

Having created a coaching-friendly context, the manager no longer has to take sole responsibility for learning. The employee is also responsible. (This should come as a great relief to most practicing managers.) When coaching is viewed through an organizational cultural lens, one begins to see why some efforts to "train managers to coach" yield disappointing results. Some organizations, while providing coaching-skills training to managers (or hiring outstanding executive coaches), actually discourage on-the-job learning, either implicitly or explicitly. We repeatedly heard comments from those in our research to the effect that "my boss asks me why I spend so much time with my people, but there isn't much he can say, our results are so good." Guided on-the-job learning requires relationships, and relationships require time.

The use of external expert coaches has appeared to be one way of working around cultural assumptions that inhibit the growth of a coaching-friendly context. (There are other, better reasons for the use of executive coaching, as we'll discuss in later chapters.) However, the failure to confront the organization's role in the learning process has two implications. First, there is some evidence that the most effective external or executive coaching interventions result when the coachee has a supportive boss who is actively and positively engaged in the coaching effort (Hunt, 2004). The converse implication is that even though such coaching may be quite expert, if it takes place in isolation, it may be less effective. Similarly, the organization may lose an opportunity to learn from the experience. Consider the following examples.

## CASE 1.1    Learning From an Executive Coaching Intervention

A well-meaning and very busy organization brought in expert external coaches on occasion to work with individual executives who were having difficulty in their roles. The coaches did a good job, and the individual executives who were consumers of the program found it useful and enlightening. In some cases, their job performance clearly improved. That is, however, as far as the program went. No effort was made to understand the implications of this effort for the organization. It might have been very useful to consider whether or not anything could have been learned about the way the organization hired executives, the challenges facing them, and why so many were running into trouble. In fact, while the executives appreciated the coaching provided by the firm, several did not feel that the organization was doing anything to address what was seen as the organization's side of the problem.

A second organization, which sponsored an active coaching program using skilled executive coaches, regularly required that coaches meet with line leadership to discuss general themes that emerged in coaching. This can provide an opportunity for organizational leaders to learn more about the strengths and weaknesses of their leadership development activities. It also provides them an opportunity to gain valuable information regarding critically important business issues. In one instance, when the organization was in the midst of executing a merger, the coaches and the head of the business unit met to discuss what the coaches were learning about employee morale, the level of employee understanding of the vision for change, and other critically important concerns. The confidentiality of individual coaching sessions and relationships was maintained, but organizational leaders had an important opportunity to gain insight into their own effectiveness and the impact of the merger on a larger group of stakeholders.

When the link between individual, relationship-facilitated, on-the-job learning and organizational learning and development has been established, we believe that a coaching organization will likely be more able to address a range of organizational-level challenges. As one example (which we will describe in some detail in a later chapter), a coaching organization may be better able to execute radical organizational transformation. Organizational change requires individual learning. One can't learn about highly differentiated radical changes, particularly those that are innovative, in the classroom or in a textbook. One learns about change by trying new behaviors and actions directed at serving the goals of the change process. In a coaching organization, individuals engaged in on-the-job learning activities and through coaching improve and refine their efforts.

# The Coaching Organization

The task of creating a coaching-friendly context and an organizational coaching capability is in our view an organizational development task. An organizational, as opposed to a skills-based view of coaching, requires an organizational action plan.

Consider the nature of the leadership required to drive the effort. The very notion of a coaching capability almost immediately calls forth the tension between a focus on today's results and the effort to build human capital for tomorrow, and between today's operational demands and the organization's larger strategy. A coaching capability ultimately begins with the organization's efforts to manage this tension.

Dave Whitwam, former chairman and CEO of the Whirlpool Corporation, describes the challenge as managing what he calls "the zone of execution." The zone of execution is the mind-set and group of activities dominating a manager's attention at a particular point in time. The tension inherent in the zone of execution is described pictorially in Box 1.1. Managers are constantly struggling with the problem of how to allocate their time. Pressing operational problems and the need to make today's numbers almost always overpower long-term concerns. The leadership of the coaching organization has to be constantly on guard for the tendency to ignore the strategic perspective completely, especially when times are tough.

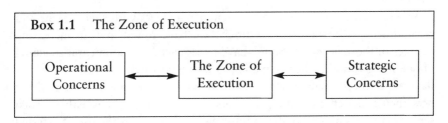

Box 1.1    The Zone of Execution

| Operational Concerns | ← → | The Zone of Execution | ← → | Strategic Concerns |

Whitwam believed that it was his job to make sure that his managers did not ignore the strategic perspective. In his view, if they were to do so, they would likely fail in their effort to transform the corporation. The Whirlpool strategy for organizational change, as we'll describe in Chapter 5, relies heavily on the use of a variety of coaching interventions. The senior management of the company has been intimately involved in leading this effort and in insisting on the link between on-the-job learning, coaching, and the goals of the business. Because of their stance, these linkages are much clearer to employees at all levels. This has, not surprisingly, resulted in significant behavior change on the part of Whirlpool managers.

The senior management of an organization must decide what they want to achieve by building a coaching capability. Coaching organizations tend to be relatively clear about the kinds of skills, behaviors, and attitudes that they believe are linked to the desired organizational outcomes. Coaching is a goal-directed activity. To what ends should employees, leaders, coaching managers, and expert coaches work? Such questions usually result in a discussion of the firm's competency model (at least in most large firms).

A *competency model* can serve as a rulebook and an instruction manual for coaches and those being coached, but it has to be widely used and widely understood. Organizations build competency models when their leaders become convinced that certain individual-level capabilities are essential to the organization's success. They may use such a model in the selection process, but unless they want to staff every position with people hired from outside the firm, they need the competency model to serve as a link between individual development and organizational need. Development requires learning, taking risks, and sometimes making mistakes, and participation in conversations about that extracts learning from experience. For useful coaching conversations around desired competencies to be widespread, senior management has to set the tone. In a coaching organization, one might see leaders telling stories about their mistakes and what they could have done differently, if they had only "listened." Senior management engages with the competency model and signals through its use that it has real meaning.

Where would you expect to find senior managers with such insight and commitment to learning? Interestingly, we have found that an increasing number of those in the "C-Suite" have experienced developmental coaching of one sort or another. Senior managers who have used executive coaches or have experienced mentor relationships openly and purposefully talk about how their experience encourages others to become more "coachable." Such senior managers may formally or informally advocate for the use of external coaches or the development of a greater internal coaching capability. As one example, Bob Nardelli, CEO of Home Depot, has stated, "I absolutely believe that people, unless coached, never reach their maximum capabilities" (Sellers, 2002, p. 96). He calls his own boss, the board chair, nearly every day for his own coaching session. When senior management decides to send a message, people are likely to listen (more so than when the message comes from human resources alone). Thus, we have come to see that the experience or lack of experience of senior managers with coaching is an important consideration when taking an organizational view of coaching.

As we found with coaching managers, coaching organizations demonstrate a strong commitment to positioning developmental coaching as a positive opportunity for good and great employees, not just for employees in trouble. Indeed, some organizations are now excluding the use of external coaches for employees with performance problems. Those individuals may be least able to benefit from such an investment and most likely to exit the organization in the process. Obviously, if there is a link between coaching conversations and the ability of the organization to deal more effectively with business challenges, it stands to reason that you'd want to engage your best talent in the process.

When used for leadership development, for instance, executive coaching in a coaching organization is strategically targeted at individuals who are going through important leadership transitions or who are expected to do so in the next few years. Coaching for such individuals is planned and coordinated, if not managed, to ensure that coachees are learning the right lessons, albeit in a fashion that allows them to tailor those lessons to their own unique circumstances. Under these circumstances, those participating in coaching are typically highly motivated and see it as a special investment in their development on the part of the organization. Learning and loyalty are the outcomes.

Compare this outcome with what could be called an "unmanaged" coaching capability: the bringing in of coaches in an uncoordinated fashion. Some managers, for instance, might decide not to deal with performance issues or problems directly, but rather hire external coaches to do so. This sends a powerful message about coaching, one that could undermine its potential as a developmental tool as it becomes stigmatized by the assumption that "if they call in a coach for you, you must be in trouble." Alternatively, some coaching dollars might be spent on individuals for whom coaching is neither necessary nor desirable. An organizational coaching capability, like any organizational capability, should be the managerial responsibility of one or more individuals.

In the coaching organization, decisions must be made about constructing linkages between individual learning mediated by coaching and organizational learning. On-the-job learning frequently leverages what is known as *tacit knowledge,* knowledge that is not codified or written down but is nevertheless essential for effective job performance, in the boardroom or on the shop floor. Knowing what a piece of equipment is likely to do in a humid environment, for instance, a "specification" not mentioned in the instruction manual, can have important organizational implications. The sharing of such knowledge can be critically important to an organization's ability to be successful in highly challenging and competitive markets or in the management of highly complex processes. The reader may recognize this as a *knowledge management* issue. Many firms have invested considerable resources in the development of a variety of knowledge management systems.

Coaching and other forms of relational on-the-job learning, however, are absolutely necessary for organizational-level knowledge management efforts to be of value. Many organizations have tried and failed to leverage technology to capture tacit knowledge (Davenport & Prusak, 2002). These efforts have failed in part because they did not take into account the human processes involved in knowledge retention and knowledge sharing.

There is a growing sense of urgency regarding knowledge management in many firms as they face an unprecedented wave of retirements that will result in the loss of much tacit knowledge (De Long, 2004). While knowledge sharing via coaching isn't the only strategy for dealing with knowledge loss, it is an important one. If a coaching capability is to be of true value at the organizational level, we believe that the linkages between the action of coaching at the individual level and the sharing of knowledge must be clearly managed.

Of course, in a coaching organization, decisions must be made about the linkages between coaching and other human resource processes. If managers are supposed to be good at coaching their reports, will the organization really refuse to promote a manager who is not a good coach even though he or she has achieved outstanding financial results? Are managers required to coach their people despite the fact that their compensation does not reward them for doing so? In organizations in which learning is divorced from management, rewards, and promotion, we are far less likely to see the development of a robust coaching capability. Organizations that really see connections between learning and success will likely reward those who promote learning.

When a coaching capability is intentionally developed and managed within an organization, coaching becomes less of a fad and more of a tool of good management. A manager shouldn't decide to work with an executive coach just because everyone else seems to be doing so. Ideally, the ground rules for the appropriate use of executive coaching have been thought through in light of the organization's needs. Support systems are provided that help individual managers assess their overall learning needs and decide on an appropriate course of action after considering a range of options.

Of course, an organizational view of coaching suggests the importance of considering how to evaluate its impact, in terms of both quality and business results. Evaluation serves the purpose of helping to clarify the goals set for the capability as well as documenting the outcomes in relation to business outcomes. Evaluating developmental activities is notoriously challenging, and such efforts at many coaching organizations are still quite rudimentary. Nevertheless, considerable momentum is developing behind efforts to refine evaluation practices; at a minimum, a coaching organization must decide how it will assess whether or not the effort has been worthwhile.

These are just a few examples of the issues that organizations aspiring to build a coaching capability should consider. Beyond these issues, a coaching capability must be managed as an important organizational asset and set of business processes. There should be a coaching strategy or plan that has been articulated and can be discussed and understood by line managers. There also needs to be an individual, or individuals, whose job in whole or in part is to oversee the coaching effort as an ongoing process, not just a series of training programs or coaching engagements. Since the coaching effort, however, is in the service of business goals as well as employee development, senior management should also remain involved. Thus, in our view, a coaching capability is more than, and requires much more than, training employees in a set of skills.

## An Organizational Coaching Capability

In the previous section of this chapter, we tried to describe some of the implications of an organizational-level view of coaching and the building of an organizational coaching capability. We can now begin to operationalize some terms. *A coaching organization makes effective and regular use of coaching as a means of promoting both individual development and organizational learning in the service of the organization's larger goals.* To make this possible, the coaching organization must develop one or more types of coaching capability. The organization must be able to access coaching resources via individuals with the right competencies who can provide developmental coaching, either as employees or consultants. The target of the coaching capability may vary from organization to organization, depending on the organization's needs and context. In addition, in a coaching organization, the coaching capability is managed so as to create value for both the individual being coached and the organization as a whole.

Not all coaching resources are the same. Each has strengths, weaknesses, and a degree of appropriateness to a particular set of goals and contexts. What they all have in common is that the coaching provided is developmental in nature. In Chapter 2, we will provide an in-depth discussion of the concept of developmental coaching in some detail. Simply put, developmental coaching is not meant to be "corrective," though it can be. It is meant to promote individual learning and development. There are four options for building a coaching capability. Many organizations deploy more than one of these approaches. We will go into each in great detail in the coming chapters.

Here, we give a brief overview and include in this discussion some of the specific challenges associated with each option. Our discussion of challenges takes two forms. There are challenges associated with building a particular kind of coaching capability. There are also challenges associated with maximizing the value of that capability as a means of promoting individual and organizational learning that also results in the achievement of business goals. Throughout the book, we will provide examples of how the organizations in our research have gone about addressing these challenges.

## Coaching Managers

The most obvious coaching resource in most organizations is the manager. The manager is involved with direct reports and their work on a routine basis. The manager is responsible for business unit performance and is typically responsible for integrating new people into the business unit. Responsibility for on-the-job learning fits logically with this role. As already stated, there is significant research evidence to suggest that managers who are effective at coaching their direct reports achieve superior business results (Buckingham & Coffman, 1999).

Important in many contexts, the coaching manager can also be viewed as the essential resource for any organization that wants to create *leadership at all levels.* A coaching-oriented manager can spot talent, that special look in the eye of an employee or that particularly influential and unexpected performance that signals to someone paying attention that "this person can help us." The coaching manager is in the best position to provide challenging assignments to talented people and to support their continued learning. The coaching manager is also in the best position to take what is learned from a coaching discussion and consider its implications for the business or for others.

Relying on managers to coach presents a number of challenges, however. For managers to serve as coaches, they must have the requisite basic interpersonal skills. They must also learn something about how to coach, either through formal or informal means. As described above, organizational leadership must signal the importance of coaching to their managers in a variety of ways, through appropriate reward systems and promotion policies. Clearly, if people are *only* rewarded for hitting the quarterly targets, then a coaching initiative will have a much lower probability of success.

There is another challenge associated with assigning managers the task of coaching, and that is the management of an inherent paradox in the role of the coaching manager. He or she must both coach and evaluate direct reports. The process of evaluation tends to inhibit the degree to which direct reports will be open about their concerns, problems, and mistakes, even those that are made in good faith. It is for this reason that the coaching manager, perhaps more than any other coaching resource, must work so hard on an informal day-to-day basis in the creation of a coaching-friendly context (Hunt & Weintraub, 2002a). As we will discuss, the tasks of the coaching manager require significant emotional maturity (Goleman, 1995).

The presence of coaching managers in organizations is for the most part an exception. If the manager is to become a major coaching resource for an organization, the organization will have to devote significant effort to achieving such an outcome. In a mature coaching organization, we would expect to find that coaching managers were not the exception (though realistically, we would also expect to find that not every manager was an effective coach).

In addition to training and the appropriate attention to rewarding coaching behaviors, senior management must also help managers and supervisors see an appropriate link between (a) the desired pro-coaching-oriented behaviors and assumptions and (b) the business needs of the organization. Managers have to possess a clear, almost line-of-sight ability to see that taking some time to hold a work-related coaching discussion is not a distraction from the tasks at hand and is not driven by the desire to be nice. They have to have a deep understanding of the business case and the business opportunity associated with an investment in coaching. More than the development of new skills, this requires new insights and new perspectives on the part of managers.

Transformational learning, on the part of both individuals and organizations, is ultimately required to build a coaching manager capability. When coaching by managers becomes an agent of both development and change, organizations begin to extract significant value from the work associated with building such a capability. This transformation can take place only when coaching is viewed as integral to the company's formula for both individual and organizational success.

## External Expert or Executive Coaches

Executive coaching is putatively a new field of activity, though some would say that organizational consultants have always done executive coaching. This type of coaching, the use of skilled external coaches paid as consultants to help enhance an executive's leadership performance, offers a number of benefits to individuals and organizations alike. The external coach can bring special expertise from a variety of disciplines that may not be available internally. The external coach also brings an external and perhaps more objective viewpoint to the discussion. The executive client can access a new perspective on the issues with which he or she is dealing, presumably free from perspectives that might be tainted by internal politics. Very importantly, there is some evidence that the experience of working with an executive coach may be one way that managers learn to coach (Hunt, 2004).

As a new field, however, there is not yet a consensus as to the definition and methodology of executive coaching. Furthermore, as what is perhaps a billion-dollar industry (Thalheimer, 2002), it is woefully underresearched by organizational scholars. As such, the marketplace of buyers (i.e., organizations), is subject to some understandable confusion. Is executive coaching a form of psychotherapy in the workplace? Or is it focused executive development coupled with a bit of business consultation? Who is qualified to be an executive coach?

The use of external executive coaches does not in and of itself imply that the executive coach is a resource to the organization. A number of challenges are associated with making executive coaching an organizational-level resource and capability. First of all, the coaches must be competent to serve in such a role. One advantage associated with the use of competent executive coaches, of course, is their expertise. Most executive coaches are psychologists, human resource specialists, or former business leaders. Many have had extensive additional training in coaching techniques as well as exposure to a variety of business issues. Those who have had experience in business may also bring with them functional or strategic expertise. However, there is no licensure requirement for external coaches at this time. "Coach certification" is available from a number of different private and professional groups, but the certification requirements and processes vary widely. Organizations take on a great deal of responsibility when they bring in any external consultant. Increasingly, organizations are taking prospective coaches through some type of qualification process to ensure consistency and a baseline of competence.

In addition, executive coaches, if they are to help their executive clients with real work, must understand something about the goals, strategy, plans, and operations of the organization. The Whirlpool Corporation experience, described in Chapter 5, illustrates value that was gained by teaching a cadre of executive coaches about the Whirlpool Leadership Model, a guide to the behaviors and competencies that senior management has identified as being essential to the company's and therefore every manager's success.

Most executive coaching is directed at those currently in leadership roles or those expecting to be in leadership roles soon. Executive coaching impacts and can be impacted by the leader's relationships with direct reports, peers, and his or her own boss or board. On a superficial level, it may appear that the executive coach is responsible only for the executive, when, in fact, the coach is working at the interfaces between many relationships in order to help the executive improve his or her ability to lead. For coaches to manage their responsibilities to organizations, they must be aware of organizations' needs and issues as well as those of executives. When viewed from this perspective, executive coaching begins to look more like an organizational development intervention than individual counseling.

There can, of course, be conflicts between the needs of the individual executive and the needs of the organization. It is for this reason that the meetings between the coach and the coachee are bounded by limited confidentiality; this helps the coach create a coaching-friendly context within which the executive is free to speak openly about his or her learning needs. We say "limited confidentiality" here because most executive coaches find it important to interact, with the executive's permission and participation, with other stakeholders, such as peers or direct reports. Through such interactions, coaches can help executives gain a more realistic picture of the impact of their actions and develop more informed plans for performance improvement.

The limited confidentiality associated with the executive coaching relationship, however, also makes it difficult for the organization to assess the full impact of coaching or to leverage issues that emerge in coaching itself for the purposes of organizational learning (Hunt & Weintraub, 2002b). As with any intervention, ideally, some effort should be made to assess the impact of the coaching process on the organization and the individual. The individual executive might have been satisfied with the coaching experience, but did his or her satisfaction translate into a positive business or organizational outcome? In addition, the limited confidentiality surrounding executive coaching makes it harder for knowledge that emerges during the coaching to be shared with others. Both of these issues are, of course, particularly challenging to manage if the organization views executive coaching as solely an individual-level intervention.

Organizations face significant challenges in trying to "manage" the use of executive coaching, particularly in light of the fact that executives find it satisfying and this satisfaction in and of itself serves to expand the market for executive coaching. To maximize the value of executive coaching, organizations must consider for whom and how it should be used, how to effect the best match between coach and coachee, how to influence the coaching process to ensure that it is working in the best interests of both coach and coachee, and how to coordinate coaching engagements and the learning and career development needs of the organization.

## Internal Expert Coaches

In response to some of the challenges cited above regarding the building of a coaching capability around managers or external coaches, some organizations have begun to build an internal expert coaching capability. In a later chapter, we'll describe how Wachovia Bank developed and managed a cadre of internal coaches from their human resource function to provide coaching services in one of their leadership development programs. The use of internal coaches appears to have some advantages. First of all, internal coaches may be less expensive. We say "may be" because to be maximally effective, internal coaches do require training and ongoing learning opportunities. As can be seen in the Wachovia example, their training requirements are not trivial.

Internal coaches are already familiar with the goals and strategy of the firm. They also have firsthand experience with the culture of the firm. Their history with the organization, even if brief, can give them insights regarding the issues likely to be faced by an executive or manager in the firm. They often possess insight as to how the firm "really works" and what behaviors are truly valued. The likely trade-off is that the firm loses the value of the more objective external perspective brought to a coaching engagement by an executive coach, though there has been no research to support this assumption.

The internal coach does, however, face a political landscape slightly different from that of the external coach. Presumably with more at stake, it may be difficult for the internal coach to "speak truth to power." The job description of the internal coach is also inherently complex. Most organizations don't require a staff of full-time internal coaches (though some do). As such, most coaches have other responsibilities. Human resource professionals, for instance, are often required to serve as "expert consultants" around a variety of strategic and compliance concerns. They are called on by senior management because of their content knowledge. Giving an expert opinion is not the same as coaching. In fact, the behavior of the expert consultant may be diametrically opposed to that of the more process-oriented coach. This creates significant challenges for the internal coach, who may have to balance a variety of role identifications in order to be effective at both.

The boundary around the internal coaching relationship shares some of the same challenges associated with that surrounding the external coaching relationship. How much confidentiality is necessary, and how much is appropriate? How should the internal coach interact with the various coachee stakeholders? Finally, given that there is some kind of boundary around the coaching relationship, how can the results of the coaching intervention be assessed, and how can knowledge gleaned from the coaching intervention be leveraged for organizational success?

## Peer Coaching

A recent focus group with a small group of health care providers in their hospital-based practice demonstrated the tremendously important resource of peer coaching. Typically in this particular profession, one learns technical knowledge in school and very little about how to apply that knowledge in the workplace. That kind of learning, the development of a foundation of the required tacit knowledge, takes place on the job. In the hospital department in question, each new hire is given a 4-month formal orientation. Everyone in the focus group agreed that by no means is that sufficient to fully orient new professionals to the hospital or their roles. What happens next? A very effective informal peer coaching capability takes over and supports the individual professional, literally for the rest of his or her career. The professionals in this group are all highly regarded, and there is no evidence to suggest that this capability is inadequate to the task (though it is easy to understand how it might look so to others, at least superficially). The peer coaching capability has been built up over the years as the culture of the department evolved.

Employees in this department are expected to seek help if they need to know something related to their jobs or organization; and employees who are asked for help are expected to provide it. Significant resources are devoted to supporting such a culture, including the provision of an up-to-date library (which people actually use) and a variety of additional online resources. People are encouraged to grow by taking on job-related challenges. The pay is relatively low, but worker satisfaction is quite high.

Researchers have known the value of peer mentoring for some time (Kram, 1988). The reality is that we turn to our peers for help for a variety of reasons. It is less threatening. Peer support is often available "just in time" to help deal with spontaneously emerging learning needs. Peer coaching can also be viewed as a form of social capital, networks of people who by virtue of their relationships with one another are more capable than they would be without those relationships. The peer network also provides support for the diffusion of knowledge from a coaching conversation to other parts of the organization.

While there are some formal peer coaching programs (Hunt, Strei, & Weintraub, 2002), as seen in the example above, an aggressive peer coaching capability is often more of a natural outgrowth of the culture within which it exists. Employees in the department cited never intentionally planned for the development of such a capability and (despite our advice) did not intend to manage that capability; and it is not clear that they are truly in a position to appreciate the significance of peer coaching as an aspect of the department's culture. This brings us to the question of the degree to which peer coaching can be stimulated intentionally. If so, can it be managed, or perhaps lead, toward organizationally desirable outcomes?

## A Coaching Capability "Infrastructure"

An organization, then, has a range of options from which to choose when considering how to establish a coaching capability. To summarize the position taken earlier, we believe that building a coaching organization requires both leadership and management. Leadership is required to establish the linkages between the organization's goals and the coaching capability, and it is also required to establish a coaching-friendly context appropriate to the organization's needs. Management is required to make and execute a series of decisions about the coaching capability, to make sure it is effective in the service of both the individual coachee and the organization.

When the decision is made to engage in coaching, perhaps by offering coaching training or by bringing in an executive coach, is the decision made haphazardly or strategically? Is thought given to what organizational-level outcomes can and should be pursued? If so, are appropriate plans and resources put into place to ensure that such outcomes are attained? In other words, there needs to be some kind of vision for what coaching can do, a leadership task, and then the allocation of resources and the follow-up to make sure that progress is made toward the vision.

Thus, there is work involved. Our main belief about that work is as old as the organizational hierarchy itself: What is seen as important gets done. A coaching capability can grow in a variety of forms, if there is a good reason for it to do so. We challenge the reader to think about the reasons for promoting coaching in his or her organization. Are those reasons aligned with the business or organization's vision, strategy, or plans? If so, you will find the existence of what we call a "coaching value chain." The exercise at the close of this chapter presents an organized approach to thinking about the coaching value chain in your organization. You may find that the linkages are clear, not so clear, or poorly articulated, representing different challenges that we address throughout the book. In the next chapter, we will more clearly describe the factors that promote the evolution of a coaching organization.

ORGANIZATIONAL ASSESSMENT **1.1 The Coaching Value Proposition**

The following exercise (see Box 1.2, "The Coaching Value Chain in Your Organization") will take the reader through the process of assessing the linkage between (a) individual development through relationally facilitated, on-the-job learning and (b) organizationally desired outcomes. If you are using this book to help you consider how to build a coaching capability in your organization, we encourage you to work through this exercise with a group of key stakeholders. You'll probably need a good deal more space than we have provided here. The exercise should create a very useful dialogue and help you consider a variety of options, which we'll begin to describe in some detail in the next chapter.

In the blocks provided, you should begin at the top, by describing the organizational goals to which you are aspiring. We encourage you to be as explicit as possible in considering the ultimate business or organizational results you are trying to achieve. In our experience, the more you can relate those goals to actual business outcomes, the more compelling people will find the logic behind the need to build a coaching capability. Many times, people respond to this question by describing, in essence, a need to build a leadership pipeline. Our question is, then, "Why is that important?" The answer to that question reflects your true aspiration.

The next two cells ask you to articulate the human resource (people) outcomes that need to be attained if you are to meet your business goals. Again, we talk in terms of outcomes, not processes yet. If you are to achieve the business/organizational goals to which you aspire, what will be required of your people? Imagine what they would be doing if they were genuinely engaged in pursuing those business goals.

In the third cell, we ask the basic strategic human resources questions: What behaviors would people display if they were to be in a position to achieve the desired human resources and organizational outcomes? What skills would they demonstrate? What attitudes would they hold? Again, we encourage you to be comprehensive, because in the next step, you'll consider the question "How can coaching help?" Think about this question in two ways. First, consider what behaviors, attitudes, and skills employees might learn best on the job. That's the traditional view of coaching. Then, consider what the organization might learn from coaching. Box 1.2 presents a very simple example from an organization that hoped to launch a major quality-oriented transformation.

**Box 1.2    The Coaching Value Chain in Your Organization–Sample**

*Desired business or organizational outcomes:*

To create greater value for our customers through shipping error-free products and, in the process, differentiate ourselves from our competitors. To this end, we are launching a major organizational effectiveness effort.

*Human resource outcomes needed to support business outcomes:*

1. Leadership will be required at all levels; direct labor and their managers must be able to proactively take ownership for quality problems before they occur.

2. We must eliminate a "culture of blame" that makes it difficult for employees to raise quality problems, let alone solve them.

3. We need to become "experts" at assessing and improving quality-related processes in all areas of our work.

*Behaviors, skills, or attitudes required to support human resource outcomes:*

1. Managers and first line supervisors will need to become more effective at leading, setting a vision, and rallying their teams to the cause of quality.

2. Managers must become more effective at spotting talent in the labor force and be capable of assuming more responsibility.

3. Managers must develop better skills in areas such as team building and coaching.

*How coaching, or relationship-facilitated, on-the-job learning, can help promote the development of desired behaviors, skills, or attitudes:*

Coaching can help managers and supervisors, as well as other contributors, improve their leadership skills "on the job." Most leadership development takes place there. Coaching can help them better understand their leadership styles, their strengths and weaknesses, and how they can alter their behavior to enhance their effectiveness. Since they need to learn to coach as well, the experience of being coached will teach them about coaching behaviors and processes. Coaching discussions can also provide important feedback on the change processes as development progresses.

Desired business or organizational outcomes:

$\updownarrow$

Human resource outcomes needed to support business outcomes:

$\updownarrow$

Behaviors, skills, or attitudes required to support human resource outcomes:

$\updownarrow$

How coaching, or relationship-facilitated, on-the-job learning, can help promote the development of desired behaviors, skills, or attitudes:

# 2

# An Overview of
# Developmental Coaching

---

In this chapter, we describe the following:

- The goals of developmental coaching
- The relationship of developmental coaching to other forms of coaching and counseling
- Who provides developmental coaching
- The core elements of developmental coaching

---

W e define *developmental coaching* as relationship-facilitated, on-the-job learning, with the most basic goal of promoting an individual's ability to do the work associated with that individual's current or future work roles. While we do believe that there is more to an organizational-level coaching capability than the act of coaching itself, that act is, nevertheless, the essential technology on which all else in the coaching organization is built. Developmental coaching can take different forms and be provided by a variety of individuals from within and outside an organization. There are some important commonalities across all of developmental coaching regardless of who is providing it and whether or not it is being provided formally or informally. In this chapter, we examine those commonalities.

# The Goals of Developmental Coaching

Developmental coaching, as already implied in the previous chapter, has multiple goals. At the most fundamental level, developmental coaching helps individual employees learn from their working experience. The practice of developmental coaching rests on the fundamental assumption that the challenges associated with work bring with them opportunities for learning. We further assume that employees, at all levels, must learn in order to be effective in their roles. This latter assumption is particularly important in economies fueled by knowledge, innovation, and creativity. In such contexts, the status quo is routinely being overthrown, and employees are either creating or adapting to a new reality.

Of course, the need to adjust to a new reality isn't driven only by the changing nature of work. We can see the same need to adapt over the course of the life cycle: as the individual enters the world of work, learns how to establish deep and romantic relationships, starts a family, and so on. When considered in the light of personal development outside of work, we get a clearer sense of how to view the goals of developmental coaching. Growth and adaptation require the individual to learn new behaviors and skills and be able to demonstrate those behaviors and skills on a routine basis. However, successful passage through any of the major stages of adult development brings with it not only a new group of skills. One feels different. One sees oneself and the world in a very different way. One progresses from feeling "in over one's head" as a new parent, for instance, to feeling at least moderately competent (at least sometimes, we hope!) (Kegan, 1994). Although our identities remain the same in many respects, development changes us.

Work role changes and organizational changes may require a comparable level of personal growth. The transition from individual contributor to first line supervisor, for instance, involves the need to learn to see oneself as a manager or leader who is responsible for organizing and directing the work of others and who works through others rather than working independently. Similar complex transitions take place as individuals progress to higher levels of management (Charan, Drotter, & Noel, 2001).

It is an interesting exercise to ask a group of professionals about the most important "coaching" relationships they have experienced. We usually phrase the question this way: "Think about the person or the people you have worked with in the past and from whom you learned the most. These are the people who left you in better shape than they found you. You think back about working with them, and you can see that you are quite a bit better at your work for having known them. You may actually feel as though you are a better *person* from having known them." Most everyone can relate to such a question (though, sadly, a few people in each group find that they cannot).

The individuals remembered in response to such a challenge include previous managers, older or more experienced colleagues, peers, teachers, sports coaches, consultants, and sometimes parents. A number of things are striking about such memories. They often bring with them a remarkable level of gratitude. They are also long-lasting memories, sometimes going back 50 years or more. These individuals are frequently remembered in the context of very powerful "peak" experiences. When describing the outcomes of such experiences, participants in our programs often use phrases such as "I learned a lot, but the more important thing is that I became more self-confident"; "I didn't realize what I was capable of"; or "Having been challenged like that, and having survived, I realized that I had been selling myself short."

Hall (2002) has captured the multifaceted set of developmental outcomes that propel a successful career. These four facets of development include the following:

- *Improved performance:* the ability to effectively accomplish required tasks. Performance is the measure that we most closely associate with an evaluation of career success. The fundamental question here is whether or not the individual has and uses the skills, or competencies, required to do the job well. As described above, as organizations and roles change, the skills required for effective task performance will likely change. We're always in the business of developing new skills. On reflection, however, we can see that having and using the skills necessary to perform a task properly is necessary but not sufficient for a successful career through time.

- *Attitude:* how one evaluates one's role and career. If I don't on some level enjoy the use of those skills or the rewards associated with using those skills (intrinsic and extrinsic rewards are both important here), then, ultimately, I may leave the role, career, and/or organization. Attitude is influenced by one's degree of motivation to use the skills required to perform, how one believes the role associated with the use of those skills is seen by others, the material rewards of the role and career path, the work-life issues involved in managing participation in the rewards, and the climate and organizational culture within which the work takes place. Self-confidence and self-efficacy influence attitude as well. The impact of attitude on career effectiveness is illustrated in Case 2.1.

## CASE 2.1    The "Anti-Coach"

A story from a successful nurse-manager in a large hospital illustrates the powerful impact of attitude, in this case self-evaluation, on performance effectiveness and career choice. In her first job after graduation, Jane experienced the unfortunate fate of working for an "anti-coach." Her supervisor, an embittered individual who felt her own career was going nowhere, managed by exception. Jane, as the new nurse, got attention only when she made a mistake. Literally, she was left to learn most of what she didn't learn in college (which was most everything she needed to know) on her own. She had no way of coming to grips with the mistakes that inevitably result from a trial-and-error learning process. She began to feel that she was not competent to do her job and was not cut out to be a nurse. This was a devastating conclusion for a young woman who had pursued a career in nursing and who still owed a small fortune for student loan repayment. She began to make plans for leaving the hospital and nursing. Luckily, however, fate intervened. Jane was reassigned to a much more supportive supervisor. She began to rediscover her reasons for pursuing a nursing career in the first place. She began to recover some of the confidence she normally felt. (She had been an excellent student, for instance.) She also began to view her own development process in a more realistic fashion. She knew she'd have to challenge herself and that she would make some mistakes. Her new supervisor also saw this as part of the normal learning process and helped her through those moments when her performance was, in fact, inadequate. Jane went on to have a successful and enjoyable career in nursing and became a well-respected leader of other nurses as well. This fundamental shift in attitude was critical to her ability to manage her career effectively. Without this attitude shift, she would not have been in a position to use the skills she was struggling to develop.

- *Adaptability:* the ability to deal with change. Performance and attitude have a short-term time horizon, addressing questions about one's ability to execute in one's current role and how one evaluates participation in that role. In the longer term, movement from one role to another, or the ability to respond effectively to changes in one's current role, requires the skill of adaptability. Adapting to changing circumstances requires scanning for external signals of change, a continuing interest in assessing those changing circumstances and one's ability to respond to those changes, the management of one's identity (see Case 2.2) in relation to such changes so that one has some sense of personal continuity, an interest in continuous personal improvement, and, ultimately, the willingness to adapt (Hall, 2002). The ability to adapt allows us to change and yet remain who we are at the same time. The adaptable person is aware of what is going on in his or her environment and actively seeks out opportunities to interact with what are seen as important changes. Obviously, adaptability requires a foundation of skills in one's existing role, as well as the self-confidence required when it is necessary to step out of one's comfort zone. Case 2.2 offers an example of adaptability in action.

---

### CASE 2.2    Everything Is Changing

John had been an executive in a financial services firm for a number of years and was very satisfied with his career and the rewards that it brought his way. He began to realize, however, that consolidation in the insurance industry, new technology, changing governmental regulations, and changing customer requirements meant that his business would have to make a fundamental shift if it were to remain competitive. He also realized that he did not have the skills to lead that effort. He had always been effective in an operational environment, managing costs while maintaining good customer service. He built a team of capable people who helped attain very good operational metrics. The time and costs associated with handling claims, for instance, showed steady improvement, an accomplishment of which John and his team were proud. Now, however, John needed to be a change agent. It became clear to him that his firm's ability to manage operations in a more cost-effective manner was replicable by others. The firm needed to build a new kind of relationship with their customers, one that would radically enhance their identity in the market place. John needed to learn how to craft a vision for such an effort and communicate that vision throughout the organization and beyond. He saw himself as something of an introvert, however, and occasionally referred to himself as an "overachieving bean counter." But he had a passionate interest in his firm and wanted to see it adapt to the changing times. He also knew that he liked a good challenge. He frequently read over the years about leadership and kept himself abreast of developments in the insurance business. John committed himself to building skills associated with becoming a more transformational leader. He was anxious about such a change and, at times, wasn't sure he was right for the job. Consequently, he sought out coaching from someone he felt could help him think about his work in a more visionary fashion. He had learned during previous developmental experiences, such as going through a difficult divorce, that trying to adjust to such a major life change by himself was a mistake. He also learned to rely on some of the better communicators within his team to spread the message as well. John took on the challenge of becoming a better leader, even though he had already won accolades for his previous accomplishments.

---

• *Identity:* an ongoing yet evolving sense of self. John, the executive described in Case 2.2, took on the challenge of adapting to significant changes in his role because of his sense of himself. Note that he had a good idea of who he was, his strengths, and his weaknesses. He was also in touch with a deep sense of commitment to his organization. He knew what he wanted. Identity refers to an individual's awareness of his or her values, interests, abilities, and plans (Hall, 2002). A career identity serves to guide an individual over time. At times, it can be easier to observe career identity by its absence, as demonstrated in Case 2.3.

---

### CASE 2.3    One Too Many Résumés

One of the authors recently worked with a very successful engineer, Tom, who was informed that his job had been eliminated subsequent to his firm's change in strategic direction. Such a turn of events should not have been a major catastrophe for this talented individual. However, he then began (against the advice of his human resources manager) to send out his résumés to a very wide variety of job openings within and outside of his organization, most of which related only marginally to his previous experience. Just as importantly, he didn't realize that recruiters and hiring managers would easily spot such evident desperation and confusion simply by looking at his résumé.

When asked why, Tom replied that he was just didn't know what he should do, so he thought he'd try whatever came along next. Though successful in his previous job from a career standpoint, he had been merely "going through the motions," as he saw it. He didn't feel any sense of commitment to his occupation or to any field, for that matter. From an occupational standpoint, he didn't have a clear sense of who he was. The lack of a sense of identity makes it very difficult to know what to do when times get tough or when times become confusing and to make the deeper commitments required to adapt to changing circumstances. Hall's (2002) work shows us that career effectiveness helps one build a sense of who one is over time, a sense of identity that isn't so narrow as to preclude adaptability, but at the same time isn't so broad as to leave one confused about where to take a stand. The engineer in this case did not end up changing his job; Tom ended up doing exactly what he had been doing, with another firm. He was still going through the motions.

---

Developmental experiences offer us broad lessons. We learn that we can adapt to change, and we learn something about how to do it. Perhaps we even learn to seek out change and its associated challenges. We also, however, learn more about who we are and about the core that we wish to preserve and take with us as we address those challenges. It is our belief that developmental coaching results in improved performance, a more positive attitude about one's work or work role, an enhanced ability to learn and adapt in general, and a clearer sense of one's identity.

Notice that the goals of developmental coaching are quite distinct from those of remedial coaching. Remedial coaching has the limited goal of fixing a performance problem. This usually involves a change in behavior, such as helping an abrasive executive control his temper through strict limit setting by his manager.

As we will repeatedly emphasize, developmental coaching helps both individuals and their organizations. The outcomes described here are of obvious benefit to the organization from a short-term as well as long-term perspective. In the short term, the organization gains an individual whose work performance and attitude are both enhanced. In the long term, the organization gains an individual more capable of adapting to changing circumstances and, as a result, more able to take on new roles and deal effectively with changing business conditions. Such an outcome is enormously important to any organization concerned about its leadership pipeline or existing within the confines of a restricted labor market. Finally, the organization benefits from an individual's sureness of identity. A clear sense of self and purpose typically promotes self-confidence, self-awareness, effective career planning, and ethical decision making, outcomes associated with longer-term organizational effectiveness.

Developmental coaching when provided by an organization, particularly when provided to current or future organizational leaders, should be viewed as an activity that has as its goal the development of the individual so that he or she can perform more effectively and authentically in the interests of the organization. Developmental coaching serves as a link between the individual and the organization. Ideally, the individual's goals and the organization's goals are sufficiently aligned such that this is a genuine "win-win" effort for both. (In fact, we would argue that in the absence of some degree of goal alignment, successful coaching is not likely to occur.)

An organizational view of coaching makes it easy to see why such a linkage must take place. Developmental experiences at the individual level don't necessarily require an organization's support. In reality, the organization can afford to be involved in development only when it serves the organization's interests as well. This is a very unique and, we believe, often misunderstood aspect of developmental coaching in an organizational context. This is not the same as an organization *imposing* skills, an attitude, and a sense of identity on an individual. When this happens, we doubt that real development can take place.

# Developmental Coaching and Other Forms of Coaching and Counseling

There are ambiguities surrounding the distinctions between developmental coaching and other forms of helping that occur in the workplace. Effective managers and coaches have always been interested in the "whole person" of the employee. Coaching discussions about career direction and work-life balance, for instance, are often extremely important from a developmental standpoint. There is then an overlap between developmental coaching and life coaching, though the goals of developmental coaching are often more focused. Confusion is likely to continue about the different roles that different approaches to coaching play in organizational life.

An exploration of the ambiguity surrounding the use of the term *coaching* is more than just an academic exercise. Managers, human resource professionals, external coaches, and those who aspire to be external coaches are often themselves quite confused about the distinction between coaching and other kinds of helping, particularly counseling. This can make it very difficult for those who purchase coaching services to qualify and manage those services. Furthermore, such confusion can act to significantly inhibit the actions of managers in particular, who may fear stepping into personal territory inappropriate to their relationships with employees.

In contrast to some other authors (see Berglas, 2002, for example) we make a sharp distinction between psychotherapy in the workplace and developmental coaching. While it is true that psychiatric conditions and personality disorders can impair work performance, we believe that it is not necessary to assess each and every coachee for such conditions. If this kind of disorder is thought to be present, the employee can be referred for help to the firm's employee assistance program or elsewhere. Indeed, if every organization required every future leader to undergo a psychiatric evaluation before participating in leadership development, very little leadership development would take place. Most employees would rightly experience such a requirement as a massive infringement on their privacy. Realistically, we must start with the assumption that the potential coachee is relatively healthy, particularly if the organization has hired or promoted effectively.

Developmental coaching addresses the individual's ability to enact a particular work role. That is why managers and others who are not expert in counseling per se can often be highly effective at coaching around specific work-related issues.

Developmental coaching in an organizational context can also be distinguished from what is often called "life coaching." The "client" in life coaching is the individual alone. Life coaching, closely related to other forms of individual counseling, may have a place in organizational life, particularly in the context of a firm's employee assistance program (EAP). In an EAP, the individual's well-being is the focus of the counselor's efforts. A "win-win" for the employee and the organization still exists, but the goals are less focused and the benefits to the organization are once-removed. EAPs have traditionally had the goal of repairing an employee's ability to perform (an indirect outcome) by repairing his or her health status (the direct impact of a successful EAP intervention). EAPs were originally designed as a vehicle for providing outreach assistance for employees with alcohol problems (Wrich, 1982). More recently, however, their focus has expanded to include the provision of a range of counseling services, including those directed at enhancing life, not just repairing the damage inflicted by illness. The relationship between an EAP counselor and an employee/client is almost completely confidential. Learning from work experiences to improve work performance is not assumed to take place. Indeed, the discussions between an EAP counselor and the employee/client may have nothing to do with work.

It is also useful to briefly consider the distinction between developmental coaching and mentoring. Again, we find that the two overlap. Developmental coaching has been found to be one of the tools that mentors use to help their mentees (Kram, 1988). Mentors and mentees typically have ongoing relationships, frequently accompanied by a sense of emotional attachment between the two. While developmental coaching is a useful tool for a mentor, it is not necessary to have a long-term, ongoing relationship to provide useful developmental coaching, as long as the other conditions, described below, are present.

Developmental coaching in an organizational context, then, unlike most other helping relationships, has to serve two masters: the individual and his or her organization. (Formal, company-sponsored mentor relationships may also be faced with this challenge.) This has practical and ethical implications. Practically, developmental coaching demands that the employee receiving coaching and the manager or expert coach providing coaching remain focused on the needs of both parties to the relationship, not just the coachee's. Ethically, the dual responsibilities of developmental coaching in the work context requires that both parties set appropriate expectations regarding coaching activities and not portray developmental coaching as an activity focused solely on the goals of the individual. Both parties need to acknowledge that the demands of the organization be considered.

## Formal and Informal Coaching

The terminology of the business-related coaching field has become a proverbial gauntlet for the uninitiated. Is there a fundamental distinction between the coaching provided by managers, peers, and expert internal or external executive coaches? It is important in addressing this question to keep in mind that the goals of developmental coaching are those described in the first section of this chapter. There are multiple pathways for achieving those goals. There are certainly differences with regard to the activities and methods of each of these coaching resources. However, it appears that there is a core set of elements common to all forms of developmental coaching, regardless of the provider.

One useful distinction is the degree to which the coaching provided is formal or informal. Coaching can be thought of as formal when the coach and coachee "enter into a written or verbal agreement that coaching will occur" (Ting & Hart, 2004, p. 117). Traditionally, formal coaching activities were associated with the work of expert coaches, while informal coaching activities were associated with the coaching provided by managers or peers. In our studies of coaching managers, we have found that a remarkable amount of developmental coaching takes place on an informal and even spontaneous basis (Hunt & Weintraub, 2002a). A manager who has developed coaching skills and created a "coaching-friendly context" can have a brief learning-oriented discussion in which the core activities of developmental coaching occur and which results in the kinds of outcomes described in the first section of this chapter: improvements in task performance, attitude, adaptability, and identity. Such activities might not necessarily be labeled as coaching. Indeed, when individuals who have been fortunate enough to work for a coaching manager in the past first learn about coaching, this may be the first time they label such behavior as "coaching." ("That's what he was doing!" frequently accompanies such an insight.) Informal coaching can take place on the plane, over lunch, or at the water fountain. In health care, informal coaching often takes place at the bedside (or, in some instances, just outside the patient's room).

The coaching manager model of developmental coaching has many strengths, not the least of which is that the coaching manager is usually involved with the coachee on a routine basis and is intimately familiar with the coachee's work. Such informal coaching is an underrated but incredibly important stimulant for employee development at all levels.

We have also found that some managers arrange much more formal coaching sessions that are equally effective from a developmental standpoint. The choice to do so often reflects the context within which the work is taking place as well as the individual manager's leadership style. In this sense, then, some managers' coaching styles closely resemble that of expert coaches. Indeed, some managers enroll in formal coach-training programs in order to add that "tool" to their set of leadership skills, and developmental coaching is now taught in some MBA and executive education programs (Hunt & Weintraub, 2004).

As we began to discuss in Chapter 1, however, one can immediately see the complications inherent in a coaching relationship between a manager and a direct report. The manager is responsible for both helping and evaluating the direct report. The role conflict that can result has to be managed if the coaching is to be effective. We will address this problem in a variety of ways later in the book.

In a developmental coaching relationship with an expert coach, not a coaching manager or peer, the relationship exists solely for the sake of the coaching activity with which it is associated. While the coaching is paid for by the organization in most cases and the coach has to work with both the coachee and the organization for the coaching to be effective, the coach is not responsible for evaluating the coachee. This can be of benefit to the employee being coached, as it can offer the individual a greater sense of psychological safety and sense of comfort in being open about his or her learning needs and the real work of learning from difficult experiences, mistakes, and challenges. Developmental coaching provided by expert coaches is nearly always formal.

The important consideration with regard to who provides developmental coaching, then, is not so much the degree to which the coaching is planned and formal, but rather the degree to which the coaching relationship is focused solely on helping the coachee and organization or whether the coach (as coaching manager) also has responsibility for evaluating the employee. The highly skilled coaching manager can be very effective as either a formal or an informal coach to direct reports *if* he or she can create a coaching-friendly context.

## The Core Elements of Developmental Coaching

There are a number of different "schools" of coaching, ranging from the behavioral to the psychoanalytic. An in-depth discussion of these theoretical coaching models is beyond the scope of this book (see Hudson, 1999, and Fitzgerald & Berger, 2002, for a more detailed review of various coaching models). In reviewing the coaching literature and from many discussions with coaches and coaching managers, it would appear that a common factor among most is that of learning from action or experience, an experiential theory of learning (Wolfe & Kolb, 1984). This is a framework that we have found quite useful and that we have also found makes sense to business leaders. As such, we will describe the underlying mechanisms of learning in a coaching context through that lens, with the caveat that it offers what may be a somewhat limited perspective.

Experiential learning theory articulates the process by which learning takes place from action. Experiential learning interventions are particularly well suited for adults who are trying to build management and management-related skills. We can learn *about* leadership from a text or in the classroom. We learn how to *act* like a leader on the job by participation in activities that require the skills of the leader.

Learning from action requires several steps, and coaching, in essence, supports the individual engaged in learning through each step in the process. Action-based learning begins when an individual takes an action in the service of a goal. To learn from that action, the individual must then assess its effectiveness. This takes place in several ways. The individual learner may have a conceptual framework or set of standards against which the action and its outcomes can be compared. The individual can then explore the gap between desired performance based on those standards or concepts and what actually took place. Both self-assessment and feedback from outside the self are helpful in this regard. Based on this assessment, the individual learner then considers what modifications to make in his or her process of working toward the desired outcome, and tries again. The process continues until the individual has mastered the skills associated with the task, or it continues indefinitely as the nature of the task evolves over time. The latter would be true in times of ongoing organizational change, for instance. The core elements of developmental coaching are listed in Box 2.1 and are discussed in some detail throughout the remainder of this chapter (Hunt & Weintraub, 2002a).

---

**Box 2.1    Core Elements of Developmental Coaching**

- A goal-directed, willing, effective coachee
- A developmental coach: a coaching manager, peer, or expert internal or external coach
- A coaching-friendly context
- An opportunity to participate in one's own learning
- A coaching relationship (time and resources to support the relationship)
- The coaching dialogue: an opportunity for the coachee to reflect on the effectiveness of his or her actions
- Feedback from beyond the self (through observation, 360-degree assessments, etc.)
- The opportunity to continue the learning process, along with appropriate support

## A Goal-Directed, Willing, Effective Coachee

Developmental coaching is driven by the learner, not the coach. The learner, in this case an employee, has a need to take a particular action, and that need involves some type of role-related goal. The new project manager (an engineer) in Chapter 1, for instance, has to assemble a high-performing team in order to capitalize on an important business goal. If she has limited experience in hiring or doesn't know how to conduct effective meetings, for instance, she'll need to learn. She is motivated to do so by her interest in being effective in her role. If she doesn't want to be an effective project manager, she is very unlikely to gain much from a developmental coaching effort. (Career-oriented coaching discussions could be useful in surfacing her distaste for the role and in helping her consider the alternatives.)

To be an effective learner, in addition to motivation, this coachee must possess at least some ability to reflect on her behavior. She must be able to accept that learning inherently involves accepting some level of incompetence in the self, albeit temporarily. She must also be able to tolerate constructively delivered feedback. Most importantly, she must have some opportunity to take action related to her learning goals.

It should be noted that the term *willing* was included in this particular element. Developmental coaching is built on the shared goals of the coach, the coachee, and the organization. If there is not some alignment of goals across those three partners to the learning process, learner-driven coaching is likely to be impossible. Through the use of coercion, an individual can be forced to comply with the directives of the organization. However, that does not mean that learning will take place (Hunt & Weintraub, 2002b). This fact has significant organizational implications.

## A Developmental Coach

As we've already stated, developmental coaching can be provided by peers, managers, or designated expert coaches. However, to be a developmental coach to others, a foundation of coaching-related interpersonal skills is essential. These skills include the ability to understand the processes that lead to the desired results. Not everyone is able to watch a team meeting in action and be able to discern problems in the process of the meeting. Untrained observers reviewing a meeting in process are more likely to listen to the content of a discussion rather than the process. For instance, they often don't notice who is participating and who is not, who is listening and who is not, how conflict is being managed, and a range of other process-related factors.

In addition to the ability to observe both process and content effectively, developmental coaches also need to naturally possess, or gain through training, the skills required to create a coaching dialogue and provide effective feedback, both of which will be described below.

Other interpersonal skills are essential as well. These include the ability to listen, the ability to ask useful questions, and the ability to create rapport, among others. Increasingly, coaches, whether expert or coaching managers, must also be able to relate to a very diverse group of coachees. Development can be greatly influenced by cultural assumptions and the availability or lack of opportunities. The skilled coach is able to understand the coachee's learning goals within a culturally diverse context.

Such foundational skills by themselves are not sufficient to make an individual an effective developmental coach. When coaching developmentally, the coach has to learn to subordinate his or her perspective to that of the coachee, at least initially. This can be particularly challenging for the coaching manager, which is one reason that more talented coaching managers are often very careful about who they hire. They frequently seek out those who have, in addition to other required skills, the ability to engage in a coaching dialogue. The developmental coach needs to be able to take a helpful and supportive, rather than a punitive, stance toward the coachee. This requires the ability to suspend one's agenda when a coaching session begins, so that the coach can see the problem or challenge from the coachee's point of view. In doing so, the developmental coach is better able to help the coachee self-assess his or her performance. The coach who looks at the challenge through the coachee's eyes is also better able to help the coachee diagnose and address the learning need in question.

Finally, to underscore the obvious, a developmental coach has to have a good sense of the nature of "development." By this, we mean that learning is a process that takes place over time, perhaps even an extended period of time. In Box 2.2, the reader will find one of the most "user-friendly" developmental frameworks (Benner, 2001; Dreyfus & Dreyfus, 1986). Most effective coaches have discerned such patterns of development even if they have not studied developmental psychology.

---

**Box 2.2    The Dreyfus Model of Skill Acquisition**

Dreyfus and Dreyfus proposed the following model of skill acquisition, a model that has been built upon by a number of researchers, particularly from health care. They proposed a series of stages through which an individual must journey to achieve "mastery." As one moves through these stages, one relies less on abstract principles (taught in the classroom) and more on the lessons of an emerging set of concrete experiences. Through development, one also is increasingly able to view a situation from a systems or holistic perspective, rather than as a bundle of seemingly unrelated details. At the same time, one becomes more aware of which components of the system are truly relevant to the problem at hand. Finally, over the course of developmental experiences, one becomes more of an involved performer, less self-conscious, and more able to fully engage with the experience (Benner, 2001). The specific stages of the Dreyfus model are as follows (Benner, 2001):

1. *The novice stage:* The novice has no experience of the situation in which he or she is expected to perform. The novice can rely only on abstract principles, rules taught in the classroom, for instance, to the extent that he or she has been exposed to such principles.

2. *The advanced-beginner stage:* The advanced beginner can demonstrate minimally acceptable performance in what is still a relatively novel context. The advanced beginner has begun the process of turning a skill into the ability to perform.

3. *The competent stage:* The competent individual has been engaged in performing the task at hand for some time, years in some instances, and has a significant backlog of lessons from personal experience in performing the task.

4. *The proficient stage:* The proficient performer is a very effective performer who is able to see situations as wholes and understand the relationships between various aspects of a situation and contextual factors, and has a sense of the current situation in a longer-term context.

5. *The expert stage:* The expert no longer relies on analysis by itself, but rather has what has been described as an "intuitive grasp" (Benner, 2001, p. 32) of the situation.

Clearly, different sorts of learning experiences, and therefore developmental coaching, are appropriate to different stages of development. The novice requires exposure to situations in which he or she can put classroom knowledge into practice, but may require a great deal of guidance. Direct observation and supervision may be indicated on a routine basis. Additional regular teaching and reinforcing of concepts may be necessary. With further development, the coachee will be able to act more independently and, indeed, will probably desire the opportunity to do so. The right mix of self-assessment and feedback may be necessary throughout Stages 2 through 4 in Box 2.2 as the coachee is increasingly able (one hopes) to evaluate his or her performance, drawing on the lessons of experience. The expert may well be in the coaching role, if—and this is not a trivial "if"—the individual can reconstruct his or her own personal learning journey. Experts do not always have an easy time when it comes to coaching because they may forget how they came to develop their level of knowledge. Even so, the expert is likely to find that the opportunity to reflect on his or her work is useful. For the more skilled individual who is continuing to face new challenges, development never really ceases.

## A Coaching-Friendly Context

The attitude of the coach, as just described, is one aspect of the larger context within which coaching takes place. The coachee must sense that it is safe to be open with the coach about his or her performance. The coachee must not be worried about a punitive response from the coach or others in the organization.

Expert coaches, whether internal or external to the organization, have the luxury of being able to create a coaching-friendly context by defining a confidentiality boundary around the coaching relationship. In most such cases, coachees have some control over what information about themselves or the coaching reaches others. Any limitations to confidentiality are agreed to in advance. As discussed previously, the coaching manager is typically not in a position to promise confidentiality.

The coaching manager will be familiar with the coachee's performance and may have to take performance issues into account in the performance appraisal. For coaching to take place within a hierarchical relationship, the coachee has to believe that his or her manager will be fair in addressing learning-related performance deficits. What does this look like in practice? We are reminded of a quote from a recent interviewee: "My boss knows how I'm doing. There's no point in trying to hide anything, making something confidential. At the end of the day, she'll be reasonable about the whole thing."

The interviewee went on to say that he was confident that if he'd mastered the key aspects of his job by the time of his next performance appraisal, his boss would not revisit every little problem that had surfaced during the steepest parts of the learning curve. She would hold him accountable for learning the job. If he did so, she would not use his mistakes to justify a bad review (and this, in turn, would make her administration of the year's salary plan easier).

Trust is thus the cornerstone of the developmental coaching relationship and the foundation for a coaching-friendly context, regardless of who is providing the coaching. The coachee has to come to believe that his or her openness is appropriate. The coach encourages trust through how he or she reacts to the coachee. Is the coach supportive and empathic? Is the coach responsive to the coachee's agenda or needs, at least within reason? Does the coach act as a role model to the coachee, by asking for feedback on his or her efforts? Does the coach respond supportively rather than angrily when serious missteps are committed by the coachee?

A coaching-friendly context results from and facilitates a focus on the coachee, not on the coach. As already noted, this does create special challenges for the coaching manager. However, our research findings are clear on this point: Coaching managers can create trust and a coaching-friendly context through their behavior. If they evaluate the coachee fairly come performance appraisal time, the coachee will not be surprised by the evaluative feedback he or she receives.

Likewise, expert internal or external coaches can lose the trust of their coachees if they ignore the coachee's agenda and needs. Obviously, designated coaches can also lose the trust of their coachees if they violate whatever confidentiality boundaries have been established around the coaching engagement. It is critically important for the executive coach to be aware of how easily trust can disappear in such a sensitive context. In our research, we have found that when coachees believe that whatever confidentiality ground rules were established for the coaching engagement have been violated, they may not believe that it is safe to discuss this perception with their coaches. They may continue the coaching for a time, but be engaged only in "going through the motions." Real learning may cease.

## A Learning Opportunity

Developmental coaching, as described in Chapter 1, leverages existing work-related challenges for the sake of learning and growth. This implies that learning is less likely to occur when an individual is not being challenged. The coaching manager offers a direct report a challenging task. The expert coach is called upon to help the coachee deal with a new assignment. (A detailed discussion of how such tasks are framed is beyond the scope of this book; see McCall, Lombardo, & Morrison, 1988, for a more detailed discussion of the kinds of challenges that appear to drive leadership development.) Note, then, that classroom teaching is less likely to serve as a driver of development than is presenting someone with a challenge. From an organizational perspective, those who are faced with challenges have the most to learn and may be among those most likely to benefit from coaching.

## A Coaching Relationship

The existence of a coaching relationship may seem obvious, based on the previous discussion of components of developmental coaching. It needs to be highlighted, however, that coach and coachee must have access to one another, in addition to having trust in one another, for coaching to take place. An organization should not expect its managers to be effective coaching managers if they don't have at least some time for doing so. If an organization designates expert coaches to aid in the development of leaders, they must address the need for coach and coachee to meet, regularly, over a period of time. This doesn't mean that coaching requires the same amount of time as long-term psychoanalysis. In our research, we have found that one coaching session can have a developmental impact. Executive coaching engagements can range from 2 coaching meetings to 20 or 30 (Hunt, 2004).

Technology is increasingly being called upon to make accessibility possible in more decentralized or global organizations in which face-to-face contact is minimal. The telephone and the videoconference, for instance, are increasingly used to facilitate the maintenance of a coaching relationship and regular coaching sessions. Although formal research on such tools is sparse (see, for example, Guthrie, 1999, for a discussion of the experience of follow-up, telephone-based coaching), anecdotal evidence suggests that for some individuals in some situations, telephone and videoconferencing coaching sessions can be very useful. Most coachees in our studies, however, have stated that they prefer the face-to-face meeting when possible.

## The Coaching Dialogue

Experiential learning requires that coachees assess their performance and then define learning needs or specific challenges related to that performance. This takes place, ideally, in the context of the coaching relationship. It is facilitated by the coach's effectiveness in supporting self-assessment and reflection. Good coaches ask useful questions that encourage coachees to look at themselves and their performance in a nonthreatening fashion.

The process of reflection is enormously powerful. We encourage readers who are less familiar with coaching to remember a time when they were talking over a difficult or troubling issue with someone who was a particularly good listener. Can you remember the benefits to you of such a conversation?

Most of us remember such conversations as having presented an opportunity to see our perspectives in a different light and in the process gain new insight into the issue. Indeed, reflection can suggest new courses of action worthy of consideration.

Self-assessment via reflection allows coachees to take full ownership for what has happened in addressing their challenges thus far. It helps coachees define learning needs and goals for themselves. Once coachees have taken ownership for their side of the challenge, they are far more likely to take action. We also encourage the reader less familiar with coaching to consider the number of times his or her advice has been ignored. People like to take their own advice. One way to view coaching is that it helps coachees learn how to give themselves better advice.

It should be noted that the process of reflection runs counter to the underlying assumptions that dominate most organizational cultures, at least in business. Too much talk is considered "navel-gazing" or "introspection" and not real work. Most business leaders have assumed until recently that a bias for action precludes spending too much time thinking about a problem. In our experience, this is a defensive stance, driven by fears associated with working in a context in which mistakes are cause for punishment, rather than conversation. People keep moving because they are afraid to stop. A bias for action is good, but it must be understood that action brings with it the need to learn. Coaching, whether by managers or experts, creates a temporal space in which reflection is encouraged. In our interviews, individuals who have been the beneficiaries of effective expert coaching consistently report that learning the discipline of self-reflection, and the discipline necessary to take the time to reflect on one's work, was one of the most positive outcomes of their coaching experiences (Hunt, 2004).

## Feedback

Self-reflection typically takes an individual learner only so far, particularly if he or she is trying to learn complex skills in areas, for example, such as leadership, project management, conflict resolution, team building, and organizational politics. Feedback from outside the self supplements self-assessment and helps the coachee develop a clearer picture of what is happening, what is working, and what is not working.

Feedback can come from many sources and in many forms in the context of developmental coaching. Coaching managers can provide feedback based on their own observations. They can talk with the coachee's peers, direct reports, or customers. Coachees, human resource development professionals, and expert coaches can rely on multi-rater feedback protocols and instruments, commonly called *360-degree assessments,* as tools for systematically accessing feedback. Expert coaches also use a variety of psychological and business-related self-assessment tools that help coachees articulate the strengths and weaknesses of their personal or leadership styles, for instance. (An in-depth discussion of the technical aspects of data gathering, feedback, and feedback-related tools is beyond the scope of this book. We refer the reader to Chappelow, 2004, for a thorough discussion of 360-degree feedback.)

We want to emphasize, however, that the purpose of feedback should be to help coachees see that which they are unable to see by relying on their own senses. Too often, we associate feedback with punishment: "Let me give you some feedback" is often a prelude to a personal attack. Feedback that is "data rich" and is directed at the individual's self-defined learning goals, however, is much more acceptable even when critical. Part of the willingness associated with being a good coachee, as described above, is having a goal that is sufficiently meaningful that one believes it is critically important to face up to one's limitations in the pursuit of that goal.

The data-gathering process has significant organizational implications that we'll discuss in later chapters. The reality is that most of us do not work within feedback-rich contexts. In the absence of feedback, we may carry erroneous assumptions about both our strengths and our weaknesses. The organization has a powerful obligation, in our view, to do everything it can to provide helpful feedback to employees at all levels.

## An Opportunity to Keep Learning

This is a broad category—purposefully so, however. For learning to proceed, the coachee needs to have an opportunity to continue to engage in activities related to the development goal. If a coachee is struggling with the challenges of building a team, ideally, through coaching, that individual will form some ideas regarding how to change his or her approach. The learning cycle can then repeat itself. Coaching managers typically support coachees in their efforts to continually engage with a challenge by keeping them on the assignment while continuing to offer coaching support. Expert coaches may make themselves available to coachees through follow-up sessions, to facilitate their continued learning.

Beyond the need to continue to engage with the learning-associated challenge, there is tremendous variation with regard to how coachees, coaches, and managers support ongoing learning. This fact stems in part from the tremendous variation in individual learning styles, learning needs, and contexts. Coaching is a highly customized activity. One coachee may "get it" after just a few discussions. She may gain an insight that helps her see the task and her role in the task in a radically different way. Armed with that insight, she may move ahead quite effectively on her own. Another coachee may be facing tremendous emotional hostility as she tries to engineer a strategic shift in her organization. She may be attacked because of her gender. She may feel tremendously alone. For her, weekly coaching sessions and the occasional late-night e-mail, extending over a period of months or years, may be appropriate to help her stay the course and keep learning from what otherwise might be a devastating experience.

The high degree of customization, coupled with tremendous variation in learning needs, styles, and contexts, obviously represents a nightmare at the organizational level. How can those in human resources be expected to manage a coaching capability, let alone determine its return on investment (ROI), under such circumstances? We will discuss the problem of evaluating the impact of a coaching capability at the conclusion of this book. The individual variation associated with coaching represents its strengths and is one of the reasons for the growing interest in the field.

## Summary

This quick overview of the goals of developmental coaching, experiential learning, and the common elements of developmental coaching has, we hope, provided the reader with an overarching framework from which to view the organizational implications of creating a developmental coaching capability. As with individuals, organizations also vary tremendously in their needs and opportunities to promote development. In the next chapter, we will provide a conceptual framework that should help the reader consider the available options for building and then managing a coaching capability at the organizational level.

**3**

# The Coaching
# Organization Assessment

---

In this chapter, we present the Coaching Organization Assessment Exercise:

- This exercise helps decision makers consider in some detail the degree to which the organization is ready for a coaching initiative.
- The factors most associated with readiness for a coaching initiative are explored through a careful examination of the organizational culture, the business context, and, in particular, the business strategy, the human resource management context, and the organization's experience to date with coaching.
- The Coaching Organization Assessment Exercise can also serve to help organization decision makers consider how to best approach building a coaching capacity in their organizations.

A s we've already indicated, the organizational context within which coaching takes place has a critical impact on the likely success of a coaching initiative and the potential value that will result. In addition, the organizational context will very likely shape the decisions that organizational leaders, human resource/organizational effectiveness professionals, and practicing managers make regarding how the organization should approach a coaching initiative. In this chapter, we more systematically articulate the factors in the organizational context that impact the process and outcomes of coaching efforts. This exercise builds on the Coaching Value Chain Exercise, presented in Organizational Assessment 1.1, at the end of Chapter 1.

We present our discussion of contextual factors in the form of a self-study exercise that, ideally, will provoke thought and discussion among decision makers as well as those charged with helping decision makers consider their options. In subsequent chapters, we will present a variety of organizational-level coaching solutions and consider how the factors articulated in this chapter were addressed across a range of situations.

As with all human resource efforts, and we do position a coaching initiative as a human resource initiative, decision makers are faced with the question of alignment. Ideally, human resource practices fit together in support of one another, have an appropriate relationship to the organization's culture, and support the organization's larger goals. An in-depth organizational assessment helps decision makers think through how a particular coaching initiative would align with and support other organizational activities.

At the most general level of abstraction, four factors appear to be important in shaping the potential for an organizational coaching initiative. The reader will note that these factors both overlap and interact with one another. The first three include the organization's culture, the business context/strategy, and existing human resource management practices. The final and often overlooked factor to consider is the experience of organizational members, particularly leaders, with coaching itself. In our experience, this latter factor can be enormously powerful in shaping the evolution of the use of coaching within an organization. The reality is that most organizations have at this point had some experience with an activity labeled "coaching." The organization's experience with coaching, if positive, can be leveraged to support additional initiatives. If negative, those interested in promoting a coaching initiative may have some repair work to do.

Our intent here is not to suggest that all of these characteristics are necessary for an organization to embrace one or more forms of coaching as a means of developing talent. However, the presence of one or more of these characteristics supports the organization's readiness for a coaching initiative. If almost none of these factors is present, then those contemplating an organizational-level coaching initiative should consider whether or not such an investment of time, money, and sweat is likely to pay off. If, as is more likely the case, some factors are present while others are absent, then a force-field analysis or other diagnostic tool for change might be appropriate. Some of the factors that are absent may have to be managed, while others can be safely ignored.

Likewise, the factors that are present may call attention to linkages that can be reinforced by a coaching initiative and other cultural assumptions, business issues, or human resource management activities. For example, organizations with cultures that strongly hold to the value of promotion from within will be able to reap considerable return on their coaching investments, by offering coaching to recently promoted managers, for instance, to strengthen the likelihood that they will be successful in their new roles. Organizations undergoing a strategic transformation will gain by making sure that they direct their coaching initiatives at least in part at those responsible for leading the transformation.

The Coaching Organization Assessment is presented in Box 3.1. A "check" by a particular item indicates both that the individual item lends support to a coaching effort and that the particular factor may also suggest an opportunity to shape a coaching program in a particular way. We first present the assessment exercise in its entirety for readers who wants to get right down to the business of assessing their own organizations. Following our presentation of the assessment tool, we offer in-depth explanations for the various items. In the close to this chapter, we discuss the implications of this assessment with regard to the options for executing an organizational coaching initiative and offer an illustration of its use.

## ORGANIZATIONAL ASSESSMENT 3.1 The Coaching Organization Assessment

Review the statements in Box 3.1. Check those that apply in your organization. Each statement is worded so that a "check" indicates that the characteristic described would work to support a coaching initiative in your organization. Because of the difficulties of describing an organization's culture, we offer several examples, where appropriate, of the behaviors or other cultural artifacts that indicate the potential presence of the underlying value or assumption described as the heading for each characteristic (Schein, 1985). We do caution, however, that *these are only examples,* chosen to illustrate the cultural issue in question.

---

**Box 3.1    The Coaching Organization Assessment Exercise**

**The Cultural Context**

☐ In general, the level of trust within the organization is relatively high, as exemplified by the following:
  o Decision making regarding employees driven by organizationally held values, business strategy, and goals rather than by arbitrary, individual judgments

- o Leaders following through on commitments
- o Sharing of appropriate business information
- o Respect for confidential employee information
- o Tolerance for reasonable levels of dissent

❑ In general, employees are viewed as ends in themselves rather than just means to a business end, as exemplified by the following:
- o Actions that demonstrate an interest in helping employees at all levels try to match their work to their interests and career plans
- o Concern about stressful or unsafe working conditions and the taking of actions necessary to deal with such conditions when possible
- o Follow-through on manager/direct report scheduled meetings
- o A tendency to view employees at all levels as assets rather than as costs

❑ In general, relationships between peers, employees, and managers are valued in and of themselves, as exemplified by the following:
- o A trend toward teamwork
- o Efforts being made to bring employees together for both business and nonbusiness reasons
- o Recognition of the importance of acknowledging relationship transitions, such as when the life of a team draws to a close or during an organizational reorganization
- o Recognition of the importance of work-life balance concerns, community involvement, and the need for special responses to special employee needs, such as crises.

❑ In general, learning is valued, as exemplified by the following:
- o The provision of appropriate formal learning interventions through activities such as providing on-site courses and seminars, tuition reimbursement, and executive education
- o Assigning work that will require learning on the part of the employee
- o The telling of stories about valuable lessons learned, including lessons learned through mistakes
- o The use of formal or informal action reviews or postproject reviews to assess "lessons learned"

❑ In general, it is accepted that employees who are dealing with challenging tasks are likely to benefit from the opportunity to seek guidance from others, as exemplified by the following:
  o Employees asking for opportunities to discuss their concerns about jobs or challenges with their managers and/or peers
  o The alternative, which would result in no check here, is the organization valuing individuals who survive and succeed with very little or no help (i.e., "sink or swim")

❑ In general, organization-specific knowledge and experience are valued, as exemplified by the following:
  o A bias toward promotion from within
  o Respect for specific knowledge, often communicated in the form of stories, regardless of position in the hierarchy
  o Discussions of "Our Company Way" (e.g., the "HP Way" [Hewlett Packard]) that imply that "Our Way" is a positive differentiator.

❑ In general, the role of "manager" and the skills required to manage (whether dedicated manager or "working manager") are valued within the organization, as exemplified by the following:
  o Promising talent being encouraged to take on managerial responsibility
  o The provision of educational and other developmental experiences specifically directed at the challenge of learning the skills associated with management

❑ In general, there is a value placed on job performance and telling people the truth about their performance, as exemplified by the following:
  o Completion of performance appraisals on time.
  o Substantial time and effort being made by most managers to make the appraisal process useful.
  o Differentiation of rewards based on performance.

❑ In general, diversity is valued within the organization, as exemplified by the following:
  o Meaningful efforts to actively recruit, select, develop, and promote women and members of various minority groups
  o The provision of opportunities to discuss the challenges associated with career management for those in minority positions
  o The provision of career development support systems for women and members of minority groups

❑ In general, innovation is valued, as exemplified by the following:
  o Open encouragement by managers to employees at all levels to give voice to their "good" and/or "new" and/or "creative" ideas

❑ In general, there is a value placed on continuous improvement, as exemplified by the following:
  o Total quality management practices
  o A culture that encourages employees at all levels to openly discuss reasonable mistakes or problems, without threat or blame

## The Business Context

### The Business Strategy

❑ The organization's strategy is relatively clear and well-known by organizational members.
❑ The organization's strategy requires a future-oriented view of the organization; in other words, the strategy is a long-term one.
❑ The strategy requires at least some degree of organic growth.
❑ The strategy requires new leadership skills on the part of the current and future organizational managers to enact the business strategy.
❑ The strategy requires large numbers of employees to develop new skills and competencies to enact the business strategy.
❑ The skills and competencies required of managers and employees to execute the strategy have been at least somewhat clearly articulated.

## The Human Resource Management Context

### Human Capital Strategy and Challenges

❑ The labor market that supplies the organization is constrained; that is, there are fewer candidates available to fill job openings.
❑ The age distribution within the organization is such that large numbers of retirements may occur in the next decade.
❑ The organization has a relatively large number of individuals moving into managerial roles from individual contributor roles.
❑ Senior leaders perceive that there is a need to build leadership and/or managerial "bench strength."
❑ The organization appeals to individuals who will likely be interested in growing within their jobs and/or careers.

❑ The organization advertises itself in the labor market place as one that encourages employee development.

❑ The organization selects talent for a broad array of competencies rather than narrowly for technical skills.

❑ The organization selects for "cultural" fit in addition to selecting for individual-level competencies.

Human Resource Management Practices

❑ The organization has competency models or descriptions of highly effective performance that inform managers regarding appropriate selection and development targets and that can help employees plan development activities.

❑ At least some senior line managers are actively involved in the development and use of competency models or descriptions of highly effective performance.

❑ The organization provides feedback to employees with regard to their levels of effectiveness in demonstrating important work-related competencies through the appropriate use of 360-degree-feedback mechanisms or other related processes.

❑ The organization has an adequate performance management system leading to effective performance appraisals.

❑ The organization strives to learn from employees through the use of tools such as employee surveys, upward feedback, skip-level meetings, after-action reviews, and other means for attaining and disseminating employee learning for the purposes of organizational development.

❑ Managers are expected to actively intervene when direct reports have performance problems and receive support from the human resource function in doing so.

❑ The compensation system of the organization encourages managers to spend time on employee development or at least does not punish them for doing so.

❑ Compensation and promotion systems encourage employees at all levels to be helpful to one another. They encourage managers to take the time necessary to develop their direct reports, and they do not encourage a spirit of unhealthy competition.

Other Strategic Human Resource Development Practices

❑ There are ongoing, budgeted executive, and/or management development programs in place.

❑ Development activities tend to focus on strategy formulation, execution, and opportunities for improvement. Development is not limited to unrelated "events" or remedial "fixes" for performance problems.

❑ Senior managers are involved in the planning and delivery of executive and management development programs.

❑ Executive education activities are used to disseminate strategy and values, build leadership skills, and/or provide opportunities for groups of managers to build relationships.

❑ The organization has regular "talent review" meetings for the purpose of assessing and promoting the development of managers and senior-level individual contributors.

❑ The organization engages in a succession-planning process.

❑ Managers are expected to consider the development of their direct reports as an appropriate and necessary activity.

❑ The organization uses 360-degree assessments for development purposes in particular.

❑ The organization has encouraged the development of formal or informal mentor relationships.

❑ The organization plans to or already does assess the business impact of training and development interventions.

## Organizational Experience With Coaching-Related Activities

❑ High-profile senior managers have had satisfactory experiences with external, executive expert coaches, and they are willing to talk about those experiences.

❑ A number of senior managers have recommended external, expert executive coaching to others.

❑ External, expert, executive coaching is generally seen as a positive for one's career; it is not stigmatized.

❑ The organization has not made extensive use of external, expert executive coaches for the purposes of assisting those with serious performance problems or for the purposes of terminating employees with serious performance problems.

❑ In general, the organization has been satisfied by coaching provided by internal human resource management and/or organizational effectiveness staff.

❑ The coaching provided by human resource and organizational effectiveness professionals is generally seen as being conducted with an appropriate sensitivity to confidentiality.

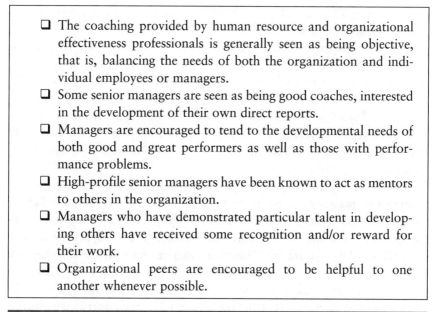

❑ The coaching provided by human resource and organizational effectiveness professionals is generally seen as being objective, that is, balancing the needs of both the organization and individual employees or managers.

❑ Some senior managers are seen as being good coaches, interested in the development of their own direct reports.

❑ Managers are encouraged to tend to the developmental needs of both good and great performers as well as those with performance problems.

❑ High-profile senior managers have been known to act as mentors to others in the organization.

❑ Managers who have demonstrated particular talent in developing others have received some recognition and/or reward for their work.

❑ Organizational peers are encouraged to be helpful to one another whenever possible.

## The Cultural Context

An organization's culture is manifested in employees' beliefs, values, and assumptions regarding what it takes for the organization to be successful in relationship to its external environment and in its integration of organizational members into a working structure (Schein, 1985). Culture is learned through participation in the organization and, over time, serves as a powerful behavioral guide. It isn't always easy to articulate such underlying values and assumptions, as they are often not discussed and sometimes not discussable. (These underlying assumptions and beliefs, however, are often reflected in and by the business and human resource practices we will discuss in the next section.) We suggest that those who are interested in exploring an organization's culture and its impact on a coaching effort spend some time talking in groups about these manifestations of culture. Consider the degree to which your organization shows the following characteristics.

### There Is an Adequate Level of Trust

Trust is a cornerstone of any learning effort, and coaching is no exception. Indeed, because coaching, whether by managers or by experts, is so personal and so intimate, a coaching effort may be more dependent on trust than are other learning methodologies. In the classroom, the putative learner can nod dutifully and still ignore really engaging with the teacher. Not so when it comes to coaching.

In a low-trust environment, it may still be possible to use expert external coaches, if what is said in the coaching engagement can remain confidential (though the outcome might not be as positive; see Hunt, 2004). In the absence of trust or some kind of safeguard, such as a guarantee of confidentiality, employees will not be open about what they don't know. And who can blame them? If you believe that admitting what you do not know will open you up to punitive career actions or emotional humiliation, it is unwise to discuss the matter.

We are quite aware that no organization is perfect in this regard. Competitive pressures, stress, personal pettiness, societal trends, the behavior of individual managers as well as the challenges of managing and working in a diverse setting lead to natural tensions that can impact the level of trust within the organization. However, organizations in which a majority of employees assume that the organization will try to act in good faith most of the time are more likely to generate the maximum return on their coaching investment, particularly if the ultimate goal of the effort is widespread coaching by managers. Organizational leaders encourage a culture of trust when they act as role models for the organization's stated goals and values, rather than as individuals attempting to manipulate the organization solely to meet their needs.

## Employees Are Viewed as Ends Rather Than as Means to an End

This assumption holds that organizational members have an inherent value and certain basic rights, regardless of their status. While most organizations cannot guarantee employment, for instance, the organization's leaders can help to promote a culture that encourages respect and takes the relationship between the individual and the organization seriously. Perhaps more important in the context of this discussion, the view of employees as ends rather than as means acknowledges the two-way nature of the employment relationship. Such a perspective suggests the value of seeing employees as human capitalists, individuals who are choosing to invest in the organization by virtue of their labor. As investors, they seek value, and the wise organization strives to maximize their value proposition beyond that of the paycheck (Davenport, 1999). Supporting employee development through coaching is one critical means of doing so. Perhaps no activity is quite so attentive to an employee's individuality.

## Relationships Are Valued

Developmental coaching is not the same as mentoring, but it is a relationship-based activity. Some organizations move people around, breaking relationships in the process, with little thought to what this does to the organization's "social capital." Relationships are the highway over which knowledge transfer takes place. Knowing whom to talk to about what, when one is in need, can be among the most valuable of competencies. Coaching requires relationship time. Coaching, particularly that provided by managers, often takes place informally. Ongoing relationships provide opportunities for individuals to get to know one another's strengths and weaknesses. Ongoing relationships also provide opportunities for trust to develop.

It is true that an excessive value placed on relationships (over performance, let's say) can theoretically inhibit direct feedback regarding an individual's weaknesses. You may not wish to offend a close friend or a direct report who has done you a significant favor. This is where the skill of coaching can be most helpful, a subject to which we will return. However, in the absence of an adequate relational context, there is little opportunity for coaching to take place.

## Learning Is Valued

It goes without saying that an organization that does not value learning will likely not value coaching. Most organizations espouse a value for learning. However, many organizations don't, or rather they don't value individual learning. If the cultural assumptions held by most in the organization support the expectation that all individuals are fully up to the tasks required of their work when they arrive on the job, they will likely view the need for individual learning as a barrier to performance. Of course, most organizational leaders will likely respond, rather quickly, that this is not true—and that in a rapidly changing business context, we're all learning, all the time. They may not, however, do the things that indicate that they truly value learning. The problem seems to be related to the conditions under which most organizations are founded and organizational control mechanisms that subsequently emerge from these conditions. The primary task of the emerging organization is survival: Find customers with a need and respond to that need in an economically viable fashion. The primary task of most organizations is not to promote learning. The control measures that are put into place subsequent to the organization's founding represent a means for accounting the critically important economic results of the business. Under traditional accounting rules, time and resources spent on learning are seen as costs—costs that ultimately weigh down on the organization's primary task.

Recent efforts to quantify the economic value of employee development from the human capital school of inquiry may lead to changes in this regard. However, even such enlightened accounting procedures are unlikely to change the basic impact of the lessons learned in the start-up phase of the organization until the organization is more mature. Learning under start-up conditions can too easily be viewed as a luxury rather than a necessity.

## Those Facing Challenges Should Seek Out Guidance

This set of cultural beliefs relates to fundamental questions regarding *how* people develop. Does development take place solely by struggle, by sinking or swimming? Or does development occur when challenges are coupled with appropriate feedback and support? Assessing an organizational culture along this dimension can be confusing.

We have known of organizations in which it would be seen as a weakness to ask one's supervisor for help with a problem: "Don't come to me with problems, come to me with solutions!" Amazingly, some of those organizations have been rather successful in making use of expert designated coaches (both internal and external) if the coaching takes place in a confidential context. (But note that *confidential* does not equate with *anonymous*. In the organizations we have in mind here, the fact that people are working with expert coaches is quite well-known.) This provocative observation reflects, we feel, the deep sense of conflict that many organizational leaders have about engaging actively in the development process and about the sense of vulnerability that by its very nature accompanies the development process. They may espouse a world in which only the strong survive and at the same time pay handsomely for coaching many individuals in their organizations.

Those who move up the organizational ladder under a "sink-or-swim" set of developmental assumptions often are able to do so because they have been successful at achieving the desired results. However, in doing so, they do not receive much guidance with regard to the processes by which results should be achieved. They don't necessarily know that their way is the best, most efficient, or most appropriate way, only that it happens to work. They don't know because they haven't really talked it over with another person. The lesson they have learned is "This is how you develop; you struggle, on your own, and you keep your uncertainties to yourself." While this may be the lesson learned by many leaders, they don't necessarily endorse the sink-or-swim approach—rather, it is what they know. So some leaders are aware that there is another way and are open to efforts (executed by others) to give a different approach a trial. They are not, however, in a position to lead that effort themselves. This factor in and of itself can create a sense of conflict for some senior managers.

Another and perhaps more subtle factor that can lead to a sense of conflict on the part of some leaders who were raised in the sink-or-swim school is their experience of vulnerability in the development process. The sink-or-swim development process encourages those who survive it to keep their own sense of vulnerability to themselves. As a result, it is difficult for them to conceive of how an intimate discussion about what one doesn't know, that is, a coaching discussion, could be appropriate. That kind of "letting down your guard" can appear threatening on both a political and a psychological level. On a political level, to discuss what you don't know with someone else creates the risk that your weaknesses will become public knowledge and undermine your credibility. On a psychological level, an admission of one's vulnerabilities to others could lead to a sense of shame and negatively impact the leader's self-image.

It is worthy of note that even the most "pro-coaching" cultures will likely experience some sense of tension over whether or not it is okay to ask for coaching support from others. This is likely to be particularly true at the higher levels of management in the organization. If there are significant examples of individual situations in which asking for help turned out well, that is a very positive indicator.

## Organization-Specific Knowledge Is Valued

*Organization-specific knowledge* refers to knowledge of products, services, and processes that are unique to a particular organization and that don't necessarily transfer easily to other organizations. It would appear on the surface that organization-specific knowledge would always be valued, but there are times when this is not the case.

When an organization is undergoing a radical change in strategy, the "old ways" may not be seen as being helpful. Rather, they can be viewed as barriers to change. Under those circumstances, wisdom, to the extent it is acknowledged at all, is usually imported from outside the organization. More commonly, however, organizational members are aware that those who have been around for a while may have valuable knowledge. Under such circumstances, there often may arise individual managers or contributors who are "natural" coaches. Their wisdom is acknowledged by many. Learning from them is seen as important.

Perhaps most commonly, however, firm-specific knowledge, particularly knowledge related to skills such as managing the political environment, handling culture appropriately, and knowing whom to ask for what, for example, is tacit rather than explicit knowledge, as already discussed. As tacit knowledge, it may be underappreciated. Even those in possession of such knowledge may not realize that what they know is actually quite valuable. In organizations that are most coaching-friendly, at least some key leaders are aware that firm-specific knowledge, both "hard" knowledge about products and processes as well as "soft" knowledge about people and culture, is valuable and that the transmission of this knowledge, often via relationships rather than the classroom, is a worthwhile activity.

## Management Is Valued

The (much-maligned in some companies) practice of management is critical to the success of a coaching initiative. Individual effort has to do with gaining results. Management has to do with helping other people gain results. In organizations in which the practice of management is not seen as valuable or relevant, coaching, as a management activity, may not be valued. Furthermore, those in management roles are not likely to allocate time toward learning processes, either for themselves or for others. As a result, their own skill sets are not likely to be strong, and unless they come by an ability to coach intuitively, they are not likely to be skillful in doing so. Furthermore, they are not likely to support the efforts of expert coaches, be they internal or external experts.

## Performance and Performance Management Are Valued

Organizations vary in the extent to which they emphasize individual accountability for job performance, typically expressed in the performance management process, as will be discussed further in the section on human resource practices. The cultural issue is the degree to which there is congruence in the organization between what is said about performance management and what really happens. Performance management, letting employees at all levels know where they stand in relation to their contributions to organizational goals, is often viewed ambivalently in organizational life. However, performance management, valuing performance, also has a significant cultural dimension. Organization members sometimes say they value performance, but they don't necessarily behave as though they do.

Discussions about performance and holding people accountable for performance is seen in some organizations as burdensome or bureaucratic. The manifestations of such a set of beliefs are plentiful. Reviews aren't completed on time, if at all. Their quality may be poor. Reviews may be done quickly, over the phone, with little or no preparation or care. Such behavior can reflect an underlying lack of interest in the managerial work of aligning individuals and the organization.

Alternatively, such behavior can occur in organizations that place such a value on relationships that organizational members are very reluctant to speak directly to one another about their performance. As discussed in the section on valuing relationships, the organization has to perform something of a balancing act in this regard. Relationships are important, yet performance is important as well. An imbalance occurs when accountability is completely sacrificed on the altar of the status quo. This imbalance can be accompanied by avoidance behavior, as described in the previous paragraph, or it can simply be manifested in a lack of straight talk between a manager and direct report about how the direct report is doing on the job.

Although we don't want to equate coaching and performance management, the two are related. When organizations believe in the value of effective performance management processes, they acknowledge that it takes work and careful attention to detail to make sure that people know what they are supposed to be doing, doing what they are supposed to be doing, and doing so by an appropriate process. A good performance appraisal takes an employee and his or her manager several hours to write and several hours more to discuss. It also takes a certain amount of courage to engage in direct and open talk about how each party to the employment relationship, the individual and the organization, are performing.

The setting and clarification of the link between individual and organizational goals provides a critical framework around which individuals can define learning goals as well as performance problems. As we will discuss in the chapter on defining success, in the absence of such clear linkages, individual learning projects, at all levels, may not contribute to the organization's progress. Organizations that value feedback also value telling employees the truth about where the organization is going and what individuals need to do to contribute.

## Diversity Is Valued

At first look, one may wonder about the possible link between a coaching organization and diversity. On closer inspection, however, it is apparent that the two are inherently intertwined. Organizations that truly value diversity, meaning building an organization that includes both men and women, people of color, and people of differing ages and is, in addition, global, creates a demand for on-the-job learning. Making a diverse organization work requires a great deal of on-the-job learning. Organizational members must learn to understand one another and be understood by one another. Leadership and teamwork, in particular, can be both more challenging as well as quite rewarding in a diverse organization. Diverse organizations that wish to be successful must in the long run create opportunities for people to learn from working with one another. Classroom learning about how to work in a diverse world is inadequate and must be supplemented by on-the-job learning.

It must also be stressed that in a diverse world, coaching can be more challenging and more rewarding as well. Diverse organizations must work very hard to make sure that expert coaches, be they internal or external, and managers who coach can manage relationships within that diverse context. This may require special training and development activities for coaches and managers.

## Innovation Is Valued

As when diversity is valued, placing a value on innovation will also require on-the-job learning if that value is to be exploited. Innovation requires change, whether it be in product or service design or delivery. Innovation challenges the status quo. Those leading innovation must learn to effectively communicate their innovative ideas to others. Beyond that, those leading change, a certain by-product of innovation, require more effective leadership skills, the kinds of skills that can be learned only on the job and with some help from managers, coaches, peers, and direct reports.

## Total Quality Management and Continuous Process Improvement Are Valued

Finally, we have noted that organizations that consider quality and continuous improvement to be of real importance create a demand for on-the-job learning as well. It is clear that disciplinary action and criticism will not root out people- and process-related errors. Indeed, such behaviors drive errors underground. Problems are hidden rather than addressed. Learning must be an integral part of the production or service process.

# The Business Context

Ultimately, it is the business context, the business policies, practices, and activities, that will likely have the greatest impact on the appropriateness and desirable shape of an organizational coaching initiative.

## The Business Strategy Requires Learning

Probably most central to the issue of whether or not a coaching initiative will be appropriate for a given organization is the degree to which (a) the business strategy requires an evolving set of skills and (b) organizational leaders believe that it is essential to a significant degree that organizational talent be "grown" instead of, or in addition to, "bought." Work that is high in learning potential is work that involves challenge and typically a change in the status quo. Most organizations have more than enough of both, but their leaders don't make the connection between business strategy and learning.

What kinds of strategic efforts are likely to promote a need for coaching? The list is quite long, but put simply, they are strategies that are future oriented (transformational strategies) and/or that rely on organic growth as opposed to growth solely through acquisitions. (We use the term *organic growth* here quite loosely. *Growth* may refer to growth in revenue or size, but it can also be thought of as an effort to become better and better at fulfilling a particular mission.) Obviously, organic growth implies that employees at all levels will be endeavoring to capitalize on new ideas and opportunities in the development and delivery of service or products and will be faced with the challenge of making the most of those ideas and opportunities. Customer intimacy, customer focus, and product leadership are just a few examples of the kinds of business strategies we have in mind here.

Regardless of the type of strategy pursued, the desired organizational goals will ultimately demand increasingly sophisticated efforts at execution. Execution requires leadership, organizational acumen, team building, performance management, and change management, just to name a few necessary skills. Depending upon the scale of the strategy and the challenges associated with its execution, many people may need to develop such skills. Furthermore, if organization-specific knowledge and values are critical to the success of the strategy, the organization's leadership has no choice but to plan on building much of the talent required internally (though during periods of growth, some talent will likely have to be imported as well). It should be noted that for the most part, hospitals, human services, and government agencies all have strategies for enhancing their effectiveness (if not growing in size) that require the development of internal talent.

This stands in contrast to strategies that rely heavily on the importation of talent, such as growth through mergers and acquisitions. It is not that mergers and acquisitions don't require learning on the part of those involved. In our experience, however, organizations that focus almost exclusively on growth through acquisition develop skills in, obviously, the management of mergers and acquisitions. Such organizations are less oriented toward the development of people, because that is not seen as explicitly related to the business strategy. There are only so many hours in a day.

As one interviewee from a financial services firm that had experienced repeated mergers over the past decade told us, "I've had seven bosses in seven years, and my chair hasn't moved." This employee had learned a lot about how to cope with changing authority relationships and changing visions. Most of that learning had, of necessity, been ad hoc and self-directed. The existence of some stability in relationships that might have allowed for thinking about the longer term was not there. Of course, many organizations pursue a blended strategy: Organic growth is coupled with some acquisition activity. Under these circumstances, employee development certainly does make sense, and, as such, a coaching initiative may be quite appropriate. Such an initiative might help to build the skills necessary to execute the firm's longer-term strategy while aiding in the integration of the merged organizations.

In addition to the content of a strategy, its articulation is also extremely important as a driver of the need for learning. It constantly amazes and alarms us how frequently the direction of the organization is for all practical purposes kept hidden from middle managers and employees. In the absence of a sense of direction that managers can comprehend and help their direct reports comprehend, people don't know what they are supposed to be learning. They may know what they are supposed to be doing today, but they will have much more trouble thinking about how to prepare for tomorrow.

Coaching and, indeed, all forms of executive, managerial, and employee development work best when the strategy is well articulated to the business unit, team, and individual levels and is stated as a set of outcomes and processes. The ability to execute the desired processes can then be somewhat easily translated into a description of the competencies required for doing so. These competencies will vary by function, level, and other contextual factors. They may not always be perfectly clear, particularly when the organization is moving into highly ambiguous but innovative areas. (One of the skills required for leaders in such a context is the ability to manage ambiguity on a personal level and the ability to help others manage ambiguity.) If the desired results, processes, and needed skill sets look at least *somewhat* clear, the opportunities for coaching, for helping people learn those needed skills, are enormous.

The importance of establishing the linkage between any coaching initiative and activities that are important to the primary task of the organization cannot be overstated. All human resource development activities must ultimately substantiate their value. As we will see when we discuss the question for understanding a coaching ROI (return on investment), the value of a coaching initiative is greatly enhanced not just when the coaching is effectively delivered to individuals who want to learn, but even more so when the coaching is targeted at helping people learn that which is important to them *and* the business.

# The Human Resource Management Context

Increasingly, we find that business strategy isn't the only context in which to look for mission-critical linkages between a coaching initiative and the needs of the business. In a knowledge-based economy, the effort to make sure that a firm has the right human capacity in and of itself can be mission critical. It can be helpful, then, to scrutinize the human resource management context of a coaching initiative as well.

## Talent Is Critical to the Organization's Success

If the organization is pursuing a growth strategy or if large numbers of retirements are anticipated, the acquisition of talent will be a preoccupation of the organization's leadership. This is particularly true if job candidates are in short supply due to labor market conditions. Either way, the development of employees who are in the firm is critical to the avoidance of a human capital bottleneck. Unfortunately, when the labor market is bountiful, particularly with individuals who have the skills the organization requires, organizational leaders can get out of the habit of thinking about talent acquisition and management.

If the organization is considering outsourcing a group or function, for instance, managers may feel that talent development within that part of the organization is less important. We could argue the case for an opposite conclusion: Outsourcing places new demands on the organization's talent, particularly given the global nature of much of outsourcing. Outsourcing also presents an interesting opportunity to an organization, that of providing access to another organization's talent. Is the development of the outsourcing partner's talent any business of the organization? Quite possibly, yes. The outsourcing partner needs to learn a variety of important skills to be able to execute the outsourcing contract. Ultimately, competition through talent will ultimately be critical to the success of most organizations.

If the organization is short on managerial talent or needs to develop greater leadership bench strength and anticipates the promotion of a large number of individuals into managerial roles, a coaching initiative may be strongly indicated. Coaching, because it is driven by on-the-job learning opportunities, may be the single most important means of aiding in the development of the skills associated with leadership. Certainly, classroom learning by itself is not likely to have a significant impact on an organization's leadership capacity.

When knowledge workers become important to an organization's success, the organization's leaders must consider the value proposition that the organization offers to current and potential employees. Does the organization appeal to individuals who wish to learn and grow? If so, a coaching initiative can contribute to this value proposition. Like other development activities, the coaching initiative sends a powerful signal of the organization's interest in fostering that development and supports an organization's advertised claim of its interest in "growing our people." We also stress that when organizations launch a coaching initiative, it is critically important in most cases to consider how the initiative's existence can be used as a signal to the outside world of its intentions in this regard. A secretive coaching program does not serve to attract candidates interested in growth.

A coaching initiative may also be relevant to a variety of selection activities in addition to recruitment. A growing number of organizations seek to hire individuals who have the right fit or possess competencies or characteristics that can't be taught. The organization that desires a team player or someone who is highly effective at dealing with conflict, for instance, should consider how it can build the search for such competencies into its selection processes. Coaching and other development activities can be very helpful but are unlikely to be sufficiently powerful to turn an iconoclast or die-hard individualist into a highly effective team player (and one should also question the appropriateness of trying to do so). Likewise, the organization that values cultural fit, the match between the individual's personality and the organization's culture, should similarly try to match employee characteristics and the organization's culture in the selection process.

After the selection process has taken place, however, much remains to be done to ensure that the "onboarding" experience of the new employee is successful. The employee who meets the selection criteria with some desirable and hard-to-teach skills will likely need to learn some new skills. If some of those skills are best learned on the job, coaching is indicated. Often, the lack of coaching by a new employee's manager sets the employee up to fail.

## Human Resource Management Practices

We begin to see, then, that organizations most likely to benefit from a coaching initiative are likely to have given considerable thought to skills as organizational assets to be refined, if not nurtured. The existence of competency models is a formal articulation of such an insight.

Competency models, descriptions of skills and other individual attributes that distinguish superior performance (Spencer, McClelland, & Spencer, 1994) are typically the responsibility of the human resource department. We define *competency,* a term we've already used, as an underlying characteristic of an individual that is causally related to effective or superior performance (Boyatzis, 1982). Furthermore, competencies include the following:

> Motives, traits, self-concepts, attitudes or values, content knowledge or cognitive or behavioral skills—any individual characteristics that can be measured or counted reliably and that can be shown to differentiate significantly between superior and average performers or between effective and ineffective performers. (Spencer et al., p. 6)

The investment of time and money required to accurately describe superior performance in key roles can be one indication of the strategic importance with which skills are viewed by an organization. It is an even more positive sign when senior line managers take significant responsibility for the stewardship of the competency model. It is one thing when human resource professionals talk in terms of the development of competency and quite another when senior line managers do so.

For a competency model to be of any use other than for selection purposes, employees must gain access to feedback regarding their effectiveness in relation to those competencies. The use of 360-degree or multi-rater feedback, particularly for development purposes, is a positive indicator of the need for coaching. Coaching can help employees who undergo a 360-degree-assessment process make sense of the feedback they receive and organize a development plan in response. We discuss the use and potential abuse of 360-degree-feedback processes in greater depth below.

Likewise, performance management practices can also be an impetus for a coaching initiative if, and only if, the performance appraisal process is effectively carried out. This requires that the manager and employee spend some quality time compiling and articulating performance data, which can then serve as the basis for a genuine discussion not only about performance results but also about skill strengths, weaknesses, and opportunities for development.

As discussed in the section on the cultural context, performance management is not typically on the short list of the favorite activities of most managers and employees. We would argue from a practice standpoint that a performance appraisal is among the most important services a manager can provide, as it serves to guide the employee as to the desired results and processes. Performance appraisal also plays an important role in the allocation of rewards and the promotion process. Finally, the performance appraisal meeting itself can serve as an important impetus to coaching discussions. Performance management and an effective performance appraisal system draw the attention of individuals to what they need to do to improve their performance. When this works well, it sends a powerful message.

Should performance management and appraisal include the use of 360-degree-assessment tools for administrative (salary and promotion, for instance) as well as developmental purposes? This has been the subject of a significant debate among human resource scholars and managers (see Eichinger & Lombardo, 2003, for a more in-depth discussion of these issues). In essence, there is evidence that when 360-degree data are shared with others in addition to the individual about whom data are gathered, raters tend to give higher scores to the individual being rated. The data then become less useful for the purposes of allocating rewards or development.

Moving beyond the simple application of 360-degree assessment to performance appraisal, in some firms, GE being among the best known, 360-degree data were used to sort out individuals into A, B, and C performers (Smart, 1999). Under such circumstances, a potential unintended consequence is that employees can feel pitted against one another. Performance ratings can then be seen as a competitive weapon rather than as a stimulus for continuous improvement (Lawler, 2003). There is no evidence that such practices actually result in performance improvement. One should consider, then, what forced ranking does to the climate for coaching. It may destroy the potential for genuine peer coaching along with creating additional tension in the manager-employee relationship.

Ultimately, 360-degree-feedback trends, along with employee surveys and other measures of organizational performance, should serve to promote both individual and organizational learning. We have been impressed with how many coaching initiatives have resulted in part from the use of such sensing mechanisms. In human resources and senior line levels, what those listening usually hear is that employees aren't sure what they should be working on; aren't sure about targets for development; don't understand career paths, if they exist at all; and don't know about appropriate opportunities for development. Furthermore, many talented employees (at all levels) will tell those in charge that they don't necessarily understand what "development" means.

Obviously, organizations in which managers are expected to develop their direct reports will likely be coaching-friendly. This is particularly true when senior managers serve as effective role models. A critical issue to consider here is whether or not they have the skills to help their direct reports develop. The expectation by itself is helpful but insufficient.

Finally, compensation systems should ultimately support performance and development and should not pit manager against employee or employee against employee. Clearly, in any performance-based compensation system, there will likely be only so much in the way of rewards to be allocated. The question here is one of balance. Are rewards seen, by and large, as being supportive of continued personal, team, and organizational improvement? If so, the reward system is likely to be seen as encouraging on-the-job learning.

## Supporting Strategic Human Resource Development Practices

Clearly, a number of the human resource management practices described above have a developmental aspect to them, particularly 360-degree assessment and holding managers accountable for the development of their direct reports. In this section, we highlight the organization's strategic positioning of development practices. A more strategic view of human resource development practices will likely support a coaching initiative.

This strategic perspective, one that links human resource practices and how the firm competes, begins the existence of an ongoing, budgeted set of executive and management development activities. This is another manifestation of the organization's commitment to development. The fact that such activities are used for strategic purposes, such as the formulation and dissemination of strategy in addition to skill building, speaks to the level of sophistication of the line and human resource leadership with regard to how to build linkages between skill building and the goals of the business.

Sending employees with problems away to "events" in order to fix those problems is just the opposite of a strategic approach to development. We discuss this further below when we look at the dangers associated with using coaching solely for the purposes of helping employees who are derailing. Any organizational activity can be stigmatized when used to fix performance problems that managers have been unwilling or unable to address.

Ongoing talent reviews speak to the active participation of line managers in the talent management process. A *talent review* is a meeting of line and human resource leaders within a business unit to discuss the current and future leaders and significant individual contributors and their learning needs. The results of a talent review can include feedback to the employee, an assignment to a coach, rotation into a particularly challenging assignment, and other developmental interventions. Talent review meetings, if they are to be effective, are held regularly. In some organizations, they take place on a yearly or 6-month basis. The routine use of talent reviews allows senior leaders within a business unit to assess an employee's progress over time.

Talent reviews are frequently associated with formal or informal succession-planning processes. Succession planning can take a variety of forms (Rothwell, 2001) but typically involves the taking of an inventory of talent in relationship to predicted leadership needs. In some organizations, specific individuals are targeted into specific slots, while in others, the intent is to ensure that the organization has enough individuals who are or will be ready to meet projected needs.

Closely related to talent development is the growing use of mentor partnerships, both formal and informal, to promote the development of specific individuals (Fritts, 1998; Kram, 1988, Kram & Bragar, 1992). Mentors, of course, make use of coaching techniques as we have described, though the mentor relationship typically has a longer-term orientation in most cases and focuses on the mentee's career above and beyond providing developmental coaching that leverages on-the-job learning. The mentor can also sponsor an individual employee's advancement through arranging for on-the-job learning opportunities such as participation in task forces and rotation into developmental assignments.

Note that we have not included the designation of a cadre of *high potentials* (often known as HIPOs) in this organizational assessment. The designation of a group of high potentials, in other words a group of individuals who are thought to be strong candidates for promotion and who as a result receive special attention, has not in our experience been a particularly strong predictor of whether or not a coaching initiative is likely to be successful. Some organizations have had good experiences while focusing on a few high-potential candidates, while others have not. The differentiator in our experience is the degree to which the organization is focusing some energy on the strategic task of thinking about tomorrow's results today and tomorrow's leadership needs today.

Finally, we have found that organizations interested in evaluating the business impact of their training and development interventions can be good candidates for coaching initiatives. If an organization has been focusing on event-based classroom development activities, they will likely discover through the assessment process that they are ignoring ongoing, on-the-job learning processes (Hunt & Weintraub, 2002a). The classroom by itself is insufficient to result in the building of meaningful skills in a number of areas and is particularly limited in its ability to promote the transfer of learning from the classroom back to the job. Coaching is the correct intervention when transfer of learning is desired.

# Organizational Experiences With Coaching

The items in this category address the degree to which coaching, in any form, has come to be seen as a useful tool within the organization. There are three different aspects to consider in this case: (1) the experiences of senior leaders with coaching, typically executive coaching; (2) the organization's avoidance of the stigmatization of coaching; and (3) positive organizational experiences with internal coaching (usually through human resources or organizational effectiveness), mentoring, and coaching by managers.

When senior leaders have had positive coaching experiences and, in particular, when they talk about those experiences or encourage others to work with coaches or refer others to coaches, they send a powerful message about the value of development. In our experience, this often occurs informally and sometimes through luck. As stated previously, coaching, labeled as such, has become something of a fad in the Western world. Not infrequently, senior managers will be susceptible to such a fad (this comes as a great shock to almost no one), and one or two will get a coach. If the coaching works out, senior managers will talk about it and others will start to imitate them. Such an endorsement in action by a senior manager or two is very helpful to any coaching initiative, though it can ultimately become a problem as demand grows, as we discuss in a later chapter.

The fact is that external coaches are expensive and not everyone needs an external coach. Usually, at some point in the coaching life cycle within most organizations, coaching starts to be "managed" as any resource might. Decisions then need to be made as to how to allocate that resource. When coaching is offered to high-potential, talented individuals who are in the right job, or who soon will be, coaching becomes associated, in the minds of the larger employee population, with career growth. This signals to those who are already doing their jobs well that the organization will help them grow even beyond their current capabilities.

Conversely, when coaching enters the organization as a remedial intervention for failing executives, quite a different signal is sent about the nature and value of coaching. Coaching, particularly since it takes place to an extent behind closed doors, can come to be seen, whether rightly or wrongly, as a signal that the organization is about to take action against a problem performer. Furthermore, coaching under these circumstances runs a greater risk of failing. Consider the case of a derailing executive who may be in the wrong job. She may be quite defensive about being assigned a coach—after all, this happened because something is wrong with her performance. Under such circumstances, the executive may be so defensive that she is unable to establish an effective relationship even with the best of coaches. The coaching becomes a ritualized activity that ultimately does little good.

Even if the coaching activity was engaged on the executive's behalf with the best of intentions from the organization's perspective, the failure of coaching may be perceived as evidence that coaching is at best a waste of time. We have interviewed a number of human resource executives who have been quite disappointed in the "results" of a remedial coaching intervention and have discouraged others (some of whom might have been much better candidates for coaching) from working with a coach.

Even when coaching for a derailing executive goes well, a variety of unintended consequences may result. If, in fact, the coachee is in the wrong job, he or she may end up leaving the company. So, now coaching becomes associated in the minds of others with providing help of questionable value to individuals who leave the company, resulting in a net loss of the investment placed in those individuals. As the CEO of a large insurance company told one of the authors, "I'm not going to pay to fix him up so he can go work for one of our competitors." Coaching then becomes stigmatized, an intervention to be avoided at all costs because of its association with failure on the part of the coachee. People come to believe, if they didn't already, that developmental interventions don't work: Good leaders are born, not made. Don't bother trying.

Finally, as many coaches and consultants have observed, coaches may be brought in to work with a derailing executive for reasons that are not openly discussed, even among those most closely involved. The hiring of a coach to work with an executive may be symptomatic of a range of other problems in the organization, such as poor selection processes (Hunt & Weintraub, 2002b). Worse yet, the coachee may never have been told that he or she is not performing adequately. A coach may be brought in to talk with an executive because his or her own boss is afraid to give honest performance feedback. Other employees observing the use of coaching under such conditions almost certainly see through such charades. They know that coaching is being used for the wrong reasons, to disguise managerial and human resource failures rather than to help with individual performance issues.

We cannot emphasize enough the dangers of the stigmatization of coaching. Nearly everyone associated with the field receives semiregular calls to intervene with a failing executive. Even the briefest assessment of the situation reveals that the organization is typically mismanaging someone with a performance problem and that a coaching failure is very likely. It seems very ironic and quite counterintuitive to propose *not* giving help to someone who might need it. In fact, we do believe that help should be offered to failing employees at any level. The place to begin such an effort is to make sure that the failing employee has been given adequate feedback from his or her manager and internal human resource professionals and that the employee's failure is not indicative of failures in other organizational systems.

This naturally leads to a discussion of the organization's experience with internal coaching. In most organizations of any size, there are individuals, often from human resources or organizational effectiveness but sometimes from line management, who are extremely good at providing developmental coaching. We have seen organizational effectiveness professionals in particular create a positive coaching context through their ability to provide effective coaching, particularly when they can do so for senior management. In a later chapter, we'll talk about the challenges associated with internal coaching, and there are many. Regardless of those challenges, however, internal coaches, even when working informally, can facilitate a developmental experience very similar to that provided by an external executive coach.

As with an appropriate and effective use of external expert coaches, effective coaching provided by human resources or organizational professionals also teaches the organization several important things. Such activities teach managers about the nature of relationship-facilitated, on-the-job development and learning-oriented conversations. This communicates the power of coaching better than any textbook. Such activities, again, signal the potential of coaching to promote growth, not just to help solve performance problems.

As just stated, internal coaches do have significant and challenging issues to keep in mind, however, as they can impact the perception that employees hold about coaching. First, the internal coach is likely to be especially scrutinized with regard to his or her ability to handle confidential information appropriately. Notice that we said "appropriately." The internal coach does have a duty to keep the needs of the organization in mind, even while trying to help an individual employee. Inevitably, the internal coach will likely find out information that could be "used" by others in the organization in a fashion that could be of some direct or indirect harm to the employee being coached.

When coaching an employee at any level who is having a difficult personal problem, for instance, the human resource professional may find that the employee's performance is impaired by a personal problem. The failure to handle this information in a sensitive manner can negatively impact the overall climate for coaching. The human resource professional in this instance may indeed have to help the employee and his or her manager address the performance problem. Assuming the performance problem was temporary and reversible, this situation shouldn't negatively impact the employee's long-term career objectives. However, if the same human resource professional found out through a coaching conversation about massive performance problems or unethical conduct, then he or she would appropriately alert other parties in the organization.

The question most employees will consider is whether or not the human resource professional engaged in a coaching discussion acted reasonably. Internal coaching, and indeed coaching paid for by the organization, should not be thought of as absolutely confidential. Coaching does not equate in that sense with counseling or psychotherapy. Most employees will understand the difference.

Similarly, the employee or manager seeking out coaching from an internal human resource professional will also likely be more responsive if he or she feels that the internal coach is willing to consider both sides of a problem. Too often, a coaching context can be soiled, if not spoiled, by internal coaches who don't have the courage to at least consider that the organization or some subset of the organization might be in the wrong. A manager might seek out coaching because he's having trouble relating to a very authoritarian boss. The internal coach will be much more effective if he helps the employee address the reality of the situation rather than try to ignore the very real limitations of others in the organization. Again, employees don't typically expect that an internal coach will always take their side when conflicts occur between an individual and coworkers, or the larger organization. But they do expect to receive an adequate and nonjudgmental hearing.

Regardless of whether or not the expert coaching is provided by internal or external coaches, it must be stressed that an additional important capability indirectly results from the process. In many cases, managers who have been coached learn to coach others (Hunt, 2004). Through identification, if via no other route, they take on some behaviors of the individuals who were helpful to them. This may be one of the most important vehicles for helping managers embrace developmental coaching as a commonly used tool in their leadership toolkits, one that is integrated with their other leadership activities.

Finally, and perhaps most importantly, one should also take note of the coaching behavior of managers in the organization, particularly senior managers, as, again, they set the standards for conduct. Do at least some senior managers actually encourage the development of their own direct reports? One can often see evidence by looking at the career outcomes for those who have worked for a particular manager. Are that manager's direct reports known for moving up to more responsible positions or for taking on important challenges?

Have at least some managers been known for holding learning-oriented conversations in addition to results-oriented conversations with their direct reports and with others? Are they known in the organizations and perhaps beyond for their service as mentors to others? Perhaps more informally, are at least some known as good people to talk with when one has an idea or an issue?

Finally, how has the organization responded to those who may invest some time in holding coaching conversations or in mentoring others? Have those individuals been recognized, even informally, for their efforts? Conversely, have such individuals been punished? We've known a number of coaching managers over the years who made it clear to us that they had to do their work in secret. They felt that coaching was the best way to build a strong team, but their bosses and peers did not share that view.

Before concluding this section of our discussion, we should also address the peer-to-peer culture within the organization. The basic question to consider when assessing the peer contribution to a coaching-friendly organization is whether or not peers are actively helping one another. In some organizations, peers are pitted against one another, through forced rankings, for instance, or through a belief the competition by itself results in the "right answer." The underlying cultural assumption in play here is that "helping peers is good for everyone." When this assumption is present, it should be relatively easy to observe frequent informal peer-to-peer coaching.

When cultural factors discourage peer coaching, it either doesn't take place or it takes place surreptitiously. It is always interesting to see in the latter case how peers can help each other discover various organizational dangers when no one else is willing to do so. The peer-to-peer relationship, unless it is defined in competitive terms, is a naturally collaborative one. Since peers do not evaluate one another, for the most part, it is relatively easier for a coaching-friendly context to take root. This is an untapped capability in most organizations, one that we'll explore later in this book. For our purposes here, we stress that when the organization naturally supports informal peer-to-peer coaching, that is yet another sign of readiness for an organizational-level approach to building a coaching capability.

## The Coaching-Friendly Organization

Having thought through how your organization stands in relation to the Coaching Organization Assessment, at the beginning of this chapter, the next question is how to interpret your responses. Most organizations have at least some characteristics that would promote a coaching initiative, and most have at least some that would inhibit such an effort. In this section, we offer a brief case example that illustrates how the organizational assessment process can help. This is a disguised case, but we run across these elements on a routine basis in our consulting work. (The results of BioTech's Coaching Organization Assessment are briefly summarized in Box 3.2.)

## Overview of BioTech

BioTech Co. is a growing medical equipment devices maker located in the midwestern United States. It is publicly traded and has been profitable for some time, though its margins have fallen over the past 5 years. The medical equipment business is rapidly changing, and, as such, BioTech must evolve strategically. BioTech had pursued an acquisition strategy for the past decade, until it found that the strategy was not paying off as had been hoped. The costs of the acquisitions and the difficulty in deriving any kind of synergy by linking with some of the acquired firms had undermined BioTech's profitability. Its core operations had also suffered due to lack of attention from senior management.

A new CEO stopped the acquisitions effort and renewed BioTech's more traditional focus on growth through internally driven new-product development and manufacturing strength. Research and development received a significant increase in budget and began the process of bringing into the firm a number of difficult-to-find (because of the experience required) scientists and engineers. In manufacturing, the firm focused on cost and quality leadership and began to implement an intensive total quality management program. The new strategy was aggressively communicated to the workforce, who reacted positively for the most part. The aggressive communications program was driven by senior management's belief that all employees would need to be fully engaged, highly motivated, and performing at the top of their game if BioTech were to be successful.

The human resource function at BioTech had previously focused its efforts on the rather Herculean tasks associated with integrating newly purchased organizations. Since the change in strategy, however, a new human resource senior management team had changed the function's focus considerably. First, they began to set up processes for sourcing the talent necessary to build up their product development pipeline. The labor market for this talent is quite tight, particularly in the regions where the firm has its two largest facilities. The value proposition they promoted to prospective and current employees emphasized the creative, collaborative, fast-paced and positive (i.e., trusting) nature of the BioTech culture. The recent employee survey suggested that this was, in fact, the way most BioTech employees experienced the firm, even those who had joined up through acquisitions.

Moving beyond recruiting, however, it became clear that the human resource infrastructure remained somewhat undeveloped. While the skills necessary for individual contributors to be successful were fairly clear (for those in R&D, be a great scientist or engineer, and for those in manufacturing, learn the skills associated with total quality management), BioTech leadership was not nearly as clear about the kinds of skills their managers would need to develop in order to lead the effort. Despite their belief in the importance of employee engagement, they were not clear with regard to their vision for the role of manager in the organization.

Of note, the senior management team and senior human resource leaders expressed the concern that their middle-manager cohort was quite weak. People had been reluctant to enter management in the past due to concerns about the relatively low status of the manager role at BioTech. Given its low status, even those interested in becoming managers were concerned that during the reorganizations that followed each acquisition, they might not be considered critical to the organization's future and would therefore be more likely to lose their jobs.

The compensation systems at BioTech were somewhat confusing. In essence, stellar performance, particularly in the scientific disciplines, would likely be rewarded. However, the previous regime had been reluctant to create a "star" culture, because they placed a strong value on teamwork. There was more concern with making sure that compensation packages at BioTech were competitive with the external environment, without much thought given to how compensation systems might support BioTech's strategy in other ways. Everyone at BioTech worked very hard. No one was rewarded for thinking about tomorrow's capabilities, however. The focus was on accomplishing today's goals.

BioTech had done little in the way of employee, management, or executive development until the past year. During that time, a major needs assessment had been accomplished, goals set, and a budget developed to support a longer-term vision for employee development. However, as stated above, the initial focus of this effort of necessity was on total quality management.

Performance management had typically not been considered a priority under the previous regime. Performance appraisals varied significantly in quality from one manager to the next. Employees were often unsure as to where they stood and how to advance within the organization. BioTech managers had a reputation for conflict avoidance when it came to performance issues. The lack of certainty with regard to effective performance and career development at BioTech surfaced as a major problem for employees on the organization's first all-employee survey, a problem that could potentially threaten employee commitment to the organization. For this reason, BioTech leadership began to consider what role coaching might play in helping to promote more effective and positive performance management and career development.

Their interest in coaching also stemmed in part from the positive experiences that several members of the new senior management team had had with executive coaching in previous organizations. Drawing on that experience, these senior managers felt that a coaching initiative might encourage employees at all levels to think about what they wanted out of their careers and might help them take a more intentional approach to their own skill development.

BioTech's only other experiences with coaching had involved the very sporadic use of executive coaching over the past decade for a few employees, typically at the upper-middle-management level, who were valued but uncertain as to their direction. These cases had generally ended on a positive note. It should be emphasized that these situations were not viewed as "fixes" for serious performance problems and most of those who had been given access to coaches in the past were still working at BioTech. Overall, however, coaching had not been seen as an important management function at BioTech to date. In Box 3.2., we briefly summarize some of the findings from the Coaching Organization Assessment.

---

**Box 3.2    The Coaching Organization Assessment at BioTech**

The following represents a summary of issues based on the case study above. In the interest of brevity, we have condensed some of the factors discussed in the Coaching Organization Assessment.

| *Factors That Would Tend to Promote a Coaching Initiative or Factors Upon Which a Coaching Initiative Could Be Built* | *Factors That Would Tend to Inhibit a Successful Coaching Initiative or That Should Be Addressed as Part of a Coaching Initiative* |
|---|---|
| • A relatively high level of trust within the organization.<br>• A cultural emphasis, apparently of long standing, on teamwork.<br>• A growth-oriented strategy that has been well communicated to managers and employees in the organization. | • (Perhaps) a cultural constraint on direct discussions about individual and team performance.<br>• Ambiguity about the role and value of management at BioTech.<br>• Lack of development of some aspects of the human resource management |

- A need to attract and retain human capital in a relatively competitive labor market context.
- A new senior management and human resource team that is actively seeking out input from employees at all levels.
- Positive experiences with coaching on the part of several senior managers. These senior managers are open to sharing their experience with others in the firm.
- Lack of stigmatization of coaching, as BioTech has not made extensive use of coaching for derailing executives or performance problems.

infrastructure, including competency, skill, and/or leadership models; lack of an acceptable performance appraisal system; and lack of a relatively clearly defined compensation program.
- Ambiguity regarding the role that managers should play in the development of their direct reports.
- Lack of widespread managerial experience in the skills on which a coaching initiative could be built, particularly those related to performance management and the giving and receiving of feedback.

## A Coaching Initiative at BioTech?

Most of those reading this case would get the impression that this is very much a firm in transition. Assuming that the current leadership has done a good job of analyzing their strategic opportunities, readers interested in leadership, human resource management, and employee development would feel comforted about the actions taken by the new leadership team, and, indeed, we felt that way ourselves. A visitor to BioTech leaves at the end of the day with the sense that "this is a good company."

The leadership is clear about their goals for a coaching initiative. They would like employees at all levels to receive good feedback regarding their performance, to know where they stand in the company, and to have some useful help in beginning to plan their own development. The leadership at BioTech views this as part of a strategy for recruiting and retaining good employees in a tight labor market. However, they also believe that the firm needs to change and to become more performance focused, while not undermining the positive aspects of the firm's culture. Stepping back to the Coaching Value Chain Assessment in Chapter 1, it seems clear that such an effort would support the direction in which the leaders hope this business will go.

This analysis suggests that, ultimately, BioTech will need a strong cadre of managers, many or most who are capable of providing developmental coaching to their direct reports. However, the assessment highlights a number of challenges that, in our opinion, BioTech must address before the organization is likely to be successful. These challenges include the following:

1. The senior management team needs to clearly define the role that managers will have in executing the new strategy. Is the role of manager to be given a higher status than was previously the case? A growing body of evidence demonstrates that effective managers are integral to business performance, particularly when employee engagement is central to effective business performance (Buckingham & Coffman, 1999).

2. What skills must managers have if they are to be effective? In our view, BioTech faces a significant management development task at this time. If the senior leaders at BioTech want middle managers to effectively engage employees, they should define the broad processes and skills required for doing so and then begin to communicate these to current and future middle managers. Coaching is likely to be one such skill, but probably not the only one of importance.

3. Once Step 2 has been completed, BioTech will be in a position to align its performance management and compensation systems in a fashion that will support coaching behavior on the part of managers.

But what does BioTech do now? The reality is that the leadership can start working on Steps 1 through 3 above and probably make some headway with regard to defining the roles, skills, and processes of the organization's managers. However, as anyone reading this book is likely to surmise instantaneously, that doesn't mean those managers will be ready to demonstrate the desired skills. There is much development work yet to be done. As the reader will perhaps also quickly guess, this a perfect opportunity for developmental coaching for those managers.

The question is this: Who should provide the coaching? Based on this assessment, BioTech has several options, including the following:

1. Identify members of the senior management team who have the motivation and skills necessary to do some coaching themselves. We already know that several have had good experiences with coaching, and

this suggests that they may have learned to use coaching in the process. Will they be willing to devote the time necessary for taking on such a responsibility? Some might do so because they enjoy coaching. Beyond that group, however, their participation will probably depend on how strategic the initiative is seen to be. If it is viewed as mission critical to interject developmental coaching into BioTech, some senior leaders, in our experience, will be quite happy to overtly build coaching time into their schedules. We have already clearly stated that in our experience, senior-management involvement is critical to the business success of any coaching initiative. That doesn't mean senior management paying "lip service" to the concept of coaching. It means that at least some senior managers must participate in coaching.

2. Make more aggressive and planned use of external executive coaches. We'll discuss in the next three chapters the form such an intervention might take. However, if coaching as a skill is lacking internally (this might be the case if too few senior managers are willing or able to coach), it can be imported to good effect. In brief, such an intervention would still require the senior management team to define the role and status of management, and either senior management or human resource management would have to define the skills the organization needs its managers to possess. Such a framework, as we will see, provides a context within which external coaches can successfully work.

3. Develop a cadre of expert internal coaches, from human resources and/or organizational effectiveness. If human resources is viewed as a helpful and trustworthy function, the talent in that area may be tapped as well. We will also describe what such a coaching intervention might look like. Again, we would stipulate that BioTech still has to define management roles and skills.

Would we recommend training a large group of managers to coach at BioTech, at this time? No. No matter how supportive the culture, in the absence of the necessary human resource infrastructure, such training may well not be as effective as the leadership, or we, would hope.

In the next chapter, we will begin to explore in greater detail the power of "defining success" as a critical foundation for any variety of developmental coaching.

# 4

# A Strategic Approach to Coaching

---

In this chapter, we describe the following:

- A strategic view of a coaching initiative
- The most fundamental outcomes of a coaching initiative that will likely strengthen an organization's overall coaching capability
- A comprehensive model for assessing a coaching initiative

M̲ost intentional efforts to build a coaching capability involve some type of initiative or program. Sometimes coaching is introduced into an organization in an informal or ad hoc fashion. Increasingly, however, coaching is introduced in a more intentional or formal way. Ideally, as we have said, such an initiative supports a business or organizational purpose. It begins when someone, perhaps from training and development or human resource management, decides to advocate for some type of coaching program. Most typically, such an initiative involves one of the coaching capabilities we have previously discussed:

- The organized use of a group of executive coaches, perhaps targeting a particular population of managers
- The development of a group of internal coaches, who may have a specific, targeted mission

- The development of a general coaching capability in a group of internal human resource or training and development consultants
- The training of a group of managers who will then be expected to provide developmental coaching
- The creation of a peer coaching program

Each effort presents significant managerial challenges that were mentioned in Chapter 1 and will be discussed in detail later in this book. Regardless of the nature of the specific initiative under way, we suggest in this chapter that the initiative be viewed from a strategic as well as a tactical perspective. In other words, each initiative has an immediate as well as a longer-term goal. The long-term perspective has to do with whether or not the initiative supports the development of a growing coaching capability within the organization. The net result of a strategically thought-out coaching initiative can be that today's coaching initiative serves as a foundation for more and better developmental coaching options for the organization in the future. In this chapter, we create a strategic scorecard against which coaching efforts can be assessed from just such a perspective.

This scorecard, then, is a bit different. In this chapter, we do not assess the coaching effort from the perspective of whether or not it supports the achievement of business results. It is a given that such a linkage is critically important. Rather, we explore the factors that appear over time to support the continued, positive evolution of an organizational coaching capability. In Chapter 5, we will give a description of a coaching initiative at the Whirlpool Corporation that was successful in part because of past decisions that were made about how coaching should be used in the organization. In Chapter 6, we will discuss the management of a coaching initiative, in this case an executive coaching initiative, in much more detail.

# The Need for a Coaching Strategy

Coaching is foreign to most organizations. For most people, the idea of sitting face-to-face with another person and talking over areas in which they can improve their performance seems unsafe, especially when that other person is the boss. Many, if not most, employees and managers don't necessarily believe that this kind of conversation will help, even though they may hold talks exactly like this daily with their peers. An intentional approach to such conversations can feel alien. It is the job of the person in charge of a coaching initiative to change that state.

What is the ultimate goal in thinking about coaching from a strategic point of view, in building a real organizational coaching capability? It certainly is not to create such a positive impact from the coaching initiative that the organization decides to provide an external coach for every employee. That isn't reasonable and would probably be a very bad idea in most instances. We will drive a stake in the ground, however, and say that, ultimately, *every employee should have access to coaching resources and should feel that he or she can make effective use of those resources. Every employee should have someone that he or she can talk openly with about on-the-job learning challenges and how to meet those challenges.* Our model employee here should ultimately be able to do so without fear of reprisal, either formal or informal. Those coaching resources should most commonly include his or her manager and peers. They may also include designated coaches from the organization's learning and development, human resources, or other functions and may on occasion, when warranted, include external experts. But the heart of a coaching capability for most situations will involve the employee (at any level) interacting with his or her immediate relational context.

This kind of outcome is not likely to be easily attained, given where most organizations begin. We have seen a number of organizations invest money and time in internal or external coaching programs that, ultimately, did nothing to support the building of a long-term coaching capability. Indeed, we have witnessed instances in which the opposite occurred: Employees became more cynical about coaching, less likely to seek out coaching, and less likely to offer it to others.

Any coaching initiative can be judged against a small set of factors that help promote such an (perhaps idealistic but nevertheless credible) outcome. Those factors are presented in Box 4.1 and discussed in detail below. We link those factors with business results later in the chapter for a more comprehensive assessment of a coaching strategy. The assessment of each factor can be made through reflecting on the underlying assumptions upon which the coaching initiative is based, with additional data being gained through the use of individual interviews and focus groups with those involved. The idea we hope to convey is that the presence of outcomes such as those described here helps to push the organization toward being one that has a *sustainable coaching capability*.

> **Box 4.1**    Coaching Initiative Outcomes That Promote a Sustainable
> Organizational Coaching Capability
>
> - Does the coaching initiative help those involved develop a better understanding of the uses and actions of developmental coaching?
> - Does the coaching initiative help those involved develop a better sense of the circumstances under which developmental coaching can be useful or not useful?
> - Does the coaching initiative promote an understanding and acceptance of the distinction between a performance problem and a learning curve (the errors that people make when they are faced with a learning and performance challenge)?
> - Does the coaching initiative promote an awareness of the critical importance of creating safe spaces within which coaching conversations, and therefore learning, can take place?
> - Does the coaching initiative help those involved build coaching skills themselves and recognition for the use of those skills?

## Outcomes That Support a Growing Coaching Capability

We now look at these outcomes in more detail. We do not claim that these factors are an exhaustive list. They were derived from our consulting practices. Each factor, likewise, will be more or less relevant to particular organizations, given their context, culture, and the state of evolution of their coaching capability.

### *Does the intervention help those involved develop a better understanding of the uses and actions of developmental coaching?*

Experience suggests to us that those who are promoting an organizational-level coaching initiative of any sort should start with the assumption that most people will not have a good understanding of what coaching really means, particularly developmental coaching. Coaching has approached "fad" status, it is true, but the phenomena behind most fads are sorely misunderstood. Developmental coaching in a modern workplace has some similarities to athletic coaching. There are many differences as well, however. This fact, coupled with clear evidence that coaching is one of the least used of all leadership styles (Goleman, 2000), means that most people don't know much about coaching.

What do we want those involved to learn about coaching? Ideally, they will gain a basic understanding of the various aspects of developmental coaching, as described in Chapter 2: the power of reflecting on experience, the role that thoughtful questions can play in gaining insight into the lessons of experience, the nature of balanced as opposed to punitive feedback, and the ongoing nature of the learning cycle in the face of a challenge. Most importantly, they will gain a real appreciation for talking about their work in the context of a supportive relationship. From successful and helpful experiences of being coached, they will learn about the technique and value of coaching. They will then be much more likely to provide effective developmental coaching to others (Hernez-Broome, 2002).

This has important implications for the management of coaching engagements, particularly those most likely to occur early in the evolution of a coaching organization. Quality and careful selection of coaches and coachees count! If initial experiences with coaching don't demonstrate effective coaching technique and generate positive coaching outcomes, the lessons learned from coaching will, of course, be confusing or negative. Case 4.1 illustrates this kind of difficulty.

## CASE 4.1    Was That Really Coaching?

During a recent research project, we had the chance to interview a young executive who had been assigned a coach to assist him in a very difficult transition period. He felt that his coach had been very helpful to him and that he had made it through this tough period in part because of that help. However, he didn't have a very positive attitude about coaching, which was puzzling. Further exploration of his experience suggested that he really hadn't been coached at all, as we have described the process here. He had gotten good advice. His coach was familiar with the organization and, in particular, some important political problems to be avoided. Instead of helping the executive find his own way through the political maze, he gave explicit direction as to what the executive should do: who he should make friends with and who he should avoid. The executive, feeling as though he had no choice but to place himself in his coach's hands, closely followed the advice he received. The result was that he became convinced that his coach was a master politician and that he, the coachee, was not. He didn't have any sense that he could do a better job the next time. When asked if he felt as though he had changed in the process, the executive said "no."

We are not suggesting here that the assigned coach did the wrong thing. Sometimes advice is very important, particularly if it is knowledgeable advice. However, advice by itself does not constitute development.

The coaching initiative overall was not hurt because of this one rather unusual case. The rest of the coaches, in fact, followed a more traditional coaching protocol, stretching their coachees to generate solutions and learn from the results of their efforts. Too many instances of "coaching" that aren't coaching, however, could result in bad experiences, leading to the creation of a negative image around coaching, or confusion.

Most organizations are introduced to coaching through the use of external expert coaches. In Chapter 6, we will discuss the challenges associated with deciding whom to choose for such an important role. For now, suffice it to say that this is a difficult decision in part because coaching is a highly unregulated activity. Most managers don't have a good understanding of coaching, and, unfortunately, the same can be said of some people in training and development or human resource management roles. The latter group needs to increase education about coaching before making such an important decision.

*Does the coaching initiative help those involved develop a better sense of the circumstances under which developmental coaching can be useful or not useful?*

The choice of potential coachee participants in any program is also important. One refrain we often hear from human resource managers is that "the people who need coaching the most just don't seem to volunteer for it." In fact, their lack of interest in or motivation for coaching may well reflect more serious problems in the fit between themselves and their current roles or organizations. Choosing individuals who "need it the most" but "want it the least" may well have the result of wasting the investment on two counts. First, they are unlikely to reach whatever goals have been set for coaching. Second, from a strategic perspective, they are less likely to help build a coaching capability (and ultimately, they may very well leave the organization).

Developmental coaching is really developmental. One of the things that surprises people the most is how poorly developmental coaching works when what is really being asked of the coachee is to comply with the demands of his or her job or to change personalities. Managers have every right to insist upon compliance with policies, procedures, job requirements, and strategies. However, when managers have to demand compliance, they should probably expect that, with few exceptions, those subject to such demands are not going to help grow the business. When coaching initiatives target development, they teach those involved the power of providing support to those who are already somewhat competent or who have a foundation for future competence. See Case 4.2 for an example.

---

### CASE 4.2    I Couldn't Believe What I Was Able to Accomplish!

Sue took over a very dysfunctional financial services group. Historically, they had been unable to accomplish their goals. The group had also become known for being a breeding ground for unresolved conflict. Her new boss advised Sue that she would have to make some changes. Several individuals in the group had absolutely no sense of the teamwork that was required of them. It was common knowledge that at least one other senior manager was technically incompetent and would have to be moved to another part of the organization. Sue had been chosen for the job because of her ability to manage change and deal with conflict. She was also someone the corporation hoped would achieve officer status in a few years. Her company had a program that offered executive coaching for managers in stretch assignments. Her boss asked her to consider taking a look at the program, not because she seemed to have a problem, but because, as her boss said, "Anyone in this role is going to need all the help they can get."

In reviewing her coaching experience, Sue reported that she could not have imagined how valuable it would be. The situation she inherited was far worse than had been described; however, her traditional approach, being very directive, was actually getting in her way. She had to learn to be directive in dealing with poor performers but at the same time also identify and build consensus among those in her group who really wanted to help her move the group ahead.

This was relatively new to her. Sue had read about consensus building but thought it was too "soft" for the kind of change management in which she excelled. This was a more senior-level group than any she had led in the past. She simply couldn't relate to them in the way she was used to. Those who felt good about the group's direction wanted to be involved in the decision-making processes: She had to learn to let them in.

Consequently, for the first time, Sue learned to let go, give tough assignments to others, and then coach them, rather than tell them what to do. She borrowed some of the techniques she had learned in her own coaching sessions. She was now a true believer in coaching and started to insist that others in her group learn to coach their own direct reports. Looking back on the experience, Sue felt that the assignment had really stretched her and though she probably would have been able to get the job done on her own, she had learned so much more through the use of coaching. She also felt that she had been more successful in building a team that could perform at a high level on a sustainable basis—and she didn't have to do it all herself.

---

This case is an example of the kind of outcome that one might expect from the appropriate use of developmental coaching. The individual involved was already a capable and committed manager. But she had the capacity do better, to learn more about her strengths and weaknesses as a leader, and to help her group achieve a high level of effectiveness by using coaching techniques.

One could ask, as we have heard, why the organization should pay for coaching for this kind of individual. She had already indicated that she could get the job done. Isn't that enough? It is enough if the only focus is on short-term results. If the mission of the organization, however, requires that it continue to remain competitive over the long-term, it makes sense to help individual employees, particularly those on whom the organization will need to depend in the future, harvest all possible useful outcomes from a particular set of on-the-job experiences. From a coaching strategy perspective, these insights help organizational leaders understand the value of coaching when it is used developmentally.

> *Does the coaching initiative promote an*
> *understanding and acceptance of the distinction*
> *between performance problems and the errors that people make*
> *when they are faced with a learning and performance challenge?*

A junior manager walked into his boss's office and explained that he was worried about one of his direct reports, who had really struggled over the past several months since being placed in a new assignment. The junior manager wanted to talk over the issue and perhaps get some ideas about how to help this employee, someone who had previously done a good job for the firm. The junior manager's boss replied, "We can't have that kind of thing going on around here. If he [the direct report] can't hack it, he's out." The junior manager began to defend his direct report, talking about his 2 years of solid performance prior to his current difficulties. His boss said, "Now you're defending him. Maybe this is your problem. Maybe you need to learn how to fire someone."

In reviewing this experience, the junior manager commented,

> You can't tell my boss about any people problems. Once you have, it is cast in stone. He doesn't have any feel for the possibility that someone can get beyond a difficult situation and figure a way out of it. He doesn't believe that people can change or learn anything.

We have been struck by how often we have heard this kind of story. The underlying premise is that people can't change. It may be a variation on the "leaders are born" theory. Such stories are probably also driven by managers' sense of helplessness. If they hear about problems, they have to fix them, and if they can't, they start to feel as though the problems are theirs.

A coaching intervention should, if at all possible, help those involved think about the idea that people can change, at least to an extent. It is true, personalities don't change a lot once we have reached adulthood. But behaviors can change. Even old dogs can learn new tricks. How many current managers and other senior-level contributors recall their own learning curves in dealing with the electronic boxes that sit on their desks (or the slimmed-down version that resides in their briefcases or pockets)? Most of us have learned to use computers in a fashion that we could scarcely have imagined 10 years ago, let alone 20 years ago. Most of us (well, some of us) have learned about the value of listening, patience, holding one's temper, and other critically important interpersonal skills. The concept of coaching is inherently built on the idea that individuals can continue learning, even when it comes to building their effectiveness in dealing with others. However, this requires the factors mentioned in this chapter: quality coaching experiences that help enhance the effectiveness of those committed to the process.

### Does the coaching initiative promote an awareness of the critical importance of creating safe spaces within which coaching conversations and, therefore, learning can take place?

The kinds of coaching outcomes discussed in this chapter require the steadfast maintenance of a sense of safety in the personal learning process. As we discuss throughout this book, one of the biggest single barriers to individual development through on-the-job learning is lack of a sense of safety in coaching-related conversations. The reality is that most employees, at all levels, are very concerned about impression management (Hunt & Weintraub, 2004) and do not believe that their bosses will be neutral and patient in judging their performance. There are two important lessons that those associated with any coaching intervention should learn about creating a safe space within which coaching conversations can take place:

• If the coaching intervention involves the use of external executive or designated internal coaches, whatever confidentiality boundaries are put around the coaching relationship should be maintained. Note that we do not say that the coaching relationship has to be confidential. However, whatever the coach, the coachee, and the organization through the coachee's manager and/or human resource professional agree to with regard to confidentiality should be honored in letter and in spirit. When this occurs, word will spread that designated coaches can be trusted. The organization's coaching capability will be enhanced.

• If the coaching initiative asks managers to create coaching relationships with their employees, the managers involved should receive a thorough education in the importance of managing employee mistakes appropriately, distinguishing between the mistakes that occur when people are learning and ongoing performance problems that may require managerial interventions other than developmental coaching. We will address this in greater detail in a later chapter, when we discuss the training of coaching managers.

Simply put, the desired outcome is that those who receive coaching believe that the purpose of coaching is to be helpful, not to be evaluative. Again, evaluation has a place, but that place has to be distinguished from the coaching context. We would emphasize here that we do not wish the reader to infer that organizations shield employees from the consequences of their actions. However, their actions should be viewed with perspective and taken into context.

This latter point is arguably one of the most confusing we have had to address. We offer one example that may be helpful: During a research interview, the CEO of a major corporation tried to describe how he manages the distinction between evaluation of his direct reports and the coaching of his direct reports:

> When one of my people doesn't make the numbers, he or she knows that there will be a price to pay. We are a publicly traded company. The whole world knows when we don't make our numbers. What am I going to do, yell at someone who fails to make those numbers? Is that going to help? I don't think so. I'll sit down and talk with the person about what they think went wrong, what got in the way. In coaching, we back it off from the obvious results and try to look at the process. My people have to know I respect them and want to help. We all know what can happen to any of us if we can't straighten things out.

In organizational life, the challenges are many, and stakes are high for most, if not all, employees. Creating a safe context in which people can talk about what they are trying to accomplish and how to improve their efforts is even more important when there are consequences for failure. Those who care about their work are always being tested in life. A "safe" coaching conversation can help someone who cares pass the test.

### Does the coaching initiative help those involved build coaching skills themselves and recognition for the use of those skills?

This outcome should naturally emerge from the ones described previously in this chapter. Having been exposed to effective coaching, gaining a better sense of when developmental coaching can work, and becoming sensitized to the learning process and the importance of creating a safety zone for coaching conversations, most participants should be better equipped to be helpful to others. We suggest that an explicit goal of most coaching programs should be that every individual who receives executive coaching at some expense to the organization should be encouraged to think about how he or she can turn that experience into a skill set so that they can be helpful to others.

Consider the alternative. What if those who have been through coaching at the company's expense do not report that they are more likely to try coaching others? What would be the implications of such an outcome? It could suggest that they need additional skills training. Fortunately, however, the research shows rather conclusively that those who have had positive coaching experiences are more likely to coach others (Hunt, 2004). If the organization does not receive some coaching capability "bounce" from the coaching initiative, it suggests that other aspects of the initiative may not have been executed in an effective manner.

## A Comprehensive Assessment of a Coaching Initiative

In this chapter, we have taken a "coaching-first" view of coaching initiatives to examine the underlying outcomes that ultimately support a growing coaching capability. To integrate the concepts from this chapter with those of Chapters 1 through 3, we suggest that the reader consider the issues raised in this chapter in conjunction with the more fundamental question articulated previously: Does the coaching initiative help the business? There are a number of possible outcomes when viewing a coaching initiative from these two perspectives. Box 4.2 graphically presents the alternatives.

| **Box 4.2**    Alternative Coaching Initiative Outcomes | |
|---|---|
| *I. A Coaching Initiative* <br><br> • Linked to business results <br> • Not necessarily supporting the building of a coaching capability | *IV. A Coaching Initiative* <br><br> • Linked to business results <br> • Supporting the building of a coaching capability |
| *II. A Coaching Initiative* <br><br> • Not linked to business results <br> • Not necessarily supporting the building of a coaching capability | *III. A Coaching Initiative* <br><br> • Not linked to business results <br> • Supporting the building of a coaching capability |

We'll start with Cell I, what some may find to be the most surprising cell. Some coaching initiatives support neither business results nor a coaching strategy. A coaching program that supports neither the development of a coaching capability nor business results typically emerges on an ad hoc basis, perhaps in response to the expression of interest from one or more employees or managers. The underlying assumptions for the development of such a program are often unquestioned (especially if they come from the boss) and erroneous. Developmental coaching is typically not the best way to deal with an employee who is truly derailing (Hunt & Weintraub, 2002a). The business is not supported. Because the program conveys a negative message about coaching and applies coaching for remedial purposes rather than developmental purposes, coaching goes to people who are not business leaders, with the result that coachees are not likely to become better at coaching and a coaching capability is not furthered.

More positively, as shown in Cell II, coaching initiatives may be designed to promote a business goal but still have less of an impact on the organization's long-term coaching capability. In an effort to promote effective decision making during a merger-driven integration of two firms, executive coaches may be assigned to key leaders. The purpose of such an initiative is to support business leaders in developing both business and personal plans during a time of change. (It is a given that some participants will not be members of the organization once the merger is completed.) The underlying assumption behind offering such a service is that coachees will be better able to make effective business decisions, as well as further their own self-interests, if they also plan their personal futures.

Although there has been no formal research documenting the effectiveness of such an intervention, the assumptions seem logical from a business perspective. Thus, the rationale may stand on the business case alone, although in reality, this kind of program may also have a positive impact on the merged organization's coaching capability (providing that some of those coached survive the process). While this may not be an important consideration in the development of the program, we argue that it would still be wise to consider designing into an intervention as many of the factors described in this chapter as possible. As we will see in the next chapter, one could argue that the coaching program initially designed to address a succession-planning challenge, from which the coaching capability at Whirlpool emerged, might fit into this quadrant.

Cell III describes what is in our experience one of the most common and problematic configurations: a program that is thoughtfully planned from a coaching strategy perspective but is not adequately connected to business results. Leadership development programs are common in most large organizations. A well-designed leadership development program frequently includes classroom activities and a significant coaching component. Participants are often carefully chosen, high-potential individuals. If properly designed, the coaching component may meet all criteria described in this chapter. The results may be quite positive from a coaching perspective, in that coachees will have a positive, developmental experience and learn a great deal about coaching themselves. However, in the absence of a tight linkage with the business needs, the programs budget, and perhaps many of the lessons learned in the program, may be vulnerable. A tight linkage is usually represented by a clearly articulated leadership development strategy that connects leadership development efforts with highly valued business goals. In the absence of a tight linkage with the business and senior line managers, those who participate will likely not have a meaningful opportunity to use on the job what they have learned in the program. What participants learned may ultimately be just as vulnerable to being lost as the program's budget during lean times.

This brings us to Cell IV, which we use as a transition point to Chapter 5. The coaching initiative described in Chapter 5 offers an opportunity to integrate most of what has been discussed in Chapters 1 through 4. Note the linkage between the coaching program and the business needs and goals. Note also the usefulness of a leadership model that serves as a bridge between the building of skills and business results. Note, finally, the evolution of coaching over the course of the previous 15 years at Whirlpool and the nature of a robust coaching capability there.

# 5

# Driving Strategic Transformation Through Executive Coaching at Whirlpool

*Joseph Frodsham, James M. Hunt,*
*and Joseph R. Weintraub*

In this chapter, we describe a major coaching initiative at the Whirlpool Corporation, which demonstrates a number of important organizing principles that we have discussed thus far:

- The power of linking coaching and desired business outcomes
- The usefulness of articulating the human processes that lead to these business outcomes in the form of a "leadership model" that offers guidance to individual coaches, coachees, and the organization
- The important role that senior managers play in making the leadership model credible
- The importance of careful credentialing and training of coaches so that the organization's point of view can be addressed
- The potential benefits of integrating coaching and other related leadership development activities

W hat happens when people visit Whirlpool Corporation's Insperience Studio in Atlanta's Buckhead neighborhood? They bring their chores with them. One man brought a bag of trash to crunch in the compactor. A family brought dough and baked bread. Jan Walters, manager of Insperience, a self-sell showcase for Whirlpool and KitchenAid brand products, sees such odd behavior as a good sign. Her company wants to change the way you buy your next washing machine. If that means bringing in a load of dirty laundry to do at their place . . . well, come on in. You won't need quarters. Whirlpool recently opened Insperience to address one of its key distribution problems: The "sea of white." "Customers go into a store, and they see row upon row of white boxes" (Kirsner, 2003, p. 32).

This is not your grandmother's, or grandfather's, Whirlpool. In 1996, then CEO and Chair David Whitwam came to the very challenging conclusion that Whirlpool, the largest appliance manufacturer in the world, had to change. The appliance business was becoming commoditized. "The decision as to how to respond was in our hands," said Whitwam. Whirlpool decided to adopt a very different strategy, one that would capitalize on its strengths in operational excellence and yet fundamentally transform the company. Whitwam envisioned a much more innovative Whirlpool, capable of building customer loyalty through a much more intimate relationship with customers around the world. Customers would experience a value proposition in their dealings with the firm that would bring them back, time and time again. This is a significant challenge in an industry struggling with long lag times between interactions with customers.

Whitwam also, as he said, "woke up in the middle of the night (!) and realized that we had to learn to lead in a different way." To transform Whirlpool, leaders at all levels of the company would have to augment their strengths as operational managers with a much greater ability to drive strategic change through transformational leadership. Given this challenge, it was clear that a significant leadership development intervention was required.

As ultimately became clear, the leadership development effort would require some traditional classroom time, as described below. However, it was equally clear that the classroom by itself would be quite insufficient as a means of achieving a fundamental shift in the leadership capabilities of Whirlpool managers. Developing transformational leaders required a set of interconnected development activities both inside and outside the classroom. Alignment across Whirlpool, a global company, required that the intervention include a set of experiences shared by all those in leadership roles.

A key element of Whirlpool's approach to developing senior leaders was a global executive coaching program directly linked with classroom executive education. This one-on-one coaching was key to equipping company leadership with the outlook and the skills required of transformational leadership by helping them apply and "embed" what was being learned in the classroom into their daily actions. The classroom experience was shared by all, and the coaching experience, which was highly coordinated, served the need to both transfer and translate learning in a global context.

## Coaching and Leadership Development Challenges

There is nearly universal agreement within and across most thoughtful firms that lack of leadership represents a real bottleneck, inhibiting organizations' abilities to change in the face of competitive pressures. A comprehensive approach to leadership development would appear to be a reasoned response to this state of affairs. However, some researchers have questioned whether or not leadership development programs deliver on their promises (Ready & Conger, 2003). The classroom, rather than the job, can too easily become the focus of learning activities, and little attention is paid to the transfer of learning from the classroom to the job (Hunt & Weintraub, 2002a). Effecting a balance between both classroom and on-the-job learning experiences seems like the most obvious response. But what should take place in the classroom? What should happen back on the job (Conger & Benjamin, 1999)? Most importantly, how can global firms coordinate a leadership development effort so as to ensure that everyone is aware of the firm's strategy and at the same time given the latitude to appropriately tailor the execution of that strategy to local conditions?

Coaching has been shown to be an effective vehicle for the transfer of learning from the classroom to the job (Olivero, Bane, & Kopelman, 1997). Furthermore, executives who have been coached often report that they are able to leverage that experience and learn to more effectively coach their own reports (Hunt, 2004). Yet significant questions remain regarding how organizations can make the best use of coaching (Hunt & Weintraub, 2002b). As described in previous chapters, if individual learning and organizational change are to support one another, coaching can't be seen as a stigmatized activity for those in trouble or as psychotherapy for the powerful. It must be viewed as an inherent part of the learning process. Whirlpool was fortunate in that regard, in that the firm had had very positive experiences with coaching and what has been described as a "coaching-friendly context."

A second challenge associated with the use of coaching as a tool for the transfer of learning is that of coordinating the coaching intervention so that it supports the organization's goals. Coaching appeals to the unique needs of the individual. As such, there is tension between organizational interventions that serve to focus the coaching and the need for the coach and the executive to have sufficient "room" to deal with unique and highly individualized challenges (Hodgetts, 2003). Managing this tension effectively is particularly important when the target of coaching is leadership effectiveness. When acting as a leader, the executive is called upon to bring his or her passion and commitment to the role. Coaching can be a venue for the executive to explore career goals and ambitions in a relatively safe context. How far can the organization intrude into the coaching context before the executive feels pressured to assume a "politically correct" but perhaps inauthentic stance?

As a third challenge, the tension between the need to coordinate and at the same time individualize coaching was particularly significant given Whirlpool's global scope. Whirlpool chose to align the inputs to the coaching effort through the use of their Leadership Model, to be described in the next section. The aggressive use of the model made it possible for executives and coaches throughout the world to tailor learning to the executives' personal and business unit needs as well as to the strategic context of Whirlpool.

## Leading the Whirlpool Enterprise: The Leadership Model

As the processes of transformation and leadership development at Whirlpool unfolded, the executive team (the senior eight officers of the firm) reasoned that leadership would ultimately be their only sustainable source of competitive advantage. But what did this mean? They had not codified what superior performance as a leader at Whirlpool looked like. This meant that too often, performance management and talent development focused on the demands of today, not the challenges of positioning the company for the future.

Working with an executive coaching firm long associated with Whirlpool, Dave Whitwam and his team began to develop the Whirlpool Leadership Model. The model articulates 12 attributes, practices, and performance descriptions that define outstanding leadership as practiced at Whirlpool. The Leadership Model is presented in Box 5.1.

---

**Box 5.1    The Whirlpool Leadership Model**

---

Attributes

*Character & Enduring Values*

Practices and remains committed to Whirlpool's set of enduring values and beliefs: Integrity, Respect, Teamwork, and Diversity. Demonstrates high integrity and develops organizations with unquestioned levels of integrity—never compromises because of the pressures of the day. Inspires and earns trust and respect as a leader. Displays behaviors that clearly show respect for others, with all their diversity. Puts the company's needs first and practices teamwork across all boundaries.

*Diversity With Inclusion*

Creates an engaging environment that leverages everyone's thoughts, beliefs, ideas, and opinions to achieve optimal results for the customer and the company.

*Confidence*

Demonstrates self-confidence and decisiveness—sharply distinguished from arrogance or egotism. Develops confidence in people and entire organizations that leads to responsible risk taking and ability to win.

*Thought Leadership*

Consistently challenges and improves thinking and decision-making processes and outcomes. Consistently offers out-of-the-box innovative thinking and sophisticated judgments that lead to results.

*Practices*

**Communications**

   Communicates clearly and with candor with all constituents. Practices active listening and two-way communications in order to enable alignment. Creates an environment that encourages and expects dialogue and debate.

**Customer Champion**

   Puts the customer at the center of every process and activity valued by the customer. Drives growth through relationship management, innovation, and the effective and efficient use of resources.

### Developing Talent

Attracts, develops, and retains top leadership and core competency talent throughout the company. Surrounds himself or herself with outstanding talent. Focuses on his or her own developmental needs.

### Management Skills

Demonstrates effective management skills in order to drive results through others. Effectively sets priorities, establishes individual and team expectations, facilitates productive meetings, provides candid feedback, develops people, delegates, and drives accountability.

### Strategy

Creates strategies that align and move the organization toward the accomplishment of the vision.

### Vision

Passionately creates a vision . . . communicates that vision persuasively, and aligns an organization around attainment of that vision. Helps organizations see beyond what is known today . . . and in the process accomplishes more than he or she ever thought possible.

*Performance*

### Driver of Change/Transformation

Anticipates the future of the business/work and creatively mobilizes resources to shape the transformation. Spends appropriate energy and resources working with the organization to drive and create transformation at all levels.

### Extraordinary Results

Consistently guides and leads the organization to extraordinary results against all dimensions of our vision, strategies, and balanced scorecard goals.

What is most noteworthy about this model is who built it and how it became the foundation for strategic leadership development at Whirlpool. Part aspiration and part empirical, the Leadership Model is not a competency model per se. However, it enjoys tremendous internal support and commitment because it draws directly on the experience of the senior management of the firm. The senior management team built it, and they own it, and for them it is connected directly to their ability to execute to the vision, aspects of which are built into the model itself (e.g., customer champion, driver of change, and diversity with inclusion). The penultimate statement of the Leadership Model, however, is the insistence that Whirlpool will be in the leadership development business, captured by the phrase "developing leaders who develop others."

Such an espoused value can, of course, generate considerable skepticism in many organizations: "Do they really mean what they say about our needing to develop others?" Jeff Fetig, now chair and CEO of Whirlpool, was asked, "What would you say to someone who made the numbers but perhaps wasn't paying much attention to developing his or her people?" Without any hesitation, Fetig responded, "That person would only be doing part of their job."

The Leadership Model represents what the Executive Committee at Whirlpool believes is essential if the company is to maintain sustained competitive advantage through its people and, in particular, its leadership. Through persistent use, however, the Leadership Model has, more importantly, become the "playbook": a guide to decision making and performance management that informs much of what executives in the firm do. It is talked about frequently, is used in coaching sessions (as described below), is part of every leader's regular performance plan, is a key element of the talent reviews that are conducted at every level of leadership, and is used to help form business strategies and plans.

Merely evoking the Leadership Model when the occasion arises, of course, doesn't result in its competent execution. Senior line management and leadership development staff designed a cascaded plan for developing leader capability on each element of the model. The result of this effort was a comprehensive program, Leading the Whirlpool Enterprise (LWE), a set of interconnected development activities that included classroom, action learning, and coaching. The first iteration of Leading the Whirlpool Enterprise, LWE I, as it was described, was rolled out for the top-100-plus officers at Whirlpool.

The program design called for all LWE participants to attend two 5-day training classes, in cohorts of 33, spread over 7 months. The first week of the program was presented by Whirlpool Executive Committee members and faculty from the Babson College School of Executive Education. Action learning projects were incorporated into this phase of the work. The first classroom session focused on elaborating the transformational vision and strategy of the firm and exploring its implications for business leadership. Participants were also introduced to the leader's role in coaching by one of the authors, Joseph Weintraub. The second classroom session was presented in collaboration with the Center for Creative Leadership, and as prework, participants completed a battery of assessment instruments, including a 360-degree assessment based upon the Whirlpool Leadership Model. The second week of LWE focused on building self-awareness and the individual dimensions of the Leadership Model.

The classroom experiences provided a carefully developed common language or map of the company's vision and strategy for attaining that vision. Participants talked about common business challenges and how they related to the Leadership Model. Both the CEO and president helped teach and facilitate these sessions. In doing so, they modeled the learning process and personally demonstrated the linkages between participants' development and business outcomes. Senior leaders described how a personal failure to listen to others' input (one anchor of the "Communications" practices component of the Leadership Model), for instance, resulted in faulty decision-making processes and costly project failures. Their self-disclosure was purposely intended to strengthen the coaching-friendly context at Whirlpool, encouraging others to be more open about their mistakes so that a deeper level of learning could emerge (Hunt & Weintraub, 2002a).

While the classroom was used to communicate a consistent message and create a shared experience for all participants, a parallel effort was made to attend to the challenges of individualizing the transfer of learning back to the workplace. At the close of the first week of LWE I, all participants completed a revised development plan called "MyPlan." Every leader at Whirlpool has a MyPlan document that is incorporated into their yearly performance plan. Within LWE, leaders revised their MyPlans to reflect session learnings and developmental goals in relation to the Leadership Model.

Between Weeks 1 and 2, Whirlpool provided each participant with an executive coach (a) to help keep the learning from the first week alive and (b) to help participants tailor and therefore embed what had been learned into their daily activities as leaders. A schematic description of coaching activities is provided in Box 5.2. The details of the various coaching activities are discussed later in this chapter.

It was hoped that working with an experienced coach would help participants strengthen their own coaching capabilities and further embed their capabilities to develop others. In line with the original leadership development plan, as the program cascades to the next level of Whirlpool leadership (below the top 100), this enhanced coaching capability can be used in formal coaching and mentoring relationships. (This is seen as a substantial challenge for Whirlpool, particularly in light of the fact that coaches and coachees are typically from different functions and global regions.) Having set the stage through a description of the business context, the leadership development context, in the next sections of this chapter, we describe the coaching experience at Whirlpool and its management in much greater detail.

Box 5.2    LWE External Coaching Support Program Flow

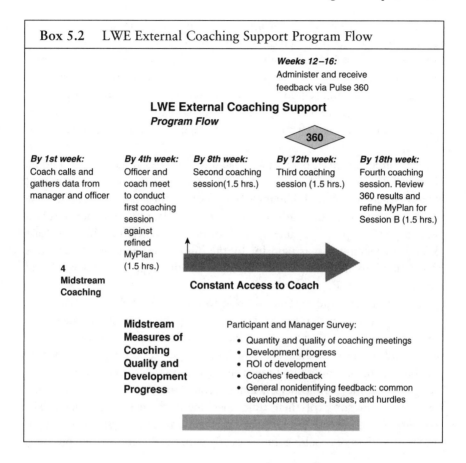

# The Context for Coaching at Whirlpool

As we've already discussed in previous chapters, in firms that have used coaching remedially, being assigned a coach can be seen as a signal of impending derailment. At Whirlpool, shared assumptions about being assigned a coach are quite different. The evolution of a positive attitude toward coaching happened "by accident," according to Dave Whitwam. Fifteen years prior to LWE, the Whirlpool board was working with the CEO on succession planning within the management team. As part of that process, for the first time, the company made use of industrial/organizational psychology services for the purposes of executive assessment. The psychologists chosen for the task also happened to be versed in the use of coaching or individual consultation to promote development planning and executive development. From the beginning, only those likely to be considered for future leadership roles were likely to be offered executive coaching. This represented a clear signal to the larger employee population regarding the intent of executive coaching. (Of course, it was also extremely helpful to the development of a coaching-friendly context at Whirlpool that the executive coaches brought into the firm at that early stage were seen as competent and ethical.)

As is often the case, over time, coaching activities began to proliferate. However, the linkages between those activities and the business were not always clearly articulated. Having come to represent a positive signal, some managers wanted to take advantage of the opportunity, whether it was a necessary and appropriate intervention or not. Executive coaching, at least executive coaching that is paid for by the human resource organization, is now limited to individuals who are in a small, high-potential pool and participants in LWE.

We should also add that in addition to the fact that Whirlpool's initial experiences with coaching were positive, a coaching-friendly context was consistent with the cultural values placed on relationships and mutual support found throughout the firm. Whirlpool employees are typically friendly and helpful to one another. Indeed, even before the current emphasis on "leaders who develop others," many senior managers at the company routinely spent some of their time coaching and mentoring others. The coaching connected to LWE leveraged this cultural support effectively, aligning the objectives of coaching more directly with the direction of the business.

## The Management of Coaching in LWE

The task of putting together a coaching program for over 100 global executives was a daunting one. Three overriding goals were attached to this part of the effort. First, the coaching had to be of a very high level of quality in all parts of the world. Second, the coaching had to be strategically focused on embedding developmental activities related to the Leadership Model and Whirlpool's organizational transformation. Third, to lessen the organization's long-term reliance on executive coaching to support the change process, each coaching engagement was to focus at least in part on helping the executive become more effective in developing others.

Fortunately, since coaching and therefore coaches had been part of the Whirlpool leadership development landscape for a number of years, assembling a team of possible coaches could proceed rather quickly. Referrals for the coaching component of the program came from current coaches (who were allowed to participate if appropriate) as well as human resource leaders. Executives who were already working with a coach were allowed to continue if the coach was willing to work within the parameters as described (i.e., to work and coach within the Leadership Model). Some coaches chose not to do so. Some coaches recommended by existing coaches were also screened out because of their unwillingness to embrace the model.

The internal certification process involved in-depth telephone and face-to-face interviews conducted around the world. These interviews had multiple goals: to educate the coaches regarding Whirlpool, LWE, and the Leadership Model and to assess their abilities and willingness to work within the Leadership Model and the logistical demands of LWE. Each coach was expected to be available to work with a number of Whirlpool executives. A thorough vetting of the coaches by Whirlpool was necessary in part because of the absence of any U.S. or global standards or professional certifications for executive coaching. (In addition, of course, thorough reference checks regarding their experience with and ability to work with senior executives were also completed.) It must be stressed, however, that the vetting was also required to link coaching to the strategic transformation under way. Even if there had been a global set of coaching credentials, this step could not have been left out. The vetting process obviously represented a major expense as well as a significant investment of time.

A number of coaches were screened out during the certification process. Follow-up interviews with LWE participants confirmed that the process had been helpful. Of note, during the LWE coaching process, negative feedback was received about only one coach, and that feedback referred to the coach's style, rather than any breach of the program guidelines. In general, the executives felt that the coaches understood Whirlpool and the tasks at hand.

In the follow-up interviews, all the coaches reported that the certification process had been helpful. Coaches reported that they liked working with Whirlpool clients because the environment was relatively supportive of coaching efforts and because once certified, they felt they could truly customize their work based on the executive clients' needs. The screening process, what might be termed an effort to manage the coaching at Whirlpool through managing its inputs, ultimately became an educational tool that left the coaches better able to understand and support the vision and strategy of the firm. At the same time, it facilitated their ability to empathize with the work of their executive clients.

The coaches who ultimately worked with LWE participants were a diverse group themselves. Some were trained industrial/organizational or clinical psychologists with extensive experience in business, while others were experienced business leaders who came to coaching as a second career. Nearly all the coaching was done face-to-face, and coaches were typically from "in country" or at least "in continent." Coaches were chosen from North America, Europe, South America, and Asia.

## Coaching Practices in LWE

Executive coaching, how to use it, its goals, and its boundaries in terms of confidentiality and reporting were described to LWE leaders in the first classroom experience. Though a serious effort was made to ensure that all participants understood the parameters of the coaching program, follow-up interviews still reported that some participants weren't clear with regard to these key aspects of the coaching process (we discuss this further below). Not surprisingly, the coaches who were quite familiar with those same parameters found that they had to review the details in the initial coaching contact with some executives.

To ensure that the momentum developed in the first classroom experience was maintained, each coach was to contact his or her coachee within the first week after the end of the first classroom experience and set up the initial appointment. The coach was also to telephone the coachee's boss. The process of goal setting in coaching involved a multiparty collaboration between the executive, his or her manager, and the coach. The executive could rely on previous 360-degree and performance appraisal data to help focus the coaching. The goals for coaching were also influenced by input from the executive's manager, who was charged with signing off on the goals to ensure that they were aligned with the firm's strategy and the executive's immediate situation.

In practice, this process was difficult at times. An executive's manager might be sitting in another part of the country, or the world. Opportunities for three-way discussions were impacted by geography and by time, as all parties were, of course, quite busy. Nevertheless, most executives found the coaching experience to be sufficiently helpful that they drove the process to a great degree. Those executives (the majority), who were able to engage in three-way conversations among themselves, their supervisors, and the coaches and who had helpful 360-degree data from which to work reported that the experience helped them clarify what they needed to work on to be successful.

Four sessions of coaching between LWE classroom sessions were paid for out of the LWE budget. In addition, coaches were expected to be available on a routine basis for telephone and e-mail exchanges, a service that was used to a considerable degree. Executives who wished to continue, and a number did, had to find funding for the effort from their own or their business unit's budget.

Finally, each participant could use a "Pulse 360," a shortened version of the Leadership Model 360-degree assessment to assess his or her progress. The participant was free to choose any of the components in the model, in line with his or her MyPlan and the work of the coaching. However, all participants were asked to assess themselves against the "driver-of-change" competency before returning for the second LWE classroom experience. Prior to the second classroom session, all participants were to have revised their MyPlan development documents based on their experiences in the first classroom session and coaching.

## The Experience of Coaching in LWE

There was widespread satisfaction with the coaching on the part of the executives. Satisfaction surveys indicated that participants uniformly recommended this component of the LWE program. A typical comment describing the coaching was made by a Whirlpool executive from the United States:

> I think that the external coaching was useful from the aspect of that all of us are a little resistant to feedback, but we need more feedback. And there is a tendency for external coaching for the feedback to be a little more reflective, and it takes [into account] the issues like the background in Whirlpool and how this is all going to play out there [i.e., the politics of it]. You can truly work on the issues and your understanding from the coach's perspective in that the only thing he wants you to do is to improve. None of what he says is couched in any politics. I think that coaching [i.e., the executive coaching received] was the best kind of coaching to get.

The strengths and weaknesses of the executive coaching model have been discussed in depth elsewhere (Hunt & Weintraub, 2002b). One of the most significant perceived benefits of executive coaching provided by an external consultant is that at its best, the executive coach can provide feedback with no hidden agenda. It is offered from a relatively objective outsider, in the interests of helping the employee improve his or her performance.

Many participants had been exposed previously to 360-degree assessments. However, such assessments by themselves, particularly if standardized, don't necessarily help the executive explore more deeply how his or her behavior may play itself out on the stage of daily life when dealing with a diverse group of stakeholders. The executive coaching was also frequently perceived, as hoped, to be helpful in embedding what had been learned into the executive's context. This comment is from another executive in LWE:

It's one thing to talk about what you need to work on and another to talk about how you come across to people on different occasions, or are aware of it in some of the other instances in which you deal with people. You may be aware of it [a problem with your behavior] in one or two different cases, but there may be four or five cases in which you're not thinking about it, and now all of a sudden when working with that coach, at least in my case, I became a little more aware of some other types of interactions that I ought to be careful about things with, and I think I made some progress with that.

The Leadership Model, and the fact that it was so clearly taken seriously within Whirlpool, was a valuable guide to the coaching process. In follow-up interviews, in no case did the executive or coach report that the use of the Leadership Model to help define excellent performance felt imposed. (Some executives did express the desire for an even simpler guide, with fewer performance attributes. However, the coaching also facilitated a focusing process that executives found was helpful. Not surprisingly, some reported that it was more straightforward to work on a few developmental goals as opposed to 12.) Rather, it was experienced as giving some shape and structure to the coaching effort. This is an important success factor when working within a culture that is used to a certain level of structure, as is the case, in particular, in most manufacturing firms. As one coachee reported,

It was a tool that we used in the coaching because everything is based on that. The Leadership Model wasn't that different from what we've used in the past, maybe more succinct, but it did give you the context of where your improvement needed to come. You picked areas from that Leadership Model to work on, and I think from that standpoint, knowing where to focus, it's very useful. It's a lot better than . . . I can remember early starting with the company, you would have appraisal reviews and you'd hear, "You've got to work on these issues," and then you'd have the next one and you'd hear, well "You've got to work on these issues," and they were different. [And you'd think to yourself] where did this come from? Here, your parameters are set, you know what you are trying to concentrate on, look for interactions between the elements and know where you are trying to go. So it basically sets your parameters, and you need that, or you don't know what you're going to be working on.

This participant's comments should serve as a reminder of the value of competency models with a manageable number of attributes that are used consistently over time and are clearly linked with the business strategy.

From the executives' perspective, the session-by-session coaching process, after the initial setting of developmental and coaching goals, was typically straightforward. As one executive from Italy described it,

I would report to her some business situations I was dealing with, and we would have an open discussion about how to manage the people involved and recognize what would be the best solution once again from a people management standpoint.

Consistent with good coaching practice, executives reported that the executive coaches offered stimulating questions far more than advice in the coaching process (Hunt & Weintraub, 2002a):

> He kind of provoked you by asking the right questions. About what is important. It was very helpful. Giving some hints. Not really advice because he doesn't have that kind of knowledge. But the methodology, the questions to provoke, were very good.

The coaching encouraged the executives to closely examine and, where appropriate, alter their behavior. It also provided a context in which the executive could develop as a person, through reflection on the self, relationships, and the larger context of his or her leadership challenges. These are practices now shown to be associated with successful executive coaching outcomes that create the most value from the executive coaching experience for the individual and organization, over the short term and the long term (Hunt, 2004).

Executives interviewed at follow-up reported that, in general, the "buzz" about the coaching was quite positive. However, the executives also reported that the coaching effort did take time and a sense of commitment:

> In my opinion, you tend to get out of that coaching pretty much what you put in. If you are open and you discuss the things that are concerning you or you are not so sure how to approach them and the like, you get very good suggestions. If you don't open up, probably you will get much less value for the money.

Not everyone is able to make the best use of coaching. The coach, of course, could also impact this process by his or her behavior. A number of the coaches mentioned the importance of providing encouragement, or "reselling" the value of coaching, early in the coaching engagement. The classroom experience was frequently motivating, but executives also found the task of trying to think and act strategically, to effect change while keeping the business going, to be daunting. It was easy to slowly but surely shy away from the challenge. Several coaches described the importance of looking out for the subtle de-motivators that impede the transfer of learning and positioning themselves with the coachee as an active and practically helpful ally in the process.

The critical challenge for executives is to learn to find some time and space to manage differently, to be able to focus on today, and tomorrow's strategy. This typically means, of course, that they need to delegate more and develop leaders to whom they can delegate. Coaching seems, when at its best, to provide an effective, bounded environment, encouraging the coachee to step back and focus on the long term.

From the coaches' perspective, a number of themes emerged. Like the executive participants, coaches found the Leadership Model to be helpful as a tool around which to focus their work. As one executive coach from Europe described,

> I worked with their Leadership Model and core competencies, skills, attitudes, and behaviors. I used that as a background. It was a very helpful tool in terms of the context of working for Whirlpool. What was helpful was to be able to work with the officers to be able to understand what these things actually mean. How do they show up in real life? It leaves some discretion about how to interpret the different components. A lot of my work was focused on helping them to understand if they were to be measured against this, what might it look like if they were being extremely good at this [particular competency].

Work with the Whirlpool Leadership Model then began with conversations between coach and coachee about how to make the model relevant to the participants' contexts. The coaches also reported the value of using the model to help participants stand back from the demands of the day-to-day operation:

> A lot of my work, even if it is with the director community, is about helping them to step back and take a more strategic overview, to understand the difference between being a day-to-day operational person and somebody who is actually at a higher level.

The dialogue around the translation from the model to reality was then tailored. Incorporating vision into one's leadership style, for instance, proceeded as follows:

> On vision, I get people to try to have the experience of creating a vision for themselves, so that they get a sense of what it is that makes a vision compelling. And then to begin to translate that into, OK, how could that look from an organizational or business point of view? Once I have done that, they find it easier to understand what it means. It is hard to grasp exactly what it is unless you could really sense it. Even at an officer level, they are extremely task oriented, focusing just on getting things done, lots of overload in terms of not having enough time.

The coaches talked of translating an understanding of the components of the model into action, addressing the ultimate strategic imperatives for the business. This component of the Leadership Model asks the participants to think about what they can do differently as individuals to enact a transforming strategic idea:

> People came out of LWE1 [i.e., Week 1] with a greater and a shared sense of what it means to create customer loyalty and customer intimacy, and the real goal for Whirlpool is ultimately to focus on its margins. Everyone recognizes that they are in an industry that has struggled mightily on these two dimensions, both on innovation but especially in terms of creating customer loyalty. And so they came to coaching with a sense that they have a mission to play a part in helping the company to get closer to the customer and create an experience that the customer is going to want to repeat. There is a rub associated with this, there is a reason that the organization hasn't been as customer focused, and so the themes associated with that tended to be issues of silo, so they didn't have responsibility, so while I'd like to do that I'm not able to do that because this part of the organization owns part of the process or production. So then OK, it sounds like we have an issue to work on about how you become influential in an organization in which you don't have ultimate authority to get something done that you now know is critically important to the way Whirlpool wants to differentiate itself.

Both coaches and executives reported that they repeatedly addressed people-development issues in coaching conversations. As one executive described, "It was a bit like a 'coach-the-coach' session. I learned a lot from being coached and from talking about how to coach in what was a very difficult situation."

LWE participants came from four continents, and their coaches came from three continents. It was somewhat surprising, then, that participants and coaches had few comments about cultural issues in the use of executive coaching. They reported that coaching is becoming more commonplace in large organizations around the globe. Increasingly, the concept is well understood. In addition, the extensive work put into finding coaches from each cultural or geographic area likely paid off in that regard, as it resulted in facilitated matching around cultural styles, at least to an extent. As one coach from Brazil said,

> Here the eye contact and shaking hands are important. We touch each other, and this is different. We need to have the coaches do this, not just what is normal in a Scandinavian environment or in the United States, where you maybe can do everything by phone. Personal contact is very important. I can work by phone, but in Latin countries we need personal contact.

## Lessons Learned at Whirlpool

The LWE process at Whirlpool continues. Whirlpool has not conducted a formal return-on-investment (ROI) study on the investment made in coaching. However, participant and Executive Committee feedback and a growing number of successful business "experiments," such as the one described in the opening of this chapter, suggest that the leadership development process overall is moving in the right direction. "Insperience" represents one example of the transformational shift that needs to occur between the firm and its customers.

More specifically, when coaching is embedded in the architecture of an overall leadership development effort, an independent ROI or comparable measurement on that one component of the program makes little sense. The participants view LWE as an overall experience. Isolating any one component is as a result very difficult, if not impossible. Nevertheless, senior line and human resource executives did spend considerable time in reflecting on lessons learned in the process. These include the following:

- A brief but well-organized coaching experience appears to have effectively supported the tailored embedment of learning for a large number of program participants. Participants received only four-to-six sessions of coaching in the interim. Coaching program goals were focused and limited in scope. This focus, however, was likely a success factor, given the limited resources made available to participants.

- According to participants, coaching created individual and organizational value in two ways. First, coaching helped each individual executive create a space in which strategic rather than operational concerns were dominant. Whirlpool, like most other firms, has to place enormous importance on quarterly results, a fact of life that inevitably pulls the zone of execution in the direction of operations. Setting the expectation that executives should use coaching and paying for four sessions of coaching encourages them to "make the time" to stop and think about not only where they are at today, but how they need to change to prepare themselves and their organizations for tomorrow.

- Not surprisingly, the coaching component of the program allowed for the tailoring of individual learning goals to meet individual learning needs. Each of the 12 components of the Leadership Model needed to be addressed within the context of the individual executive for embedment to take place.

- An equally important outcome, the strengthening of participants' ability to coach others, was fostered by the experience of being coached.

Many executives, particularly those who had not had a previous executive coaching experience or who had not worked for a coaching manager, reported that they got actionable ideas about coaching from their experiences in LWE. In addition, a number of executives actively solicited "coaching about their coaching" and used the coaching sessions to explicitly deal with tough coaching dilemmas in their current work context. However, participants varied with regard to their confidence about being an effective coach to their own people going forward. Several expressed the need for more support in this regard. Several participants also noted that in addition to the coaching itself, several classroom activities in both sessions of the LWE classroom experience also helped them build coaching skills.

- A carefully and meaningfully articulated leadership model can serve as a critically important tool, helping to organize the learning goals and activities of executives and the activities of executive coaches. The aggressive communications about the model to executives and coaches paid off, without interfering with the more "organic" aspects of the coaching relationship. The Whirlpool Leadership Model, in part because it had source credibility, rather easily made sense to Whirlpool executives and was rather easily linked with the firm's strategy. This has important implications for other organizations struggling with how to manage coaching engagements. Some organizations are now focusing solely on credentialing to ensure the quality and alignment of coaching. While Whirlpool did spend considerable effort on credentialing, the Leadership Model was largely responsible for the alignment of coach, executive, and organizational strategies.

- The careful selection and orientation of coaches is critical to the success of the process. Although a great deal of effort was put into orienting coaches, particularly to the Leadership Model and ensuring their buy-in (which was accomplished), even more could be done.

- Most executives had a fairly good understanding of the goals and processes of the executive coaching as provided. As with the coaches, however, more can be done to ensure that they understand how to make use of this valuable resource. In addition, it is critically important to orient executives to the confidentiality boundaries of the executive coaching. Many of the executive coaches were chosen purposefully because they had some familiarity with Whirlpool, perhaps having served as coaches previously. Their familiarity, however, caused a few executives to question the degree to which what was discussed in the coaching sessions would remain confidential.

- Global and cultural issues seem particularly important in terms of the style of interaction but less so in terms of the content, given that the content was organized around the Leadership Model. The lack of culture as a barrier to the transfer of learning seems to have been further facilitated by the use of coaches from "in country" or "in continent" whenever possible. Interestingly, from culture to culture, there was little variation among coaches with regard to their understanding of the link between the coaching, executive development activities, and the need for business results. The practices of highly effective executive coaches seem fairly consistent across the globe. What does vary, however, are how issues are discussed, particularly the use of face-to-face versus telephone interviews. Though executives from all cultures expressed a preference for face-to-face coaching, those from Latin America were most adamant about its importance. At the same time, they also acknowledged that in a global company, there is an enormous need to learn how to coach remotely.

• Perhaps most importantly, Whirlpool's cultural tradition of being coaching-friendly provided a context within which coaching would be seen positively by participants and used as such.

The Whirlpool experience, though quite positive, still raises a number of questions regarding the strategic use of executive coaching:

• How much is enough? The single biggest complaint of participating executives was that four sessions was not enough. Some, in fact, continued coaching, paying for it out of their own budgets. The literature shows that a relatively small number of coaching sessions, when coupled with a 360-degree-assessment process, can result in measurable change (Smither, London, Flaut, Vargas, & Kucine, 2003). It is clear that the executives found it useful to stop and focus on strategy and transformational leadership and that it helped them step back from daily demands. Would more coaching help to embed the executives' abilities to do this on their own? That question remains to be answered.

• When to coach? Whirlpool made the decision to start participants' LWE experience by looking at organizational-level leadership and then moving to the personal dimension of leadership, using coaching to bridge the gap between the two. A number of executives and several coaches suggested that movement in the other direction might have been helpful. In future LWE streams, Whirlpool plans to reverse the order of the sessions, with the first classroom period focusing on the introspective and more personal elements of the Leadership Model and the second session focusing on the organizational aspects of the model. This should result in greater exposure to self-assessment data and feedback from classroom teachers and peers prior to the formal embedment-coaching experience.

**6**

# Building and Leading
# a Coaching Capacity

---

In this chapter, we describe the following:

- The need for leadership and management in the building of a coaching capability
- The phases of organizational coaching capability development
- Competing mental models of coaching with which the coaching leader must contend
- The role and tasks of the coaching practice manager

---

The building of a robust coaching capability, like that described at Whirlpool, does not happen by itself. As with most aspects of organizational life, these outcomes are achieved when specific individuals are tasked with making them happen and then exercise the management and leadership skills necessary to mobilize resources, build a coalition of stakeholders, develop an action plan, and follow through with an operation that meets the demands of those stakeholders.

Much has been written about the use of coaching in organizations, but little has been written about the leadership and management of a coaching capability. The exceptions are *Executive Coaching: A Guide for the HR*

*Professional* (Valerio & Lee, 2005) and the often-cited *Executive Coaching: Practices and Perspectives* (Fitzgerald & Berger, 2002, which has a number of articles by those who manage executive coaching activities on behalf of organizations). In this chapter, we draw on the writings of these authors and our own research in an effort to construct a more complete model of the challenges associated with creating and managing a coaching capability within an organization.

## The Need for Leadership

As we have discussed, in many organizations, the evolution of a coaching capability begins with the introduction of expert coaching, typically provided by executive coaches. A good experience with an external coach serves to teach one or more organizational members about the role that coaching can play in leadership and employee development. Once coaching has been introduced into an organization, there are two basic paths that its evolution can follow.

One path, an *unmanaged,* ad hoc path, can ultimately lead to the rejection of the process and the organization's failure to build any kind of coaching capability. As with any change effort, one of the unintended consequences of failure is the crippling of future efforts. The second path is a *managed* path. A coaching strategy or vision that links one or more varieties of coaching and organizational needs leads to an action plan; the action plan is executed, results are measured, and adjustments made in follow-up, accordingly. The planned path allows stakeholders in the organization to make sure that coaching supports the needs of the business as well as the individuals involved.

Although the field of coaching is relatively new, interviews with a number of those involved in organizational coaching have led us to believe that there are certain regularly observable, perhaps predictable, phases in the evolution or attempted evolution of a coaching capability. We present these in the next section. The notion of regularly occurring phases in development is helpful, in that it suggests that certain forces for change are likely to be present at certain times, as well as certain risks that need to be carefully managed.

## The Organizational Evolution of a Coaching Capability

### Stage 1

Coaching is introduced into the organization. As discussed, this may well take place by accident. One individual or a few individuals work with a coach, believe that the results are helpful to them, and encourage others to try coaching themselves. Typically, the coaches are external, expert (ideally) coaches. As demonstrated at Whirlpool, a growing interest in coaching can develop momentum very quickly if senior people are among those involved in coaching.

However, coaching can also emerge from the middle of the organization when it is introduced by influential middle managers and/or human resource professionals in response to a widely accepted organizational need. In such cases, as discussed, it will likely be seen as credible if it is perceived as effective. In one financial services organization, for instance, we found that coaching by expert external coaches, which was essentially confidential in nature, served as the perfect "cultural" compromise. In this organization, frank, learning-oriented discussions between employees and managers were not frequent. In fact, they were considered to be potentially dangerous. "If I talked with my manager about one of my direct reports who was having trouble, my manager would really want me to do something about it right away. We could *not* just talk, and problem solve. And if I didn't take action quickly, at some point, my own manager would," was the perspective offered by one middle manager there.

At the same time, this firm, though relentlessly action oriented, did have a supportive, paternalistic culture, and its leaders were not averse to spending a bit of money on employees, particularly middle managers. Confidential expert coaching in the service of employee development was quite acceptable and allowed managers to deal with issues that everyone knew were difficult but no one knew how to address. (Of course, if this particular organization were to become "stuck" at this phase, organizational learning would be minimal. They would never address their inability to have coaching discussions between managers and employees. We return to this problem later in the chapter.)

In Stage 1, we have observed the important role played by a "champion" when coaching emerges from the middle of the organization. In essence, the champion plays the same role that an executive who is satisfied with coaching may play. The champion sees coaching as a real opportunity for individual and organizational development, and begins to "evangelize." If he or she is credible and influential, others, including those in senior management, may listen and provide resources and support.

In Stage 1, coaching catches on. It develops real, though informal, support. Other employees beyond the early adopters begin to use the services of expert external or internal coaches. The number involved increases, and people feel for the most part well served if the needs of key stakeholders are addressed. However, it should be stressed that at this point, coaching is likely not to be seen as an organizational capability. It is seen as a "good idea, imported from the outside." As an activity, it may also be quite misunderstood. At the organizational level, it may be the case that no one knows what to do with it.

### Stage 2, Managed

One or two individuals, often from within the human resource or organizational effectiveness functions (not necessarily the champions described in Stage 1) are aware of coaching as a vehicle for promoting individual and organizational development. They are glad to hear that individuals within the organization have found coaching to be helpful. They then begin to consider how they might use coaching in a more planned fashion and begin to see it as a "program" or a function that needs to have some goals and procedures/processes to ensure that it is working properly.

These individuals may be seen as interfering with the organic use of coaching as a tool, but actually their actions are quite appropriate. Of note, we have also observed in some instances that the human resource professionals who ultimately came to guide the coaching initiative actually capitalized on a coaching failure. They were involved in some type of damage control subsequent to a poorly executed coaching engagement and intervened to help others see that coaching needed to be managed, not discarded, in the face of failure. If such individuals have sufficient credibility, they are in a good position to say, "See, we have to get this thing right." In doing so, they are actually able to breathe life into the coaching effort.

Good human resource professionals are acutely aware that that which is not managed carefully can quickly be seen as a fad. They may convene a group of stakeholders to deliberate with regard to how they might use coaching to promote a business goal, perhaps on a pilot basis. In doing so, they are positioning themselves to discover and, ideally, confront a range of strategic and tactical challenges (discussed later in this chapter).

### Stage 2, Unmanaged

Coaching continues to proliferate as a response to coachee satisfaction and demand. Costs go up. Issues with quality control may begin to emerge. A coach breaches confidentiality or submits an exorbitant bill. Coaching is offered to individuals with serious performance problems. It is seen as failing to help those individuals, undermining the credibility of coaching as a useful tool. Coaching becomes a victim of its own success.

In our experience, though, the most common failure of the unmanaged, though popular, coaching effort is a failure to establish a coherent connection with the business. The symptoms of this failure are comments such as the following:

- "They just go into their coaching session and talk, I have no idea what it's all about" (from the manager of an executive coachee).
- "I know it has to be confidential, but shouldn't someone be keeping an eye on what's going on?" (from the human resource manager of a manager in coaching).
- "We're spending a lot of money on coaching, but I'm not sure we see any results or even any connection with what we're facing. This stuff is fine when times are good, but we can't afford the luxury these days. We have enough benefits for our people already" (from a chief financial officer).

This last comment in particular is quite telling. Coaching is not a benefit. It should not be viewed as a retention tool, like health care insurance. Coaching is a tool that promotes individual performance in current roles, preparation for future roles, and organizational effectiveness, now and in the future. When, out of confusion, coaching is viewed as a benefit, its life expectancy may be quite short! In Stage 2, unmanaged, coaching continues to proliferate while a growing body of line managers shake their heads and wonder why. But they don't express their concerns, yet.

## Stage 3, Managed

A coaching program (or programs) results from the deliberations that took place at Stage 2. The coaching program may rely on internal or external coaching resources, but regardless, it has certain characteristics. First, it has a job to do, as we have discussed. It is "hooked" with a program or a desired outcome that is seen as important to the organization. At Whirlpool, coaching was hooked to their formal leadership development efforts. Stage 3 managed external or internal expert coaching programs are targeted at good and great performers, those with high potential or those who hold mission-critical roles, not at those with performance problems. Plans begin to be made for engaging managers as coaches so that on-the-job development activities can disperse widely throughout the organization.

In addition, Stage 3 managed coaching programs confront a range of important operational issues, including assessing the quality of coaching and coaches, the length and scope of expert coaching engagements, diversity in the pool of expert coaches and coachees, working across geographies, and establishing metrics for evaluating outcomes. The Stage 3 program likely has a set of policies and procedures that guide the work of coaches and coachees.

In addition, as needed, one is likely to find an appropriate internal marketing or educational plan to ensure that key stakeholders are aware of the program, educated as to its purpose, and engaged in a constructive fashion.

### Stage 3, Unmanaged

A new vice president for human resources enters the scene. (We don't know why such tasks always seem to fall to a new HR vice president, but they do.) She asks about the amount of money being spent on expert coaching and looks for some measures of the impact of the coaching. She might also inquire with regard to the diversity of coachees and coaches. Is coaching being provided to some deserving individuals and not others? If such questions are not answered appropriately, the vice president may restrict or eliminate coaching, even though some good coaching is taking place and some of the coaching is positively influencing the business—though, of course, she doesn't know that. If she is uninformed about coaching and its potential, her opinion of coaching may be shaped by this experience, and she may become a more or less permanent opponent of coaching.

Why would a new vice president oppose the use of coaching? The new vice president has what appears to be an out-of-control item in the budget (or line managers' budgets, as they are just as likely to fall victim to the lure of Stage 2). She also isn't sure what the firm is getting for its money. If she is sophisticated regarding coaching, she may push the organization to cycle back to Stage 2, managed. Or she may allow the organization to move to Stage 4, unmanaged.

### Stage 4, Managed

The coaching program continues to demonstrate its ability to deliver results in meaningful ways. The results are captured through an evaluative process that may include measures of return on investment (ROI) as well as assessments of behavior change and qualitative assessments of organizational impact. An important item on the agenda of those responsible for the coaching capability will likely be to grow that capability by using designated internal coaches, training managers to provide developmental coaching, and creating peer coaching networks. Those responsible for coaching, as good businesspeople, want to keep pursuing quality results and lowering costs at the same time. They also, in most cases, would like to support the evolution of the organization's culture into one that is maximally adaptable and "learning-friendly."

Those responsible for coaching continue to look for cost-effective ways of supporting this culture shift. If they have not done so already, they begin to plan for the wide-scale development of coaching managers. In this process, if they are to become more successful in coaching their direct reports, they assess not only the training needs of managers but also the impact of the organization's culture and reward system on such an effort. Change management strategies may be required if the latter two factors are at issue, as we'll describe in Chapter 9.

The Stage 4 managed coaching capability is also likely to be a facilitator of organizational learning. At the World Bank, for instance, coaches are brought together with line managers and human resource professionals to discuss issues that emerge in coaching (without violating confidentiality, of course). A number of the World Bank's coaches were involved in a coaching and development intervention that was targeted at "team leaders." They met with those responsible for the overall team leader program to discuss the role of the team leader and provide feedback on how the role and the training for the role evolve. Likewise, coaches who have worked with a number of individuals from various regions throughout the World Bank have met with vice presidents and senior human resource officers from those regions to discuss common concerns that have emerged from the aggregate of coaching engagements, again, without violating confidentiality.

These engagements are promoted and managed by a specific individual within Executive Resources who is responsible for the overall coaching program. Our interviews with various stakeholders to the coaching program at the World Bank revealed that this type of organizational learning activity created value for participants that went above and beyond that which was created through the success of individual coaching engagements.

### Stage 4, Unmanaged

Coaching is considered a "frill," and little attention is given to the process by which individuals develop on the job. A "sink-or-swim" culture remains intact. There is very little hope of developing coaching managers.

Although we do not have data on the relative frequency with which these differing paths are followed, it is our guess and fear that the unmanaged rather than the managed path is the more common of the two. In a recent Web-based seminar in which we presented some of our ideas about coaching to a human resource professionals industry group, with representatives from over 50 firms, including some of the best companies in the United States, 60% of participants reported that coaching in their organizations is unmanaged and is largely provided to derailing executives.

George Hollenbeck (2004), a noted coach and coaching researcher, has observed a similar trend, though he takes a more macroeconomic view of the evolution of coaching. In Hollenbeck's view, the fundamental driver for the proliferation of coaching is the daunting set of challenges associated with modern leadership roles. Once it was apparent that coaching had something to offer leaders, the demand soared. The hint of growth in demand created a strong growth in the supply of coaches as MBAs with an interest in helping people and psychologists driven from their therapeutic roles by managed care (in the United States) turned their attention to what appeared to be a lucrative market: executive coaching. Ultimately, "Everyone had to have a coach," as the press has suggested. The end of the dot-com era and the crash of the market served to put the brakes on the growth of coaching as organizations found that they had to do more with less.

Hollenbeck's argument has some merit, but coaching did not die the same death as the "dot-bomb" companies. It is still going strong in a number of firms but in a different fashion. The management of coaching was not in our view a consequence of constrained budgets, though this was, of necessity, a factor. Rather, good businesspeople were asking tough questions about input, output, and throughput processes and unwilling to spend money, or at least as much money, on faith alone.

## Why on Faith Alone?

This is fundamentally a question of leadership. Leaders put forth appropriate and adaptive visions for action, but, of course, they must educate those who are uncertain, and they must deal with alternative visions, including those that can undermine their best efforts. Coaching, it appears, confuses people. Managers don't necessarily know what to make of the process and may be reluctant to exercise their input in an assertive fashion. As is clear from our previous analysis, we don't believe that is the most effective route to go. It may be helpful, then, to review the "deeper background" from which coaching has emerged. It is our hope that this discussion will surface underlying assumptions that people hold about coaching and allow those assumptions to be "reality checked." Line managers and human resource professionals should not be so hesitant in trying to apply an appropriate level of managerial discipline, particularly when that discipline is exercised in a strategic fashion.

As Hollenbeck has suggested, the growth of the coaching industry seems to be the result of some important trends in, first, Western and, now, the global culture. It's gotten tougher to be a leader. It has become much harder to "wing it." Though they may not always admit it, those who are struggling with leadership and other complex roles appreciate helpful guidance.

Traditionally, guidance has been provided by parents, relatives, and members of family-oriented social networks. When necessary, individuals have also turned to religious leaders, teachers, and physicians for help. At the beginning of the 20th century in Europe, society witnessed the growth of more explicitly defined, psychologically oriented, nonreligious professional helpers, the first psychoanalysts. Of course, the task of psychoanalysts, who are mostly physicians, is to treat the sick—to repair the broken individual when the support of other helpers is not adequate for the challenge.

Psychotherapy caught on, particularly in the United States, after World War II. By the mid-1950s, psychoanalysis had assumed the status of a fad in some U.S. cities and subcultures. While in many or perhaps even most cases, analysis and therapy did deal with psychiatric conditions, the reality is that the therapeutic methodology can be helpful for those without psychiatric impairments, to the extent that it can help the patient, or client, gain insight into needs, motives, dreams, stresses, and the like. Psychotherapeutic methodology can also help clients plan and implement behavioral changes. Indeed, *The Handbook of Coaching* (Hudson, 1999) lists the following individuals as providing a theoretical foundation for coaching as a discipline: psychoanalysts Freud, Adler, Jung, Erikson, and Gould, among others. The original ideas of the founding psychoanalysts, at least some of those ideas, turned out to have applicability far beyond the psychiatric clinic.

However, psychotherapy was not to be the source of expert guidance sought out by the general public en masse. First of all, because therapy was used to treat those with psychiatric problems, it was also stigmatized. Yes, many people made use of therapy for help with personal transitions and work-related stress, for instance, but they did so in private. If they did not wish to share their experiences, they did not have to. Psychotherapy is almost completely confidential.

Second, as a health care service, psychotherapy is predominantly funded through insurance or government health care agencies. Downward pressure on costs has served to encourage regulators to limit access to such services. At this point in time, most insurance companies insist that psychotherapy be limited to "medically necessary" conditions. Few individuals can afford the expenses associated with funding therapy on their own.

So, while psychotherapy may be considered inappropriate for those who are more or less psychiatrically healthy, what has been learned from psychotherapy that can be applied to the problems of *living*, lives on. Coaching is something like psychotherapy, in that it involves two people, one more experienced and presumably more skilled in coaching, working together for the purpose of helping the coachee or "coaching client" address important challenges in his or her personal or working life. Coaching also takes place under more or less confidential circumstances.

This underlying connection between coaching and psychotherapy in form, if not substance, unfortunately evokes a mental model, that of healing the sick, and this is actually quite inappropriate to the task of coaching, which is essentially a developmental one. No one can say for sure who actually first used the term *coaching* in organizational life. It has always been our assumption that the term was originally used to try to capture something that was somewhat like counseling or therapy, but different. The word *coach,* of course, is much more closely associated with athletics than with business. Consider the differences between the mental model of coaching evoked in an athletic context and the mental model most of us hold of psychotherapy. Box 6.1 exposes significant differences between the two.

| **Box 6.1** | Athletic Coaching Versus Psychotherapy | |
| --- | --- | --- |
| *Characteristics* | *Athletic Coaching* | *Psychotherapy* |
| Goals | Improved performance and winning. | Return to the level of previous performance. |
| Visibility of the work | Very public in almost all cases. | Rarely public, confidentiality assumed and protected. |
| Measurement of outcomes | Both individual and team performance are measurable. External monitoring of outcomes is routine. | Can be difficult to assess progress. Many intervening variables. Little, if any, external monitoring of outcomes. |
| Stakeholders | The individual and the team. | The individual and perhaps the family. |
| Participant drivers | Motivation and ambition to improve. Those with some potential are likely to profit from coaching. Success builds on success. Those who have experienced success may very well want more. | Illness and pain. Success means that pain is alleviated and normal functioning is returned. That is what is desired by the patient. Once that has been achieved, in most instances, the patient will be satisfied with the outcome, and therapy will cease. |

We suggest that although athletic coaching and developmental coaching in the workplace are quite different in many respects, the underlying characteristics of both are quite similar. Furthermore, *workplace developmental coaching is more similar to athletic coaching than it is to psychotherapy, even though coaching and psychotherapy appear to have more in common.* Why is this important for those who would build a coaching capacity? In our experience, one of the most important underlying tasks of building and leading coaching capacity is to make sure that the mental models that support that activity are appropriate.

Indeed, there is still significant confusion with regard to the boundary between coaching and therapy. Berglas (2002), for instance, has proposed that those who provide expert coaching without having had the benefit of intensive training in a mental health discipline run the risk of harming their coaching clients. This fairly radical proposition has generated a good deal of controversy. While his position is considerably outside the mainstream, it is symptomatic of (a) the fact that coaching is popular (the article appeared in the *Harvard Business Review,* one of many published there about coaching), (b) the mental model that many (though by no means all) hold about coaching is a psychiatric one, and (c) there is real confusion about who should be providing expert coaching services and the appropriateness of their qualifications.

A more appropriate coaching mental model supports the following:

- Coaching is for both the person and the organization.

- The organization's stake in the coaching capability as well as its responsibilities for the individuals involved require the organization to be an active participant in the coaching process.

- Since coaching has to benefit the organization as well as the individual, the coaching effort has to pay its way, from an organizational standpoint. The team needs to win, or at least increase its chances of doing so.

- Coaching sessions may be confidential so that coachees can feel free to explore difficult issues without the risk of retaliation, but coaching itself is not a solely individually focused, private activity.

- Those involved with coachees, particularly their managers and human resource professionals, have work to do. They should not expect that they can pass off the case to "the doctor" and wash their hands of further responsibilities.

- Participation in coaching should bring with it neither guilt nor shame.

- Those in coaching are expected to improve their performance. Some are expected to improve their performance a great deal.

- Coaching should not be "medicalized" or equated with psychiatric treatment, despite the fact that insights from psychology and psychiatry can be valuable in coaching under some circumstances.

- The coachee is quite free to disagree with the coach and, indeed, to terminate coaching. It is very unlikely that termination of coaching will result in serious or immediate threat of harm to the coachee.

We have gone into this rather deep review of the mental models surrounding expert coaching because it is our view that *the Number 1 task of those responsible for promoting a coaching effort is to counter inappropriate mental models that surround coaching and promote appropriate mental models of coaching that are truly developmental.* This task involves promoting a new vision about coaching and development and actualizing that vision through concrete steps. In the next section, we provide a more grounded view of what this really means. This description, again, makes the assumption that the organization is most likely to begin the process of building a coaching capability through the use of some type of expert coaching intervention.

## The Rise and Role of the Coaching Practice Manager

If some "one" is to be in charge of building a coaching capability, that person must address the issues discussed above, as well as the usual business challenges: obtaining funding, getting management support, staffing, marketing, and so on. Increasingly, this challenge falls to individuals whose work, if not job title, is *coaching practice manager* (CPM). The formal managerial tasks of the CPM, as described by Susan Ennis, herself a former CPM, are listed in Box 6.2 (adapted from Ennis, 2002; we have changed or made additions based on our research as well).

| Box 6.2 | The Tasks of the Coaching Practice Manager |
|---|---|
| *Step 1:* | Link coaching to the business strategy, involving appropriate stakeholders in the process. In doing so, create a business case for funding for that capacity. |
| *Step 2:* | Design the program or intervention prior to coaching. |

| | |
|---|---|
| *Step 2a:* | Align key stakeholders, including the manager's potential coaches, regarding the developmental nature of coaching and their roles in the coaching process. |
| *Step 3:* | Identify a pool of potential coaches, based on the task requirements of the coaching program or intervention. |
| *Step 4:* | Screen and qualify potential coaches. |
| *Step 5:* | Orient external coaches to the coaching task and train internal coaches. |
| *Step 6:* | Create a process for assessing potential coachee needs and match coachees with coaches if coaching is seen as an appropriate intervention. |
| *Step 6a:* | For individual situations in which coaching is deemed inappropriate, help those screened out of coaching make other arrangements to support their developmental needs. |
| *Step 7:* | Support ongoing coaching engagements (at the individual level) and the larger coaching program. |
| *Step 7a:* | Coordinate coaching program activities with other employee development or leadership development activities associated with the coaching program. |
| *Step 8:* | Measure results (of both individual coaching engagements and the program effort as a whole) and communicate results to appropriate stakeholders, including coachees, coaches, human resource professionals, and line managers. |
| *Step 9:* | Reassess results to determine whether or not they are aligned with the business strategy as described in Step 1. |

The steps described in Box 6.2 are managerial tasks. Leading the effort to build a coaching capability requires promoting a positive vision of developmental coaching. The effective CPM in our view uses the managerial tasks associated with building a coaching capability to promote that vision, as well as making sure that the coaching program operates smoothly.

Rather than walk through each of the tasks in Box 6.2 one by one, it may be more helpful for the reader to see the work of the CPM firsthand, through a short case. The reader should note that this case is not set in a large corporation, but rather an emerging one. We tend to associate progressive management practices with very large organizations, but smaller companies need them just as much, if not more so. Case 6.1 presents the story of Summer Turner, who manages executive coaching at Omgeo LLC. (This is a real company, and real names are used.)

## CASE 6.1    The Management of Executive Coaching at Omgeo

Omgeo LLC plays an important role in the financial services value chain, providing posttrade, presettlement operations. Omgeo serves more than 6,000 investment managers, broker/dealers, and custodians in more than 40 countries. They currently have approximately 500 employees, located in 15 offices. Their vision statement reads, "the globally recognized leader in orchestrating connectivity and trade management in securities processing."

Despite its relatively small size, Omgeo has had a commitment to leadership development almost since its inception. Early in the life of the company, executive coaching became an integral part of its leadership development efforts. When coaching was first introduced at Omgeo in the form of expert executive coaching, some managers were skeptical or resistant. They knew little about coaching. However, the initial positive experiences of several senior managers began to enhance the reputation of coaching as a leadership development tool and clarify the distinctions between executive coaching and therapy, counseling, or life coaching. Phase 1 was well under way. Fortunately for Omgeo, they took a managed approach early. Not the first CPM at Omgeo, Summer Turner has been the program manager for executive coaching for the last 3 years.

As of this writing, there were 30 to 40 managers receiving executive coaching at the company. There are three different tiers of coaching at Omgeo, directed at three different segments of the employee population, each with different but clearly articulated goals. Coaching is made available to members of the senior management team, to individual managers (typically middle managers) involved in formal management development programs, and to those individuals likely to move into significant leadership roles in the near term. Expert executive coaching is typically not made available to individuals experiencing significant performance problems. Coaching for serious performance problems is provided by the employee's manager and by human resource staff. Coaching is seen by the company in part as recognition of and reward for already-competent performance. Coaching is also positioned as an investment that is made with some attention as to the likelihood of significant payoff for the company.

When Summer first came to Omgeo, the coaching effort had already been under way for some time. The linkages had already been established between coaching as a developmental intervention and the needs of the business. Target populations had been defined. Though the role that coaching has played at Omgeo has changed somewhat as leadership in the company has evolved, those linkages have proved to be sufficiently strong to survive a number of challenges.

On a day-to-day basis, the administration of executive coaching engagements at Omgeo varies slightly from situation to situation, but across all three tiers, there is a basic process in place. At Omgeo, as well as a number of larger firms, that process is quite personal. Summer works with potential coachees to assess the appropriateness of coaching, to facilitate the defining of the initial coaching goals (if coaching indeed appears to be appropriate), to match coach and coachee, to provide follow-up support during the implementation of coaching plans, and to evaluate coaching and coach effectiveness. These tasks are performed through direct, usually face-to-face, contact between Summer and the executive coaching client.

One can see from this list of activities that significant work is required to effectively support an executive coaching capability. In a larger firm, this might be a full-time job, but in the case of Omgeo, Summer's portfolio includes other functional activities, particularly the running of related leadership and management development programs. The advantage of integrating these through one individual is, of course, that coordination between the programs, which should support one another fully, is facilitated.

The coaching program at Omgeo is well-known to the employee population. The marketing of the program, which might be a challenge in larger firms, now takes place largely through word-of-mouth or through informing managers during other classroom-based management or leadership development activities. The most consistent source of referrals into the program are, as we have seen, managers who have had positive experiences themselves. The lack of a stigma associated with seeking out coaching plus the company's general emphasis on employee and leadership development serve to create an appropriate level of demand for coaching, though access to coaching is carefully managed.

The individual interested in accessing coaching must seek out Summer as the "gateway" to participation. She holds an individual interview with each prospective coachee for the purposes of determining whether or not coaching is an appropriate intervention and, if so, to develop an action plan based on that decision. Given the popularity of coaching within Omgeo, on occasion, requests for coaching are deemed inappropriate, and the decision is made not to begin a coaching engagement. The company supports other types of educational activities that may, in fact, be more appropriate to the particular individual's development need.

Managers who seek out coaching may, of course, lack a full understanding of its nature, of the indicators for coaching, of alternatives to coaching, and of the responsibilities of being a coachee. The initial interview thus serves as a critically important educational tool that is conducted in a fashion that in many respects models what would ideally take place in a coaching engagement. Issues, rather than immediate solutions, are first explored, tentative goals are set, and action planning takes place.

The discussion between Summer and the prospective coachee addresses the competencies the coachee hopes to develop. This dialogue is aided by the existence of a widely understood, firm-specific competency model. (There are distinct competency profiles for both middle- and senior-level leadership positions.) As was the case at

Whirlpool, the ability of the employee and, in this case, an internal coach (Summer) to work with a definition of success, such as a competency model, facilitates all aspects of the coaching process. When the prospective coachee is less familiar with the competency model, Summer uses the interview as an opportunity to help the employee better understand the model and the connections between planned individual development and the needs of the business.

The effort to define an initial set of goals has multiple purposes. In addition to helping to assess the need and plan for the coaching, this early, tentative definition of goals is critical to the task of assessing individual progress and aiding in the evaluation of the coaching program itself. Summer works with the prospective coachee to define at least one or two very tangible and observable outcomes that the coachee is hoping to attain, outcomes that can be observed or measured. The coachee may also work on less tangible or less visible goals (such as building self-confidence) and is encouraged to do so if they relate to the business and to the competency model. However, one or two goals have to be quite concrete.

The potential coachee, for instance, might come in with the stated goal of "building communications skills." After discussing the situation in more detail, the coachee and the program manager narrow down the tentative developmental goal to that of "improving listening effectiveness." This process of clarification in and of itself may be helpful to the coachee. Regardless, once the goal has been tentatively described, the next challenge is to articulate how improved listening effectiveness might, indeed, lead to a desired *concrete, observable* outcome.

The company's online 360-degree assessment (more about that below) is a helpful tool in that regard. If, as in this case, the coachee's listening effectiveness was related to employee morale, productivity, or intent to stay with the company, such factors can be measured through the 360-degree process. Reports from the coachee's manager are also acceptable.

While Omgeo's approach to coaching concedes that through the process of coaching, there may be some shift in goals, the initial meetings between Summer and the prospective coachee are designed to help the coachee establish a clear focus for the work as well as remind him or her that this is an investment that must pay off for the company. If the payoff is not clear, then coaching or counseling should be a private matter for the employee to consider and fund. The plan for coaching that results from this process has to be approved by the coachee's manager.

Finally, the initial interviews should provide insights that will aid in the process of matching coach and coachee, if coaching is indicated. Summer has spent a great deal of time assessing the coaching pool's competence, through individual interviews with coaches and the use of reference checks and endorsements from previous clients. In her screening interviews with prospective coaches for Omgeo, she works to answer the fundamental question: What is this coach best at developing in other people? Given the challenge of defining coaching goals and outcomes, it isn't always easy to define coach expertise. She refers no coach to the matching process who has not been certified as to his or her competence, allowing the coachee to focus more on subjective factors, such as personal style, during the matching process.

As Summer described,

> One of our coaches has a great deal of expertise. Her primary specialties are in working with women in executive roles . . . [aiding them in] navigating that landscape. Sometimes it is a different landscape if it is a predominately male-led environment, because the rules and the norms have been established by men. If you are with only a few or no other women, how do you operate the best in that kind of environment? You have to learn how to influence others to get the work done. She [this particular executive coach] is highly competent in that area. The reason she is so competent in that area is in part because she is so good at developing influencing skills in people.

Such coaching expertise can easily be applied to the task of helping men as well as women become more adept at influencing others. This process of defining fundamental coaching skill sets helps Summer make more conscious, less intuitive decisions regarding which coaches to suggest to a particular coachee (though most CPMs still hold that intuition helps as well).

The coaches are also trained in the Omgeo competency model and the company's Career Development Plan. Summer is responsible for this training process. (The Omgeo Career Development Plan document supersedes what used to be called the "Coaching Plan." The name was changed to clarify that developmental activities are not limited to coaching. The company's value system holds that employees are responsible for their own development. Each year, they complete a Career Development Plan, using the language of the competency model. The plan is reviewed on a regular basis with the employees' managers.) The coaches, then, are prepared with a shared language regarding desirable skills at Omgeo as well as the use of the Career Development Plan as a tool to support skill development that is aligned with the company's needs. Indeed, the last question on the career development plan is outcome oriented in this way: "How will this plan benefit Omgeo?"

Each potential coachee is given the names of two or three coaches, with appropriate documentation of their backgrounds, who appear to have the requisite expertise for the particular coaching engagement. Summer encourages the prospective coachee to be honest in his or her reactions to a particular coach during the initial exploratory interview with the coach:

> Do you think you can establish trust with this person? If you are giving a big presentation and want some feedback, would you be comfortable with this person sitting in the back of the room? I want the coaches to screen for fit.

Once the match between coach and coachee has been set, coaching begins with a rapport-building process between coach and coachee, and the further articulation of coaching goals. The assessment portion of the coaching engagement aids in this process. In addition to the online 360-degree-assessment instrument mentioned above, most coaches also use various self-assessment tools, for instance, to assess personal style. Omgeo does insist that regardless of the manner in which it takes place, feedback from key stakeholders in the coachee's environment must be included in the coaching assessment process. An interview-based 360-degree assessment (in which the coach interviews key stakeholders either in person or by telephone) may substitute for or be used in addition to the online 360-degree-assessment instrument.

The coaching assessment process culminates with a discussion of the feedback between coach and coachee. This process results in further refinement of goals and strengths. Once again, an effort is made to concretize the goals and connect them with the business needs, via the competency model. Success criteria must be finally defined during this phase. As stated above, at least some outcomes must be concrete and observable. The final plan for coaching, including the success criteria, has to be approved by the coachee's manager. Coaching is paid for out of the coachee's manager's budget, not the learning and development budget. This level of accountability ensures that coaching goals and organizational needs are in alignment.

While the need for coaching and coaching goals must be aligned with the needs of the business, the confidentiality boundary around the coaching interviews themselves creates a safe nonevaluating space for candid coaching discussions. Any information sharing requires the coachee's consent and frequently the coachee's participation. Only goals and basic measures of activity are monitored throughout the coaching process.

Coaching progress is assessed in two ways, formally and informally. Ideally, the Career Development Plan is revisited by the coachee and his or her manager every quarter. For individuals working with a coach, progress in coaching would naturally be one focus of the Career Development Plan discussion. In addition, Summer engages in a routine informal evaluation of coaching through quarterly meetings that she holds with each coachee. These may be very brief meetings. The intent is not to pry into the content of coaching discussions, but rather to hear the coachee's reflection on the coaching experience. When the coachee is involved in a classroom-based leadership development or management development activity, he or she may also inquire about the interaction between the two projects. In those instances, the employee's questions may be more focused with regard to whether the learning efforts are sufficiently coordinated.

Organizational learning via the executive coaching program is facilitated through periodic meetings between Summer and the coaches. As at the World Bank, the coaches are asked to participate in group sessions, during which time they are encouraged to share "themes," not confidential information, regarding issues that emerge in the company. These conversations allow for feedback regarding coaching management; the state of the workforce, particularly those who are involved as coaches; and the implications that issues raised through coaching may have for the business and changes under way there. Such sessions also allow coaches to support each other's coaching efforts through the sharing of concerns and ideas that might enhance their effectiveness.

As appropriate, information from these sessions is fed upward to senior management. Senior management also receives routine reports on the number of individuals in coaching, the goals of coaching, and Summer's assessment of the progress within the coaching program as a whole. The Omgeo competency model is the tool against which coaching progress is measured.

When asked, "What does it take to be an effective manager of the coaching program?" Summer replied,

> The diagnostic piece, sitting down with someone who says, "I want to work on this" and talking with them about whether or not this is really most important or have they talked with their manager, defined the problem accurately . . . that kind of diagnostic questioning to get at the core issues. That, of course, has a coaching impact itself. Clarifying goals and opportunities for coachees is another piece of it, drawing the connection between our competencies, the goals and objectives, and our vision/strategy and people's individual success criteria and how it benefits the business.

## Managing the Coaching Capability

As the story of Summer Turner and Omgeo suggest, the CPM is vigilantly involved in the creation of *shared individual and organizational value* through the coaching process. By ensuring the appropriate inputs (coachees and coaches) and processes (coaching processes and the involvement of others) are in place and exercising quality control through the monitoring of outputs, the CPM is in a position to align individual and organizational goals. This is, from our perspective, what is required to maintain the credibility of the coaching effort and program. We now isolate some of the key tasks of the CPM and note in more detail how value is created. Some of the issues raised here have been addressed in previous chapters, and some will continue to surface throughout the remainder of the book.

### Before Coaching

The prework requires, above all, establishing a rationale for coaching in relation to the needs of the organization. This becomes the ultimate goal of the coaching intervention and the goal to which coaching can be managed by the practice manager. We will explore this further in Chapter 8, when we look at how Wachovia Bank began their internal coaching program. At Omgeo, those linkages were for the most part already established by the time the current CPM took on that role. The missions of coaching are (a) to support senior managers in doing their work, which often means managing change; (b) to have coaching serve as an adjunct to ensure transfer of learning in a classroom-based management development program, not dissimilar to what we saw at Whirlpool; and (c) to support the development of high-potential managers. The latter two, of course, can interact. Success is measured by participants' success. The link between coaching and participant success is assessed through qualitative evaluations. We discuss this further below and in the last chapter.

The coaching program itself is planned to meet these three goals. In the case of Omgeo, expert coaching was indicated given the high risk/high reward nature of the goals involved. Obviously, however, defining the proper expertise, as the case shows, requires very careful thought. We discuss that further below.

## Educating and Aligning Key Stakeholders

The need to educate and align stakeholders to the coaching program refers to the need to bring affected line managers and human resource professionals into the process early and maintain their support for the long haul. This can be done informally, as at Omgeo, or formally, as is the case at the World Bank. The manager of the coaching program at the World Bank convenes an advisory board twice each year. The advisory board is composed of senior line managers, senior human resource professionals, and other key individuals, many of whom have made use of the coaching program as either coaching clients or as managers of coaching clients. The advisory board reviews the program's overall performance, offers advice and input, and considers the coaching manager's forthcoming plans. One key topic is that of working to integrate the activities of the coaching program with other executive development activities. Advisory board members also serve as individuals in the larger community who can speak for the program with credibility.

The manager of the coaching program at the World Bank, Nina Mickelson, also uses many informal strategies to gain the ongoing participation and support of stakeholders. She actively seeks the involvement of line managers and individual contributors whenever the occasion lends itself, such as when a new coaching program initiative begins. She has regular contact with line managers around coaching engagements, seeking their input and advice. This activity takes considerable time, but one of the lessons of organizational life that should never be forgotten is the value of networking, of building support proactively. This display of program leadership ensures real alignment between stakeholder and program goals.

One important goal of building stakeholder credibility for the coaching initiative, particularly as it involves the use of expert coaching, is to encourage the managers of coaching clients to appropriately involve themselves in coaching engagements under way. The systems view of coaching strongly points to the importance of the manager of the coaching client in assisting in the goal-setting process and providing ongoing coaching, acting the role of the coaching manager to ensure that learning from coaching is being transferred to the workplace. Of course, the manager of the coaching client is the individual most likely to have assigned the coaching client to the challenge he or she is using to drive the coaching in the first place. In our research on effective coaching engagements, we were clearly able to show that the positive involvement of the manager of the coaching client was a key success factor (Hunt, 2004). Yet because coaching may be somewhat mysterious or confusing to many, it may be essential for the CPM to "evangelize" about the importance of this involvement. At Omgeo, as we have seen, this is a requirement of the coaching engagement.

## Qualifying Coaches

The question of who should coach is obviously of critical importance. As we have discussed, expert coaching is an unregulated activity. In the next chapter, we'll describe how internal expert coaching programs have grappled with this problem. Various professional organizations, such as the International Coach Federation (2005), have attempted to set standards for the competencies and training ideally required of the expert coach. However, the larger community of organizations that fund coaching has not reached any consensus on a set of standards or accreditation procedures. This means that, ultimately, the selection and qualification of coaches is up to someone in the organization.

The stakes in this regard are high. Poorly delivered coaching can negatively impact individual executives and their organizations as well as poison the water for future coaching initiatives. It is critically important to remember that expert coaching that takes place within an organizational setting is quite different from expert coaching delivered to an individual in a confidential setting.

The expert coach in an organizational context, whose role it is to facilitate employee or leadership development, must serve two key stakeholders: the individual and the organization. Expert coaching is thus a systems-oriented intervention. The following definition of executive coaching, applicable to both external and internal executive coaching, captures this perspective:

> Executive coaching is an experiential, individualized, leadership development process that builds a leader's capability to achieve short- and long-term organizational goals. It is conducted through one-on-one interactions, driven by

data from multiple perspectives, and based on mutual trust and respect. The organization, an executive, and the executive coach work in partnership to achieve maximum impact from the coaching effort. (Ennis et al., 2004 p. 21)

The authors of this definition have engaged in a reflective exploration of the competencies required to effectively practice such a definition of expert coaching (Ennis et al., 2005). These are presented in detail in Appendix A. They include four knowledge areas, a skill set, and a set of personal attributes. These include the following:

• Psychological knowledge, including an understanding of personality, personality style, and the interaction between the person and his or her environment

• Business acumen, including an understanding of the various business functions, the role of strategy, basic financial savvy, operations, information technology (IT), quality, and other business-related trends

• Organizational behavior and development knowledge, including an understanding of organizational structure, leadership, teamwork, roles, and the place of power and politics

• Knowledge of coaching theory, including various schools of coaching and how coaching facilitates personal change

• Coaching skills required to build and maintain coaching relations, including development of a contract at the commencement of a coaching engagement, assessment and development planning skills, change management skills, and termination skills

• Personal attributes, including mature self-confidence, positive energy, assertiveness, interpersonal sensitivity, openness and flexibility, goal orientation, partnering and influencing abilities, positive orientation toward continuous learning, and integrity

While our articulation of these competencies must be considered hypothetical at this time, it does have face validity. The effective expert coach does not have to be a psychologist, but does have to possess many of the skills of the psychologist. That by itself is not enough, however. The effective coach must have a solid understanding of business realities and organizational life, as well as individual- and systems-level intervention skills. Of course, certain coaching engagement requirements will require more or less expertise in specific areas within the model, as Summer Turner, at

Omgeo, described above. Likewise, specific coaching initiatives may require more or less expertise in specific components of the model in Appendix A as well.

The qualification of coaches requires the development of a rigorous process (though we say this knowing that as with all selection processes, it is likely to never be perfect). Résumés and applications, behavioral interviews, and references are all indicated. Given that the need for particular coaching skills may not always be predictable, a reactive, last-minute approach is not indicated. We suggest that if an expert coaching capacity is desired by the organization, this key component of selection of external and internal coaches (more about the latter in the next two chapters) be given adequate time.

## Orienting Coaches

It goes without saying then that once selected, external and internal coaches require appropriate support. That begins with orientation to the coaching task, the business, and the organization's culture. As we have seen at both Whirlpool and at Omgeo, a critical element of the orientation is familiarizing coaches with the competency models in use. Coaches need to learn the language of the firm and, above all, to understand the developmental needs of the firm, so that they can help the coaching client work toward meeting those needs. Again, we would say that this is mission critical. As with any other worker, the expert coach can do what is needed only if he or she knows what is needed.

## Assessing the Need for Expert
## Coaching in Individual Cases

While we can offer advice regarding the tasks of the CPM with some confidence in the case of the previous items, the task of assessing the need for expert coaching in individual cases is more challenging, and even less research has been completed to guide us in this regard. At Omgeo, Summer Turner spent some time with each potential coachee in this activity. Here are the basic issues involved in managing this task as we see them today:

• If the coaching program is linked to a particular, usually classroom-based, leadership development activity, it may be the case that everyone in that activity will be given the opportunity to work with a coach. In essence, the organization is saying that everyone should give this a try. So, is the decision to coach or not to coach moot in this case? Yes and no. Yes, because it may make sense to try this approach if the participants in the overall program have been thoroughly screened and if they have been briefed on the role of coaching in the larger program, as was the case at Whirlpool and Omgeo. However, in our research on such activities (at other firms) we have found that even if thoroughly screened and briefed, some may not make effective use of coaching, for reasons that we discuss in the next section. The CPM and other key stakeholders simply need to be ready for this reality.

• When making individual assessments of whether or not to support an expert and therefore costly coaching engagement, we strongly suggest that those in charge look for the factor we have called "coachability" (Hunt & Weintraub, 2002a). Coachability implies a demonstrated interest in learn- ing, an open mind, and an ability to accept feedback, including difficult feedback. Not everyone fits such a description all the time, for a variety of obvious reasons.

• We have also found that the "learning potential" of the potential coachee's situation is also very relevant. Is the coachee engaged or about to be engaged with challenges that require learning? In the absence of those challenges, it is not clear what factors would drive the coaching (Hunt & Weintraub, 2002a).

• Finally, it is important to remember that coaching is driven by an experiential model of learning, as we have discussed earlier. As such, a cer- tain level of conceptual understanding of how to construct responses to a challenge is necessary. The classroom is a great place to learn about leadership, for instance. It can be quite useful to learn the basics of project management before taking on the leadership of a major project. Coaching would help with the latter.

## Matching Coaches and Coachees

Most CPMs we have interviewed make the match between coach and coachee after a thorough interview or two with the prospective coachee and based on thorough knowledge of the cadre of qualified coaches from which they can select, as the Omgeo case study indicated. Many freely admit that intuition, after a thorough immersion in the situation, plays a role. It is for that reason that CPMs follow up with the coaching client to assess whether or not the match has "taken." Furthermore, at Omgeo, as with several other firms of which we are aware, the coachee can be given greater control over the process by selecting from several possible coaches. (Obviously, the latter process can take some time, though it may be worth it.)

What do we know about the match between coach and coachee? In our research, we found that three factors were involved in making an effective match between coach and coachee. The first we called *credibility* (Hunt, 2004, using a term first coined by Hollenbeck, 1996). Credibility here refers to the degree to which the prospective coachee believes that the coach can actually help. This raises a tough question: If the coaching has yet to take place, how can the coachee know for sure what the outcome will be? The coachee must rely on referred credibility. The endorsement of the CPM or some other individual who is trusted by the coachee means a great deal. The coachee, particularly a naive coachee, must take it on faith that a potential coach knows what to do, when, and how. The coachee is initially in a very vulnerable spot.

The second and third factors we found were personal style and background. Neither of these was surprising. *Personal style* refers to characteristics such as assertiveness. Some coachees prefer that the coach "tell it like it is." Others prefer a more open-ended approach. *Background* refers to the accumulated career knowledge of the coach. A coachee moving into a major senior-management role, for instance, might find his or her sense of comfort with the coach enhanced by the knowledge that the coach had once been through a similar transition. Again, the argument is made that the CPM needs to have fairly in-depth knowledge of the coachee and potential coaches if the match is to be a successful one.

## Supporting Ongoing Coaching

The coaching may or may not require much in the way of ongoing support once under way with a motivated or coachable coachee and an effective coach in a well-constructed match. In our experience, the most important need for support comes if the coaching is not going well or if the coach and coachee are having a problem in the relationship. We have encountered such cases often enough that we would encourage CPMs to check in on all coaching engagements, at least informally, as is done at Omgeo.

## Coordinating Coaching and Related Employee or Leadership Development Activities

Again, we have seen the value of this activity in the Whirlpool case study and will see it most clearly when we examine the internal coaching program at Wachovia in Chapter 8. As we have already stated, coaching can greatly enhance the impact of the classroom or of rotation assignments. In our view, it greatly potentiates the organization's and the individual's investment in those assignments.

## Measuring Results

The measurement of results takes two forms. The CPM must, of course, develop a mechanism for assessing the impact of individual coaching engagements. Were goals attained or not? As we saw at Omgeo, the careful articulation of goals can greatly aide in this process. Beyond that, however, the CPM must also address the question of whether or not the overall coaching program investment is meeting the needs of the organization. As with all human resource development activities, there is considerable debate with regard to the appropriate measures to use in this outcome. We will discuss this in somewhat greater detail in the closing chapter.

## Closing Thoughts on the Management of the Coaching Capability

We have tried to make a strong case for the importance of placing a qualified individual in the role of overseeing the coaching initiative. Obviously, this is a most challenging role. The CPM has to be part coach and part change agent. He or she has to be adept at organizational politics, building stakeholder support, and educating others. The CPM has to know when to say "no" and be able to manage coaching as an important, but not free, resource. The CPM must, of course, also be good at assessing coaches, coachees, and the context of the coaching. Those in senior management ultimately responsible for creating a coaching capability would do well to make this selection with care. In the next two chapters, we'll consider how these factors are managed when the coaching initiative that is chosen involves the use of expert internal coaches.

# 7

# The Internal Coaching Capability

In this chapter, we describe the following:

- The distinguishing features of an internal coaching capability
- The goals of an internal coaching program
- The selection of internal coaches
- Internal coaching program guidelines
- The development of internal coaches
- The evaluation of internal coaching programs

As we have seen, it takes considerable effort and resources to develop and maintain an effective executive coaching program that relies on outside experts. Nevertheless, when an organization is devoid of coaching capabilities or when the coaching context is too unfriendly, the external expert coach or an external executive coaching program may be necessary. Likewise, when the organization needs specialized coaching skill, over and above an existing coaching capability, turning to resources outside the organization makes sense. If the organization, for instance, is sending an executive on an international assignment for the first time, coaching can help to ensure the success of what is often a risky leadership and career transition. This type of coaching assignment may require specific coaching skills not available from internal coaching resources.

Over the past decade, however, as an understanding of the value of developmental coaching has grown, some organizations have naturally begun to consider the strengths and weaknesses of relying on an external cadre of experts as their sole coaching capability and to consider alternatives. The use of expert *internal* coaches represents one such alternative. In this chapter, we discuss the issues associated with building an internal expert coaching capability and review what at this stage appear to be best practices. In the next chapter, we will offer a much more detailed example of a specific internal coaching program at Wachovia Corporation.

## What We Mean by "Expert" Internal Coaches

It is useful to revisit the concept of expert coaching in this regard, to see how it applies to internal coaching capabilities. Frisch (2001) defined internal coaching as "a one-on-one developmental intervention supported by [the coachee's] organization and provided by a colleague of those coached who is trusted to shape and deliver a program yielding individual professional growth" (p. 242). Upon review, this seems like a sensible definition. Frisch continued, "The simplest definition of internal coaching may be a tautology: being formally viewed by organizational coworkers as a coach makes it so" (p. 242). Unfortunately, we have to agree with that statement as well. Sometimes all it takes to be viewed as a coach is to call yourself one. However, being viewed as a coach by others does not mean that one is capable of delivering a "program" yielding individual professional growth, that is, being an effective coach.

The central question in any discussion of a value creating internal coaching capability, we believe, has to do with the role of expertise. Many human resource and organizational effectiveness professionals provide informal developmental coaching. Some line managers do as well. This is all to be encouraged, without question. However, we typically would not expect informal coaching by human resource professionals or coaching by managers to result in a focus with the same depth and with the same level of skill on the needs and unique context of the coachee as coaching that can be provided by an expert.

The coaching manager, as we will discuss in Chapter 9, focuses on helping the coachee, most often a direct report, learn from experience and apply what has been learned immediately. This certainly has longer-term implications for an employee, but the focus of the coaching manager is the present or the near-term future. Similarly, informal coaching offered by the effective human resource professional is likely to be directed at helping the employee deal with immediate learning challenges: managing a difficult employee, for instance. The expert coach, while leveraging immediate experience, can potentially help employees address longer-term or more difficult development challenges, such as those associated with transitioning into a new role or the development of skills requiring the coachee to work very far from his or her "comfort zone." This requires a much more in-depth assessment, a more focused contracting process, involvement of stakeholders, and follow-up coaching over an extended period of time.

Are these distinctions rigid? No, they are not. As has been reported elsewhere, expert executive coaching is more likely to be effective when the coachee has a manager who also provides effective coaching, in the moment (Hunt, 2004). We are arguing, rather, that an organization can maximize the impact of various kinds of coaching interventions by tailoring those interventions to meet somewhat differentiated needs. An internal coaching capability has the ability to address longer-term development issues, much as does an external executive coaching capability. We discuss what we know about the mission of the typical internal coaching program below. Going forward, however, we will assume that under "best-practices" circumstances, internal coaches make use of significant coaching expertise, such as that described in Appendix A, and it is this sophisticated skill set that gives them the greatest opportunity to create value for their organizations and their coaching clients.

## Why Expert Internal Coaching?

Why should organizational leaders consider an internal as opposed to an external coaching capability? As we find so often in the study of developmental coaching in an organizational context, decision makers have little in the way of robust research to guide them in making such choices. One of the more common reasons cited for creating an internal expert coaching capability is to reduce the costs associated with expert coaching (Frisch, 2005). We can't say with 100% confidence that this argument has merit, for two reasons. First, the reasonable costs associated with an external executive coaching engagement can vary so widely. Second, the standards for the conduct of coaching also vary so widely.

Anderson (2003), in a study of the return on investment (ROI) of an executive coaching program, reported the costs per participant for coaching and the management of the coaching program for a group of 43 executives as $6,000. The nature of the coaching was not fully described, however. We suspect that figure is low, particularly in light of the sums that some more widely known coaches charge for working with senior executives. The reality is that because of the ambiguities surrounding market-based arrangements for the provision of external coaching, we just can't say how much a coaching engagement should cost, and as a result, the purchaser of those services can't tell, either.

Not to belabor the point, then, but the "fact" that internal coaching is less costly than external coaching reflects an untested assumption. As we will see, internal coaching is an enormously challenging undertaking. Organizations that take a strategic view of their coaching capabilities will likely want to staff coaching positions with real talent; and such an approach, whether drawn from a regular employee or outside consultant, brings with it certain costs. In-depth coaching, in particular, may take time, and there are only so many hours in a day.

Expert coaching talent also needs to be nurtured through a program of development. As such, we would suggest that organizations considering the development of an expert internal coaching capability be prepared to make a substantial investment. Minimizing costs may have the unintended consequence of minimizing effectiveness. We need much more research on the question of cost shifting before we can conclude with certainty that internal coaching is cheaper than externally provided coaching.

There are, of course, other reasons for considering the use of internal expert coaches in lieu of, or in addition to, external coaches. When the coach and the coachee are both from the same organization, they are likely to be more intimately aware of the organization's goals and business models and the issues associated with both. Both participate in the same culture (albeit they may not always participate in the same subcultures within their host organization). Both are likely to have at least some exposure to the same or similar political challenges associated with service in that culture. Indeed, both may know some or all of the same key players within the organization's context.

The shared experiences of coach and coachee may facilitate a greater ability to address important cultural, political, and strategic issues. The coach may be able to offer a second set of eyes to help the coachee interpret his or her reality more effectively. The coach may be able to respond with concrete advice based on organization-specific knowledge. Finally, the coach may be in a position to actually observe the coachee in action, in a somewhat less intrusive fashion than might an external coach (Frisch, 2001). Based on such firsthand observations, the coach may be in a much better position to provide effective feedback to the coachee.

Of course, each of these potential advantages can also represent a potential disadvantage. The coach may empathize too readily with the coachee and become more of an ally than an objective observer (Smith, 2005). The coach, being a participant in the organization's culture, may be blinded by the culture. The advice offered by the coach may be less objective as a result.

The internal coach must face a whole host of political challenges as well. The internal coach may have to take positions that are less popular with some key organizational actors. The internal coach, by virtue of his or her position in the organization, may have interests that actually conflict with those of the coachee or key stakeholders to the coachee's world. Finally, the coach, because of his or her closer involvement with the coachee, must address concerns related to the psychological boundaries that create a coaching-friendly context.

The coachee still has to be able to trust the coach, even though the coach's role, depending upon its nature, may create the potential for a perceived conflict of interest. The internal coach may be involved in decisions that directly or indirectly impact the coachee. The coachee must be able to assume that the coach's behavior and actions, at least in the context of the coaching, are in the interest of the coachee.

As with every aspect of the challenge of creating a coaching organization, building an internal coaching capability can be done from a strategic perspective or an ad hoc one. The strategic perspective should meet the standards outlined in Chapter 4: A strategic approach to building a coaching capability results in (a) a better understanding of the nature and use of developmental coaching for most or all of those involved, (b) a better understanding of when developmental coaching can be helpful, (c) a better understanding of the distinction between learning and a performance problem, (d) a heightened ability to create safe spaces within which learning-oriented dialogues can take place, and (e) an overall increase in the ability to coach on the part of participating coachees.

An ad hoc approach to the development of an internal coaching capability may by its very nature yield such results; an ad hoc approach also entails significant risks. There has been an explosion of knowledge about coaching over the past two decades. A coaching "career" has become attractive to many people, including those employed in other, sometimes unrelated, jobs. On a number of occasions, we have heard stories of individuals with an interest in coaching being given permission to "start coaching" based on their interests—"Seems like a good idea." In some of those instances, fortunately, the results have been truly strategic. In others, they have been disastrous. Ineffective "coaching" given to the wrong people at the wrong time can make subsequent efforts to build a coaching capability the target of much skepticism, as in Case 7.1.

## CASE 7.1    Sam the Coach (A somewhat fictitious story)

Sam was seen as being very influential at AgriBus Co. He was well liked by the firm's owners (a family) and had a certain level of credibility because of his success in various business functions over the years. As his career progressed, he became more interested in the "people" side of the business. Always thought of as being "good to talk with," he naturally drifted toward establishing helping relationships with a number of employees. Sam enjoyed this aspect of his work thoroughly and decided to take formal coursework in personal coaching. He located a reputable coaching training institute and studied for the next 2 years on a part-time basis. With the firm's owner's approval, he developed a small number of coaching clients among middle-level managers in the organization. The coaching focused almost solely on the personal development of those clients rather than on their development within their working roles. This led one coaching client to reassess his career activities and subsequently leave the organization.

While this created some concern among the firm's senior management, overall, they were impressed with Sam's skills and asked if he could spend more time coaching others on a more formal basis. In particular, they asked him to help the new sales manager, Joan. Joan had been with AgriBus for only 1 year but already had a startling reputation for being hostile and demanding of her direct reports and untrustworthy among her peers. She justified her actions by extolling the need to "be tough" and "shake things up." Sam was asked to help her "deal with her rough edges" by the firm's owner. (The firm had no competency model or plan for developing leadership talent.) While his coaching addressed her personal concerns and career aspirations, it did little to change her behavior. Her own manager continued to be unwilling to confront her behavior and ultimately expressed the sense that "this coaching is useless." Ultimately, it was. Joan got a better job with a competitor and then threatened to sue AgriBus. She accused the firm of pressuring Sam to divulge information from their coaching sessions. (The firm had no guidelines for the use of coaching or for the execution of coaching-related activities.) Sam's career as an internal coach came to an end.

Sam's case (actually a composite of several similar cases) illustrates the challenges associated with the role of internal coach. First, firms that choose to develop an internal coaching capability still have to manage that capability. They need to think through, ideally, in a proactive fashion, what they are trying to accomplish and the implications of the plan. Once they have a guiding plan or strategy in place, they need to make certain that they target coaching appropriately, not haphazardly. They also need to carefully credential coaching providers and assess their strengths and weaknesses. Not all coaches are created equally (in fact, none are). In this case, for instance, they might have considered Sam's relative inexperience at coaching and the severe nature of the presenting problem. Of course, they could also have asked themselves whether or not this was a situation appropriate for expert coaching or if it could have been more appropriately dealt with through the performance management process, by the supervisor.

Regarding the last point, firms must also assess the context within which the coaching takes place. As we have seen, the supervisor of the coachee plays a critical role in the outcomes of expert coaching interventions (Hunt, 2004). The reluctance of Joan's manager to function as an active participant in the coaching ultimately doomed the effort. Yet we would have to ask, under this ad hoc approach to program development, whether Joan's manager was educated as to an appropriate coaching process.

Ultimately, the organization needs to manage an internal coaching capability through guidelines or policies that are adequate to provide support and a sense of appropriate safety for those involved. Internal coaching may look like a free ride to an organization that finds it has a protean coaching capability in the form of a motivated, credible employee such as Sam. Consider the following Case 7.2, and note the differences.

## CASE 7.2    The Management Effectiveness Business Partner

Steve Leichtman is vice president for human resources and management effectiveness consultant in a large financial services firm. He works directly with the heads of two businesses. He describes his responsibilities to his business partners as being "to help them achieve their business objectives in the near term and grow their skills and competencies in the longer term." Steve is a midcareer executive with a long and successful track record as an internal organizational effectiveness professional. In several previous jobs, he developed a significant skill base in the provision of internal expert coaching services. Coaching activities now consume approximately 30% of his time. Steve stresses that he actually sees himself as a "businessman" who uses coaching in the service of his and his organization's business goals. He talks the language of his business, financial services, and embraces the values of the firm. These factors all help Steve build credibility with his audience.

Upon entering his current role, Steve spent considerable time building a trusting relationship with the heads of the two businesses and developing a strategy to help them promote the success of their businesses. All agreed that "people management skills" were critical to their success, yet at the same time they agreed that there were significant organizational deficiencies in this regard. Coaching was a logical response in the context of this organization and its culture. This is a fast-paced firm in which people are much more likely to engage with on-the-job learning strategies than with classroom-based approaches. The organizational need and context, then, served to drive the coaching initiative. Coaching became a means to an end, not an end in itself. The goal being an important one, the business leaders became active participants in the building of this coaching capability.

At a tactical level, Steve has found that coaching from an objective, data-driven perspective (i.e., one that relies on a thorough assessment) to be of most value to coaching clients. From a cultural standpoint, this is fortunate in that those in his current organization place great stock in the value of data. The approach he suggested to his business partners was consistent with the organization's culture.

The coaching plan involved the use of a 360-degree management effectiveness assessment tool and follow-up coaching for the purposes of building formal, work-oriented, and useful development plans. The leaders of the two businesses and their direct reports began the process themselves. They went through the 360-degree assessment and coaching process in a very public fashion. Everyone would be involved, and, as such, the organization avoided the trap of focusing coaching resources on problem performers, with all of the risks such an approach entails.

Through this process, the leaders developed a hands-on feel for what coaching could do, dealt with concerns and risk factors regarding the process, and modeled the creation of an environment that encouraged people to view coaching as a useful development tool. Subsequently, this process cascaded through the organization, ultimately involving over 60 individuals. (Steve has subsequently developed a team of internal coaches, including several senior human resource professionals also trained in coaching to address the needs of this large number of executives.) This initial coaching process served both to focus employee development efforts and build longer-term coaching relationships between Steve and those involved. Follow-up coaching, both formal and informal, is in the service of executing to both business and development plans.

Steve is able to leverage his close proximity to his coachees. He is in a position to appropriately but discreetly support observed behavioral changes or address the lack thereof, through observation and feedback. At the same time, however, Steve is very aware of the challenges of maintaining trust as an internal coach. As such, even given his close proximity to his coachees, he is very careful to manage the boundaries around coaching activities. For instance, he avoids becoming part of a triangular relationship between a direct report and his or her boss. Like the external executive coach, the internal coach has to manage multiple stakeholder relationships effectively by clearly and consistently delineating the goals of coaching relationships and the boundaries surrounding those relationships. Steve states,

> I work with the managers of those being coached, primarily to understand their perspectives on my implementation of the coachee's development plan. I do not, however, share my coaching conversations with the coachee's boss . . . . I leave that sharing up to the coachee [and encourage it].

So far, Steve, his organization, and his coaching clients are pleased with the results, and he has run into little skepticism. Steve is sensitive as to how coaching is viewed and may not describe his work with certain clients as "coaching." He believes that he is seen as someone who is trying to do the right thing and who is experienced in leadership development. From a results standpoint, development plans are in place for nearly 60 individuals and are being taken seriously. Extensive follow-up coaching is taking place to support the execution of those plans.

---

As we have repeatedly stressed, trust is an essential ingredient of developmental coaching. The external coach has the advantage of being seen as an outsider and, as such, "trustworthy" by virtue of his or her lack of contact with some key organizational players (the more key players with whom the external coach is involved, the less this advantage is bestowed). The internal coach must establish and maintain "personal trust" based on his or her conduct and despite his or her participation in other organizational roles (Hall & Otazo, 1995).

Was this an ad hoc effort to build a coaching capability in Steve's business unit? It certainly began with one individual's vision for that capability. There was no designated "coaching function" in this case. However, Steve's ability to connect his vision for coaching with the business goals of senior management, coupled with a systematic rollout of a *developmental* coaching protocol, for all managers, illustrate the strategic nature of the effort. As such, it offers some important lessons. The internal coach, particularly the internal coach who is promoting a strategic approach toward building a developmental coaching capability, needs to be viewed as someone who has the following characteristics:

- Has the best interests of the organization at heart
- Understands the organization and its business and is a true business partner
- Has a robust coaching-related skill set and is able to articulate the nature of developmental coaching to other stakeholders.
- Is truly engaged in helping others succeed and is seen as a resource
- Avoids at all costs the use of information to enhance his or her personal position within the organization
- Is clear about confidentiality or its limits with all parties and educates coaching clients with regard to the limits of confidentiality on a proactive basis
- Serves on occasion as a resource for individuals with performance problems, but for the most part is seen as a developmental resource (not a "signal" that one is on the way out) to good and great employees who are likely to be most able to take advantage of the coaching effort and at the same time contribute to the organization's goals.

# Critical Issues in Building an Effective Internal Coaching Capability

In this section, we build on Steve Leichtman's experience as well as using insights from the existing literature and examples from the ongoing buildup of an internal coaching capability at the National Aeronautics and Space Administration (NASA). These examples, as well as that of Wachovia Corporation, to be discussed in much greater detail in the next chapter, suggest the importance of considering the following issues:

- The specification of the internal coaching program's purpose, goals, or mission
- The selection of individuals who can serve as internal coaching resources
- The development of policies or guidelines for the internal coaching practice
- The ongoing professional development of those chosen to serve as internal coaching resources
- The evaluation of an internal coaching program

We now discuss each of these considerations in some detail.

## The Purpose of the Internal Coaching Program

As mentioned above, in our view, experience suggests to us that an internal coaching capability is most likely to be of value if it can apply real coaching expertise to longer-term developmental challenges. For Steve Leichtman, the internal coaching program had several goals, including (a) to help the organization's employees do their jobs effectively and (b) to address a longer-term need to promote management development, particularly the "people skills" that were deemed to be important to the organization's success. Research to date suggests that such a defined purpose is consistent with those found in a number of other companies that use an internal coaching capability.

Robertson, Higuchi, and Huff (2004), in a study of Canadian firms with an internal coaching program, found that the most common goals were to improve management behavior and/or develop leadership talent. McDermott, Levenson, and Clarke (2005), in a study of 55 firms with coaching programs, found that internal coaches tend to be used more often for those at the vice president level down through middle management and for the leadership development of high-potential employees. The same data show that external executive coaches were more likely to be used for senior vice presidents and CEO-level employees. This research appears to support the assumption of many who have considered internal coaching programs that it is difficult for the most senior-level employees to receive coaching from someone who essentially reports to them (Strumpf, 2002) and that organizations are trying to use internal coaching programs in contexts that are slightly less politically sensitive.

McDermott et al. (2005) also found that internal coaches were more likely to be used for derailing executives than were external coaches, though this was not the bulk of the work done by internal coaches. Interestingly, they found that while the use of external coaches for derailing executives had a negative impact on employee morale (as we would predict), the use of internal coaches was less likely to have such an impact. It may be more palatable to organizational members to devote already-existing resources to the resolution of a performance problem than to bring in "expensive consultants."

In summary, then, the most common and perhaps most reasonable mission for an internal coaching capability is to improve the leadership effectiveness of middle- and upper-level (but not the most senior) managers in a fashion aligned with the perceived needs of the organization. Certainly, the need for a coaching intervention for this group is evident in most organizations. Middle- and upper-level managers need to not only expand their leadership toolkits as they move up but also do so in increasingly complex contexts. They will likely have to work cross-functionally and exert influence up, down, and out, with key, powerful stakeholders. The knowledge of the culture and politics that the internal coach brings to the coaching task seems particularly well suited to such a learning challenge. At the same time, the internal coach may be less likely to bump up against overwhelming political issues inherent in working one level down from the CEO.

The NASA coaching program (which provides coaching by external and internal experts and promotes coaching by managers) was initiated as a part of the agency's Strategic Human Capital Plan, a response to a U.S. federal government response to the president's management agenda that states that "agencies must make better use of the flexibilities currently in place to acquire and develop talent and leadership" (NASA, 2005, p. 3).

This larger goal cascades down as subgoals that encourage the development of a climate of open sharing of information, which promotes, among other outcomes, personal growth and includes a variety of strategically designed training and development programs, including coaching and mentoring. The mission of the internal component of the coaching program has expanded over time (C. Williams, personal communication, July 28, 2005).

NASA is quite a decentralized organization, with major semiautonomous centers across the United States. Leadership development services are guided from NASA headquarters in Washington, but execution is tactically managed at the center level. As such, there is a need for both coaching expertise and coaching practice expertise at the centers. The internal coach supports the credentialing of external coaches and managing the matching process between external coaches and coaching clients. In addition, the internal coach may often provide more informal and in-the-moment coaching, as well as taking on formal coaching engagements. There has been a trend for internal coaches to work at lower levels than external coaches in the centers when taking on formal engagements, consistent with research cited above (C. Williams, personal communication, July 28, 2005).

The missions of the internal coaching program at NASA are thus multifaceted, but they are quite strategic. The internal coaches are ultimately responsible, by virtue of their expertise, for maintaining the overall integrity of the expert coaching program, as well as providing coaching services themselves. They are, as such, "practice managers" for the individual centers, as we described in Chapter 6. The potential value of the internal coaching cadre for the performance of this task was not initially recognized, but recognition has grown as the overall coaching program has matured (C. Williams, personal communication, July 28, 2005).

Robertson et al. (2004) found that the "internal coaching role" was codified in the form of a job description in nearly 50% of the companies in their sample. This reflects a positive development in that the tasks inherent with the role can be made explicit and therefore more easily be aligned with the program's goals and the organization's goals. A well-written job description for the internal coach can, of course, greatly facilitate the process of selection for internal coaching roles, our next concern.

## Selection of Internal Coaches

The selection of internal coaches who can provide expert support requires the consideration of two factors: competence and credibility. We address the competency requirements first. The competency model for executive coaches generally is articulated in Appendix A.

While this model is very preliminary, the list of skills and attributes included seems appropriate for the expert internal coach as well. We realize that this comprehensive list sets a high standard for internal coaching programs. We suggest, however, that given the importance of the tasks assigned to an internal coaching capability, a robust skill set would simply be a nonnegotiable requirement. (We concede that no one is perfect, and an individual may enter the internal coaching role possessing some, but not all, of the desired competencies. We discuss the continued development needs of internal coaches below.)

Consider one task of leadership development work, that of helping high-potential employees and managers prepare individual development plans. Consider whether or not the process is really effective in your organization. Effective individual development plans, those that are outcome oriented rather than activity oriented, are actually challenging to build. In most organizations, research suggests that the process is essentially a waste of effort and money because it is poorly executed and there is little or no follow-up (Eichinger, Lombardo, & Stibler, 2005). Data-driven development planning is a highly challenging task and requires a sophisticated skill set.

The challenge of establishing credibility can be more subjective. Robertson et al. (2004) found that most internal coaches had jobs beyond coaching in their host organizations and that they tended to come from human resource or organizational development functions. Thus, the internal coach is likely to be someone who has been visible to many others prior to taking on the coaching role.

As mentioned above, the internal coach has to be seen as someone who invokes a personal, rather than role-based, sense of trust. This has to do in part with how this individual is known for handling sensitive information. It also has to do with whether or not he or she is seen as someone who has been an effective performer and is knowledgeable and helpful to others and to the organization. The coachee who is naive to the coaching process is in no position to assess the competencies of a potential coach, particularly early in a coaching engagement. He or she will be looking at something else, the coach's general demeanor or presence, personal style, and credibility. Credibility is often a function of reputation and is typically bestowed by consistent, helpful, and ethical conduct over time, as well as by some familiarity with the business issues faced by the coachee (Hunt, 2004).

How can organizations best assess talent for competence and credibility? An organization attempting to assess internal coaching talent, just as with external talent, have three choices: It can rely on an external certification of coaching skills, build up its own competency model and certify individuals against that model through a combination of interviews and references, or work with some combination of the two.

As we saw when discussing the selection of external executive coaches, certification of coaches by groups such as the International Coach Federation (ICF) is seen as helpful in some organizations. NASA requires everyone chosen as an internal coach to have training from an ICF accredited program (see Box 7.1 for a brief overview of ICF competencies).

**Box 7.1    International Coach Federation Competencies**

A. Setting the Foundation

1. Meeting Ethical Guidelines and Professional Standards: Understanding of coaching ethics and standards and ability to apply them appropriately in all coaching situations

2. Establishing the Coaching Agreement: Ability to understand what is required in the specific coaching interaction and to come to agreement with the prospective and new client about the coaching process and relationship

B. Co-Creating the Relationship

3. Establishing Trust and Intimacy with the Client: Ability to create a safe, supportive environment that produces ongoing mutual respect and trust

4. Coaching Presence: Ability to be fully conscious and create a spontaneous relationship with the client, employing a style that is open, flexible, and confident

C. Communicating Effectively

5. Active Listening: Ability to focus completely on what the client is saying and is not saying, to understand the meaning of what is said in the context of the client's desires, and to support client self-expression

6. Powerful Questioning: Ability to ask questions that reveal the information needed for maximum benefit to the coaching relationship and the client

7. Direct Communication: Ability to communicate effectively during coaching sessions and to use language that has the greatest positive impact on the client

D. Facilitating Learning and Results

8. Creating Awareness: Ability to integrate and accurately evaluate multiple sources of information and to make interpretations that help the client gain awareness and thereby achieve agreed-upon results

9. Designing Actions: Ability to create opportunities with the client for ongoing learning, during coaching and in work-life situations, and for taking new actions that will most effectively lead to agreed-upon coaching results

10. Planning and Goal Setting: Ability to develop and maintain an effective coaching plan with the client

11. Managing Progress and Accountability: Ability to hold attention on what is important for the client and to leave responsibility with the client to take action

SOURCE: Adapted from ICF (2005).

Note that the ICF competencies focus on the coaching process at the interface between the coach and coachee. Unlike the list of competencies and attributes found in Appendix A, the ICF competency descriptions do not address the abilities associated with expert executive coaching in an organizational context. To address such skill requirements, NASA has also articulated additional requirements for those in internal coaching roles, described in Box 7.2.

---

**Box 7.2    NASA Competencies for Internal Coaches**

- Tested Experience: The coach must have the appropriate level of corporate experience to understand the developmental, political, and environment needs of the employee.
- Skilled at Problem Diagnosis: If diagnostic instruments are used, the coach must be appropriately certified to administer those instruments to assess gaps, help identify blind spots for the individual being coached, determine outcome measurements (scorecards for accountabilities, pre- and post-assessments to measure 360-degree feedback), and facilitate communications and feedback.
- Results Oriented: The outcomes of the coaching relationship should specify how the coaching success would be measured, evaluated, and realized by individual performance improvement and NASA mission impacts. In addition, a coaching agreement for the employee should be established up-front and refined throughout the coaching relationship.
- Knowledge and Application of Coaching Competencies, Including Interpersonal Competencies: The coach must demonstrate knowledge through past experience and application of competencies previously identified.

SOURCE: Adapted from NASA (2005, p. 8).

Of note, when NASA began the process of building an internal coaching capability, they did not have a sufficient number of internal coaches who were, in fact, trained as coaches. As such, this has become a developmental goal for the overall program and is further discussed below.

## Guidelines for an Internal Coaching Practice

The purpose of guidelines or policy statements for any coaching capability is to ensure that the coaching activity is aligned with the goals and needs of the business. As has been discussed in Chapter 6 and elsewhere (Hunt, 2004), there is some tension between the need for the coach and the coachee to have an open space within which to customize the learning experience and the need to manage the process so as to ensure that the work is aligned with the organization's needs. At the same time, employee development should be aligned with the talent needs of the organization.

At NASA, this process is managed on a personal basis (NASA, 2005), similar to what we found in the case of Omgeo, in Chapter 6. NASA guidelines require some assessment of the situation at the input level and periodic reviews as coaching progresses. External and internal coaching are both available to potential coachees. Requests for coaching are reviewed in a collaborative process with a human resource professional at the Center level, described as a "Center Coaching Point of Contact." Prior to this meeting, the employee interested in coaching must complete a brief questionnaire regarding his or her goals and background. Goals established during this period are then tracked through periodic and closing evaluations. We'll see an example of a very focused guideline set for an internal coaching capability in the next chapter.

Strumpf (2002) has recommended that organizations using an internal coaching program develop an explicit confidentiality policy. Clearly, coachees need to understand the confidentiality boundaries of the internal coaching experience, just as they might for the external coaching experience. As discussed in Chapter 6, however, the boundaries around expert coaching are not the same as those that might surround counseling provided by an employee assistance program (EAP). EAP counseling is typically shielded by confidentiality boundaries equivalent to those that surround the doctor-patient relationship.

Expert coaching requires the participation of a variety of stakeholders, including the coachee's manager and perhaps others as well. An interview-based, 360-degree assessment is a very public event, involving peers, direct reports, customers, and the coachee's human resource manager in many instances. Internal coaching, given that it is provided by an organization's employee, may be particularly vulnerable to intrusion from senior managers. This can occur out of ignorance if the confidentiality policy is not made clear to all those involved. Attempted intrusions can also occur out of malice as well. It is for this reason that we recommend that the confidentiality policy be clearly documented and that it receive a "sign-off" at the highest possible level (the firm CEO and/or vice president of human resources).

To summarize, the internal coaching program should have guidelines or policies that can help all stakeholders clearly understand the following:

- The developmental nature of the coaching involved
- The appropriate candidates for developmental coaching
- A means of assessing the coaching process and outcomes
- A confidentiality policy

These, of course, are in addition to an articulation of the program's goals or mission and the guidelines for the selection and the development of internal coaches, which we address in the next section.

## The Ongoing Development of Internal Coaches

Strumpf (2002) has suggested four strategies for the ongoing development of internal coaches: promoting self-development, selecting appropriate coaching assignments, partnering with external experts, and creating coaching networks. The development of internal coaches requires the same three components as development more generally: challenge, assessment, and support (Van Velsor & McCauley, 2004). Internal coaching programs are still rather new, and, as such, the implementation of development programs appears to vary widely. In the next chapter, we present what we believe is a "best-practices" example that includes most of these elements. We would argue, however, that this is one area in which internal coaching programs may be most at risk, as the development of employees requires the investment of firm resources. When the firm hires outside consultants, it can assume that consultants will take care of their own development needs and build in the costs of doing so in their fee structures. The same is not true of internal coaches. Let's look at how Strumpf's (2002) four development components can be actualized.

Support for self-development can include reading, attendance at conferences, and participation in activities in which the coach's conceptual toolkit is expanded. The requirement for external certification can serve as a driver for these kinds of activities. NASA's requirement that internal coaches receive ICF certification represents such an example. ICF certification requires certain specific classroom activities in addition to participation in supervised coaching engagements. However, organizations using certification as a driver for development activities should also consider what to do after the certification process is complete.

The selection of appropriate cases is analogous to the selection of appropriate development assignments. Early in their careers, it may be helpful for coaches to work with lower-risk coaching clients. Later in their careers, once they have achieved mastery over routing coaching challenges, they will likely learn more from more challenging assignments. This often means that they will be working with more senior individuals. As we saw in Case 7.1, it can be a mistake to create a mismatch (in that instance, a very challenging client with a less experienced coach). While development does involve making mistakes, if the mistake is too significant, careers can stall as a result.

Partnering with external experts appears to represent one of the most common developmental strategies used by internal coaching programs. The internal coaches at NASA participate with external coaches, as part of a coaching "community of practice" in which they can compare their experiences in that rather unique context. The Wachovia coaching program described in the next chapter requires that internal coaches with active cases participate in a group supervision experience with a more experienced, typically external, coach. The purposes of this activity are twofold. First, it offers the program an ability to exercise some quality control over the work in process. Second, however, such a structure also supports individual coaches' abilities to learn from their ongoing experiences. As Strumpf (2002) has said, "Credibility for internal coaches hinges in large measure on their consistently practicing what they preach, and for this reason, continuously examining and improving coaching performance is key" (p. 232).

These partnership arrangements naturally create the potential for the development of a "community of practice" in which experienced coaches share their work with the explicit goal of continuous improvement. An experienced cadre of both internal expert coaches and external expert coaches working together seems particularly appropriate for meeting the developmental needs of more senior coaches. The distinction between learner and teacher tends to disappear in communities of practice. Both NASA and Wachovia are actively supporting the evolution of such communities by creating events that bring experienced practitioners together for the purposes of helping their organizations learn from the coaches' experiences, through providing appropriate classroom activities to draw the coaches' participation and by providing a safe space for peer-to-peer development dialogues.

# The Results: Do Well-Run Internal Coaching Programs Yield Different Outcomes?

The answer to this question is, at this point in time, we simply don't know. In this chapter (and in the next), we have tried to share with the reader how best-practice organizations are attempting to build robust internal coaching capabilities. Their goal appears to be that of building a capability that will deliver expert coaching services. One could, of course, quarrel with this designation. After all, in every "best-practice" organization we have studied in this regard, the internal coaches have had other duties beyond that of coach. One would presume, then, that their roles require other forms of expertise as well.

Indeed, as we will discuss at the close of the next chapter, the expertise of technical or content-based consultants, such as those found in human resources, may at times appear to conflict with the expertise of process-oriented coaches. Regardless, can we expect internal coaches who have a few formal coaching cases at any given time to be as effective as an external executive coach who may have had 20 to 30 open coaching engagements at any given time for a decade or more? The answer to this question is made more complicated by virtue of the fact that some of those in internal coaching roles may have had external coaching practices at other stages in their careers.

What does the research tell us? The only study that we have been able to locate to date that included an assessment of outcomes from coaching engagements in which both internal and external coaches were used reported no distinction between the two (Hall et al., 1999). In fairness, however, this was not the focus of their study. When assessed against the kinds of coaching outcomes discussed in previous chapters, it seems clear that internal coaching, properly conducted, would likely have a look and feel quite similar to that of coaching provided by external consultants. The exceptions are as we have already noted. Trust issues must be aggressively addressed. The internal coach must be able to manage the political challenges associated with the role. (Of course, one distinction at the programmatic level appears to be that of mission: internal coaching programs may be more likely than external programs to provide services to middle- and lower-level senior managers.) On the positive side, the internal coach has certain advantages in that he or she has access to the organization's culture and perhaps a better feel for the business realities faced by the coachee. Finally, the internal coach may be in a better position to access data about the coachee's performance under certain circumstances.

We suggest that effectively provided internal coaching should be capable of promoting improved performance, attitude, a strengthened sense of identity development, and adaptability in the face of change (Hall, 2002). The qualifier here is "effectively provided." Clearly, that requires well-honed, senior talent (as in the case of Steve Leichtman) and/or an extensive investment of resources into building a program that will result in the selection, guidance, and support for well-honed talent to serve in the role of internal coach. In the next chapter, we will look at one example of the latter, in the Wachovia Corporation.

# 8

# The ELP Internal Coaching Program at Wachovia Corporation

*Colleen Gentry, James Hunt,*
*Ellen Kumata, and Joseph Weintraub*

In this chapter, we describe the following:

- An internal coaching program in a major financial services institution
- The factors associated with the program's success, including the program focus, the careful selection of coaches, the training of coaches, and the linkages between the internal coaching program's mission and the business needs of the organization
- The training and development of coaches in some detail
- The challenges of assuming a formal coaching role for the functional human resource management leader

The internal coaching capability at Wachovia Corporation is an integral part of a larger development program, the Executive Leadership Program (ELP). ELP is an integrated classroom and practice-based development activity for high-potential future leaders from throughout the corporation. The task of the internal coaching program is to facilitate individualized development planning, drawing heavily on a 360-degree assessment of participants' leadership competencies. Approximately 55 senior human resource (HR) professionals serve as coaches in ELP.

The design of the internal coaching program also supports a larger strategic vision for coaching at Wachovia and draws on the lessons learned from all aspects of the effort to execute to that vision. Not surprisingly, one of the most important lessons learned in the development of an organizational coaching capability is that any coaching program design has to be consistent with the goals and culture of the organization. Nevertheless, all coaching programs, whether internal or external, must address a number of key challenges having to do with defining the mission of the program and the selection, training, and development of coaches. In this chapter, we describe these challenges in relationship to the buildout of Wachovia's internal coaching capability in some detail.

The experience at Wachovia suggests the value of carefully scoping an internal program by linking the program with a very clear task. The opportunity to serve as a coach was not seen as a developmental assignment, given that the program's success was essential to the business as well as the long-term viability of coaching at Wachovia. An extensive training program was required of those participating as coaches. An investment was also made in the coaches' ongoing development. First and last, the program was intimately linked with important business drivers for Wachovia, including the need for an expanding and highly diverse leadership pipeline. We start with that part of the story.

## The Wachovia Executive Leadership Program

Wachovia Corporation is headquartered in Charlotte, North Carolina. With 93,000 employees, it is the fourth-largest bank-holding company in the United States and the third-largest full-service brokerage firm, based on client assets.[1] In addition to organic growth, the corporation has also grown through merger activity, the largest being the merger of First Union Corporation and Wachovia Corporation, in 2001. Such a substantial increase in the sheer size of the corporation created a long-term and ongoing need to intensify thinking about and acting on the development of a substantial leadership pipeline.

Both legacy corporations had different experiences with coaching and leadership development. Legacy Wachovia had made considerable use of external executive coaching and had also developed a cadre of internal coaches. In contrast, leadership development programs at legacy First Union had focused on efforts to create a more diverse leadership pool. Legacy First Union had had little experience with coaching for the purposes of leadership development.

The ELP had actually been pioneered in legacy Wachovia, with a coaching component not dissimilar to that which we describe here. However, the merger required a rethinking of existing efforts from both legacy firms. Coaching had to establish itself as a legitimate activity to legacy First Union leaders (who constituted the majority of those in leadership roles in the newly merged organization), who, while not necessarily against the building of a coaching capability, simply had less familiarity with the concept and what it could offer. The internal coaching program thus had a complex set of requirements when viewed strategically. Its success was critical to addressing a major business need, the accelerated development of a *diverse* leadership pipeline, as well as the credibility of future coaching efforts, given that this would be a highly visible program.

## The Decision to Build an Internal Coaching Capability

Fortunately, much of what had been learned through the initial efforts at legacy Wachovia could be used, with appropriate modifications, in the new Wachovia. The choice to build an internal coaching capability to support this effort, as opposed to using external coaches, was driven by a number of factors. One factor, of course, was costs. As discussed previously, an internal coaching program appears to compete effectively from a cost perspective with the use of external coaching resources in a well-defined, time-limited, managed coaching initiative. However, internal coaching is not a panacea from a cost perspective. Wachovia found that there were significant costs associated with building an internal coaching program as well, as will be clear from the investments discussed below.

There were, however, additional drivers that supported the development of an internal coaching cadre. There was an explicit desire to partner with senior HR generalists as one way of educating the larger community about the value of coaching and the need to approach coaching from a developmental and strategic perspective rather than a remedial perspective. Bringing some of those HR leaders into the coaching program could obviously be of help in that regard. Through their participation in the internal coaching cadre, they would be well positioned to assess and respond to a wide variety of situations in which coaching could be a useful tool.

There was also a strong desire to leverage the knowledge that the internal coaching cadre could bring regarding Wachovia's emerging culture and the challenges associated with development in that culture. It was felt that those familiar with the culture of the firm would be well positioned to help high-potential employees learn to more effectively work within the culture to achieve the desired business results. Finally, given that the time span of the coaching engagements themselves were to be relatively brief, ease of access between coach and coachee was a consideration.

## Program Design Elements

As discussed in previous chapters, a coaching capability ideally works with a set of learning goals or competency requirements thought by organizational leaders to be important for current and future success. These serve to guide assessment, goal setting, and evaluation within the coaching process for the coach, coachee, and the coachee's manager. At Wachovia, as was the case at Whirlpool, a leadership model served this function. Cambria Consulting was engaged to build the leadership competency model for the new Wachovia, a function they had played in legacy Wachovia. There were significant changes from the leadership competency model that had been developed for legacy Wachovia, however. The leadership model developed for the new Wachovia Corporation balanced both internal and external factors (see Box 8.1). These served to define the learning goals for ELP and provided a framework for linking individual development and Wachovia leadership effectiveness.

---

**Box 8.1    The Wachovia Executive Leadership Model**

1. Creating vision and direction

2. Executing on strategy

3. Communicating effectively

4. Assessing, leveraging, and managing risk

5. Focusing on customer satisfaction

6. Developing high-performing teams

7. Creating partnerships

8. Demonstrating integrity and personal excellence

---

ELP participants were carefully chosen. They included only individuals who were seen to have significant leadership potential for the future of the corporation. Experience has shown at Wachovia, as elsewhere, that a high level of participant motivation and organizational commitment is essential if the most value is to be gained from the corporation's investment in individual development. It was hoped that those chosen to participate in ELP would have a significant commitment to improving the organization as well as their own skill sets. An effort was made to avoid using the program as a vehicle for attempting to repair badly damaged careers or those almost certain to leave the corporation when the chance arose. Of course, these participant criteria served to enhance the "coachability" of those participating in the coaching as well (Hunt & Weintraub, 2002a).

ELP itself is a process rather than a series of events. The program extends over a number of months, depending upon scheduling. All told, participants devote 12 days to in-class activities. A discussion of the classroom content is beyond the scope of this report, but the topics covered are aligned with the leadership model and the needs and directions of the business. Wachovia's CEO and Operating Committee are involved as "executives in residence" and support the ELP faculty in developing the participants throughout. As such, ELP has a high level of visibility throughout the organization.

In addition to traditional classroom-based activities, each participant completes a 360-degree assessment using the Wachovia Executive Leadership Model. This activity forms the basis for personal development planning. It is at this point that coaching becomes relevant to the participants.

Participants are assigned a coach from the internal coaching cadre who provides 20 to 40 hours of coaching, spread over the course of 6 months, depending on the needs of the ELP participant. This, of course, represents a significant investment of time and energy, with the goal of assisting the participant in individualizing lessons learned in the classroom to his or her unique needs and context. As such, the matching of coach and coachee is made carefully, based on an extensive data-gathering process involving the coachee.

ELP participants are also oriented to the coaching activity in the classroom by the coaching practice leader at Wachovia. She briefs the ELP participants on what coaching is, how it can help, and its role within ELP. She emphasizes to the participants in ELP that unlike typical HR initiatives, the *participants*, not the coaches, are responsible for driving their own coaching engagements. This places maximum responsibility for the effectiveness of the coaching on the coachee. It is a given that those participating in ELP are busy. They need to make the time and put in the energy required to keep the coaching sessions from becoming interesting but ultimately useless rituals. This orientation encourages the participants to really work on their development and use the coach as a tool in the process rather than seeing the coach as a leader of the process.

The coaching task is then clearly defined. In the training for internal coaches, this coaching activity is distinguished from coaching related to career transitions, acclimation, the development of a leadership agenda, and other kinds of coaching goals. While each coaching engagement may touch upon a variety of issues, particularly those related to diversity given the corporation's larger strategic concern with this issue, coaches are asked to help the coaching stay focused on development planning, particularly as it emerges from the 360-degree-assessment results.

## The Internal Coaches

Although there is widespread interest in a variety of coaching activities in the HR community within Wachovia, the opportunity to participate as a coach in the program was not seen as developmental in nature. Only seasoned HR professionals were recruited. Some had significant experience in organizational-development-related work. Over half had been through Wachovia's Diversity Practitioner Development Program (an intensive yearlong experience) and had expert knowledge in that strategically important area. Most importantly, those chosen were able to demonstrate a high level of self-awareness, a factor that serves as a foundation for a number of the competencies described in ELP.

The opportunity to engage an ELP participant in a 360-degree debriefing coaching session was an "add-on" for those chosen and completing the training. They would do coaching in addition to their regular work duties. Thus, coaching represented a potentially challenging addition to their workload. Nevertheless, there was an enthusiastic response to recruiting efforts.

Part of the appeal of the role of internal coach was that it gave people an opportunity to use their skills in a new way, working with an individual in a customized fashion that was nevertheless very results oriented. However, the fact that this is an "add-on" for coaches does create a risk factor that has been closely monitored. The coaches have to respond quickly when a coaching opportunity emerges. If they are too busy with other activities, their ability to respond may be compromised and service to the client may suffer. It is important to stay in close touch with the coaching cadre around this issue and to be understanding of the fact that some coaches may have to opt out of the coaching role for a time.

There was also a concern that despite their expertise and seniority, internal coaches would not be given the same level of credibility as external executive coaches. Certainly, at Wachovia, credibility is also an important success factor in coaching effectiveness, and so it is an important factor in the selection of internal coaches. This meant that it was critically important that the selection process be rigorous. If coaches were chosen for political reasons, as a place to "park" an individual HR professional whose career was in decline or simply because that person held a leadership position in the HR organization or as a reward for past performance rather than for a person's current and potential coaching competency, the quality of coaching offered by the program could be compromised. The criteria for selection thus focuses on current and potential competency to do the job. This seems to have done an adequate job of safeguarding the credibility of the program to date.

As already stated, the strengthening of a diverse leadership pipeline was seen as an essential goal by the leaders of the corporation. As such, an additional requirement for selection stipulated that candidates were required to participate in a series of diversity-related workshops and learning activities at which they address, among other things, the biases associated with consulting/coaching related to gender, race, sexual orientation, and dominant and subordinate group memberships.[2]

A final risk factor considered in the choice of coaches has to do with the all-important ability of the coach to "speak truth to power." Much of the objectivity that organizations hope to gain from the use of external coaches stems from the ability (ideally) to be honest, direct, and unbiased in the feedback they provide. It can be tough to provide such high-quality feedback to someone with whom you have a complicated set of interdependent relationships. From the coachee's perspective, an intertwining of relationships could impede the development of a coaching-friendly context. Imagine talking over serious concerns about your weaknesses with someone who next week may be consulting with your business unit leader about whether or not you should be promoted. The potential for role conflicts is obvious and may be even more severe than those experienced by the coaching manager.

Wachovia addressed this challenge in a fashion quite different from that executed by Steve Leichtman in Case 7.2, who formed an alliance with line management leaders to ensure that the program's interests were aligned with theirs. His work, though highly focused, did not take place in the context of a larger executive development program. He also had access to decision makers at the highest possible level on a routine basis.

Wachovia addressed this challenge by arranging coaching assignments such that no internal coach ever works with someone from her or his own business unit. It is our experience that this offers the best of both worlds for coach and coachee. Coaches still have familiarity with Wachovia culture and strategy, a strength of the internal coaching model. At the same time, they have some psychological and political distance from the coachees and their contexts. From the coachee's perspective, a sense of safety is bolstered by the understanding that the coach will not likely be engaged in making decisions about the coachee's future, at least in the near term. In fact, feedback from coachees suggests that they experience an internal coach from another business unit as though the coach were an external executive coach.

## Training and Support for the Internal Coaching Cadre

The goal of the training of the internal coach cadre is to provide them with the guidance and skill enhancement necessary to execute the tasks of their role with the highest-possible level of quality. As a leadership development activity itself, it was our intent to create a development *process* for coaches, rather than rely solely upon event-based trainings, though the latter were also used. The program for coach development extended over roughly 6.5 months and included the use of readings, training workshops, and an ongoing "Coaches' Coaches" support function, to be described below. Upon selection, each internal coach begins his or her training with a 2-day coaching workshop, conducted by Cambria Consulting. The ELP Coach Development Process is presented in Box 8.2.

---

**Box 8.2    ELP Coach Development Process**

1. Coaches are selected by HR directors within Wachovia, based on the criteria described in the text. In addition, candidates should have been exposed to at least two assessment tools from a list of personality assessment tools, such as the Myers-Briggs Type Indicator™, and attendance at an appropriate diversity awareness workshop.

2. Selected coaches are notified by the Executive Coaching Practice (ECP), the function within Wachovia responsible for managing the program. The ECP outlines expectations for the role to those selected.

3. ECP conducts four "virtual training sessions" in which the context of the coaching, the coaching model and process to be used, and details of the expectations of coaches are outlined. Through these sessions, coaches' questions are surfaced and addressed.

---

4. ECP simultaneously sends out 6 monthly reading packets to participants with a variety of articles on a variety of carefully chosen topics related to the types of coaching they will be performing in this role (i.e., 360-degree debrief coaching and development planning). They also receive additional readings and self-assessment materials in the area of diversity so that they can get a better understanding of how far-reaching their coaching can be while still working within the defined goals of the program.

5. All ELP coaches are required to attend a 2-day workshop during the 6-month prep period on *Introduction to the Enneagram and Applications in Coaching,* a personality assessment system in wide use throughout the corporation.

6. These activities all lead up to the ELP coach workshop, cofacilitated by the leader of the Executive Coaching Practice and a partner from Cambria Consulting. This 2-day, face-to-face workshop again covers the coaching model, expectations, ELP, the 360-degree assessment (how to use and understand this tool and explain it to others) and diversity concerns in coaching. The phases of the coaching model presented in this workshop are described in Box 8.3.

7. In addition, participants are introduced to the continuing education component of the ELP coaching program, which is described further below. They hold their first meetings with those with whom they will be following up in the continuing education and support process.

8. Of note, participants are not automatically "passed" into the cadre if they complete all this work. Expectations are set at the beginning of the process that participants must show up and actively participate. Coaches who fail to attend parts of the various programs are removed from the potential cadre.

The selection and orientation process is thus lengthy and extensive. Throughout, experiential activities such as role-plays are the main vehicle for instruction. The process clearly requires a very great deal of motivation on the part of those interested in coaching. Goals are rigorously set, and a process for achieving those goals is set forth. It is obviously impossible to anticipate every challenge that the coaches will face. Furthermore, coaching is inherently customized learning at the individual level. As such, the coaches will still have to use their experience and intuition, as well as their skills, if they are to actively help coachees. The anticipated phases of the coaching process utilized in the ELP coaching program are described in Box 8.3.

---

**Box 8.3    Phases of the 360-Degree Debrief Coaching at Wachovia**

*Phase 1: Getting Started*

This phase addresses the relationship building and initial goal setting necessary for the coaching to commence. The goals of the coaching are discussed as well as the parameters of confidentiality and the commitments required of each party to the coaching engagement.

*Phase 2: Gathering and Analyzing Information*

In the buildup to the actual goal-setting phase for the coachee, 360-degree data are reviewed, and the coach also makes contact with the coachee's immediate manager. An additional interview-based, 360-degree assessment is not performed. However, a variety of self-assessment tools, such as the Enneagram, may be used.

*Phase 3: Deciding What to Do*

Drawing on 360-degree data, self-assessment, and coaching conversations, coachee, manager, and coach define the developmental goals for the coming year.

*Phase 4: Making It Happen*

Follow-up coaching is directed at helping the coachee execute the development plan.

*Phase 5: Evaluating and Sustaining Progress*

As the coaching proceeds, coach and coachee explicitly evaluate progress toward developmental goals and discuss plans for sustaining positive change in the future. At this point, momentum has been established around the action plan, and the coachee is transitioned to the manager and the HR generalist for ongoing support.

---

# Ongoing Support and Development of ELP Coaches

Given the unique nature of each coaching engagement, the challenge of putting concepts into action also suggests a requirement for coaching. To support the Wachovia internal coaching program, a cadre of Coaches' Coaches (C2s) was developed. In groups of 10, the internal coaches work with a more experienced internal coach. During monthly conference calls, coaching engagements and challenges are reviewed. The internal coaches then have the opportunity to receive support from one another as well as their C2s. The Wachovia executive coaching practice manager supervises this group of senior internal coaches. These sessions are mandatory for active coaches, those who have a current coachee with whom they are working. In addition, C2s provide the executive coaching practice manager with a "systems-level" view of what is happening with the ELP itself, making it possible to track organizationally significant trends (such as those relating to diversity) and intercede when appropriate to ensure that coaching engagements are successful.

In addition, the Wachovia executive coaching practice has created a coaching "community of practice." Annually, internal coaches and external coaches working with Wachovia meet jointly to discuss what they have learned about the leadership development issues of the corporation and about coaching within Wachovia. This represents a significant venue for organizational learning, allowing the group of coaches to compare their experiences with individual leaders with the leadership goals of the corporation. This information is then appropriately shared with key stakeholders, such as the Operating Committee, including the HR director and the leadership development and organizational development functions, to inform corporate-wide strategy and interventions.

The annual gathering of the community of practice also serves as an additional vehicle for supporting both internal and external coach cadres. Internal and external coaches make proposals for providing development to each other, and other external educational opportunities are also provided. The annual community-of-practice meeting helps generate additional enthusiasm and momentum for the coaching practice.

## Comments on Being an Internal Coach From HR

It is logical to look to the HR function as a source of internal coaches. HR professionals routinely engage with line managers and employees about development. Informal coaching is one of the most important tools of their trade. Nevertheless, the role of the HR professional is complex. He or she may have to manage a high-profile compliance issue one minute (such as a sexual harassment claim) and the next talk about staffing and recruiting needs and the next engage in a high-level strategic-planning activity. In this section, we briefly describe lessons learned regarding how to help senior HR professionals engage with the coaching role.

HR professionals bring considerable expert knowledge to their various tasks and are often called upon to render expert opinions. The requirements for effectiveness as a content expert and a developmental coach are, however, quite different. Content expert HR professionals are routinely confronted with demands to provide that expertise in telling other people what to do. They must be action oriented and often work with a sense of urgency. Developmental coaches fundamentally guide coachees in seeking out their own solutions to self-determined developmental challenges. They may offer advice, but one of the most important activities of developmental coaches is to assist their coachees in reflecting on action and coming up with their own responses. The developmental coach often operates in a way that is the opposite of the action-oriented manager. Thus, the effective internal HR coach must be able to transition comfortably between these very demanding yet very different roles and sets of role requirements.

Internal coaches at Wachovia cite as helpful in this regard the relatively high level of structure in the program, the ongoing support systems such as C2, and the intensive training they receive via their participation in the program. In addition, the change in venue offered by the fact that they are coaching outside their own business units supports this role transition as well. When working outside their own business units, internal coaches can't typically jump in and take action.

Finally, internal coaches cite significant personal rewards and satisfaction that accrue from their participation. Exposure to other parts of the business and the careful selection of ELP program participants (meaning that most coachees are eager to engage in the coaching activities) make the opportunity to step back and reflect on coachees and their contexts very satisfying. Coaches frequently receive positive feedback from other coaches, because they are able to help coachees (and themselves) engage with the role of learner.

There has been no evidence to date that coachees have been reluctant to engage with internal coaches with an HR background. It is possible to imagine a problem complementary to that described for the coach, the fear on the part of the coachee that the coach, as an employee of the company, could possibly take action that would harm the coachee. The coaches and coachees report no such concerns. In fact, the intensity and importance of the connection between the coach and coachee, as reported through channels such as C2s, has surprised the coaches. It does seem clear, however, that it is important for the coach to take the time to build rapport and explain to the coachee the level of confidentiality associated with each coaching engagement. It also appears critical to demonstrate an ongoing level of integrity in the coaching process in order to safeguard the coaching-friendly context.

## Evaluation of the Program

The internal coaching program has rather quickly established a high level of credibility within the leadership ranks of the new Wachovia Corporation.

Anecdotal evidence from senior managers and ELP participants points to satisfaction with both the process and the outcomes of the coaching effort and the investment required to make these happen. It should be stressed, however, that satisfaction alone is not sufficient to substantiate the ongoing investment required to maintain a quality coaching effort, either internal or external. Ultimately, behavior change and business results are necessary. Wachovia is now involved in a major effort to systematically gather data regarding various coaching practices in that regard.

What are some of the limitations of the coaching program described in this chapter? Perhaps the most important limitation has to do with the level of competence that can be sustained by the internal coaching cadre when coaches are engaged in only one coaching engagement at any one time due to the constraints of their schedules. As described previously, this is an "add-on" assignment for these very senior individuals. As such, they may find at times that they are unable to make the commitment required of a coaching relationship. It is necessary, then, for the coaching practice manager to be concerned about both maintaining the competence levels of those who coach and the need to refresh the cadre of coaches as some move on. External coaches have to take personal responsibility for maintaining their competence themselves (though some firms, such as Wachovia, actively help them out in that regard). Internal coaches need their host organization's help to keep their skills sharpened to maintain their motivation to participate as part-time coaches.

# Notes

1. Company Facts as of October 1, 2005: http://www.wachovia.com.
2. Elsie Y. Cross Associates, Inc.

# 9

# Building a Coaching
# Manager Capability

In this chapter, we describe the following:

- The indicators for building a coaching manager capability
- The rethinking of management jobs necessary to facilitate managers' integration of coaching into their leadership skill sets
- The cultural shift necessary to promote a culture that truly values learning and therefore supports individual managers taking the time necessary to provide developmental coaching

I magine a scenario in which all members of an organization have access to someone who can help them learn on the job, improve their performance, help their organization, and grow their careers. Wouldn't that be great? Everyone does have access to someone who should be doing just that: his or her manager. Case closed. Well, perhaps not.

But what if this rather idealistic vision were actually possible? What would that mean from a business perspective? It would probably mean the following for employees:

- They would be more engaged.
- They would do a better job.
- They would enjoy their work more.
- They would find work less stressful.
- Their firms would benefit through enhanced profitability, productivity, customer satisfaction, and employee retention (Buckingham & Coffman, 1999).

This scenario seems ideal, and yet, for the most part, it does not happen. In this chapter, we describe some of the issues that are raised by this important but largely untapped opportunity. In Chapter 10, we'll describe one organization that chose to enhance its ability to provide developmental coaching through its leadership ranks, Children's Hospital Boston.

## Can Managers Coach Developmentally?

We start out with this question because it has been put to us, particularly by expert coaches. Referring back to the developmental model of coaching presented in Chapter 2, we see no reason why managers can't coach their direct reports, or peers, for that matter, in a fashion that results in development: performance improvement, a positive attitude, adaptability, and a clearer sense of identity, that is, individual strengths and weaknesses (Hall, 2002). But does developmental coaching provided by even the most talented managers create the same kind of developmental experience as being coached by an expert executive coach? The reality is, we don't know. The research just has not been done.

Anecdotally, it is not hard to obtain data on the impact of a good, "coaching-oriented" manager on an individual's development. Just ask a room full of workers. As we found when we did so at Children's Hospital Boston, most, but not all, can quickly point to a relationship with a boss that made a very significant impact on their development in their jobs and as individuals.

In a study of the impact and outcomes of 15 successful executive coaching engagements, coachees reported the following outcomes (Hunt, 2004):

1. They developed a "bigger picture" or a more systems-oriented view of their organizations and their roles within the organization through the process of reflecting on emergent learning opportunities. In other words, coaches helped them step back and assess the situation before acting in the face of new challenges.

2. They developed more effective leadership behaviors. This was often associated with working on the specific goals for which coaching was initially sought.

3. They became more effective at coaching others.

There were reports of other positive outcomes as well, but these three were most frequently cited by the study respondents.

We might say from this data that the second outcome was probably most related to improved performance in the here and now and the first outcome to a better understanding of self and others and a greater ability to see problems from multiple perspectives. This would suggest that executive coaching may have somewhat longer-term implications than developmental coaching that takes place between employees and talented coaching managers, but this is only a hypothesis at this point. Again, anecdotal evidence suggests that both short-term and long-term gains accrue to those subject to either developmental coaching from their managers or from expert coaches.

There is a further reality that cannot be ignored. If managers could be encouraged to really coach their direct reports in a developmental fashion rather than in a compliance-oriented fashion, many, many more people would have access to such coaching. No organization can hire an expert coach for everyone.

## The Major Differences

Assuming that we are comparing developmental coaching provided by a talented manager and developmental coaching provided by a well-trained and effective expert coach, there are significant differences. These differences impact the nature of the coaching contract between coach and coachee, the management of a coaching-friendly context, assessment of the coachee's strengths and weaknesses, the ongoing coaching process, and the management of accountability for results. We look at each of those factors briefly before discussing what organizations could do if they wanted to build or grow a coaching manager capability.

### The Coaching Contract

The contract between the coachee and the expert coach has one overriding goal: the coachee's development within his or her role and organization. The simplicity of a single, though challenging, goal allows them to focus their relationship and the activities within it accordingly. The contract between the coachee and his or her manager is multifaceted. The coachee is much more dependent on the coach in this case for work assignments, quality of working life, and evaluation of his or her work, a subject that we address further in the next section. The manager and coachee must be able to shift roles within their relationship. This requires a good deal of flexibility on the part of both. It also requires a higher level of trust and more effective communications, and different role relationships are adjusted "on the fly."

Luckily, the roles don't always conflict, though they can. The coaching manager can make a work assignment that promotes learning and development, for instance. Nevertheless, the coaching manager is responsible for the performance of his or her business unit. As such, decisions may be made regarding the coachee that are not in the coachee's best interests.

## The Coaching-Friendly Context

The expert coach is duty bound to try to protect the coachee's interests in the coaching relationship as long as ethical considerations (e.g., the coachee threatens violence) don't intervene. There is limited confidentiality surrounding the coaching relationship that serves to further protect the coachee. Ideally, this makes it easier for the coachee to be open about mistakes and problems. However, this confidentiality is limited, and, as we discussed in Chapter 6, others must be drawn into coaching from time to time, including the coachee's manager. Indeed, including others in coaching contributes to the success of expert coaching engagements. The manager who is involved appropriately in the expert coaching activity is in a position to provide real-time feedback to the coachee, which the external expert coach may have no access to (Hunt, 2004).

The relationship between the employee and his or her manager is not a confidential one. The coaching is typically public, though it may take place in individual meetings between the manager and the employee. If the coachee is unable to ultimately improve his or her work performance, the manager, no matter how inclined to behave in a developmental way, will have to coach for compliance. This can ultimately mean that the coachee is terminated. In our experience, most employees are willing to take that chance if they believe their managers are fundamentally trustworthy and fair. Good and great performers, the bulk of workers who are unlikely to be terminated for cause, are in better positions to be open to their managers about work-related issues as long as the boss does not retaliate against them for doing so. Clearly, some managers have been able to create a sufficient sense of safety that their employees have turned to them for developmental coaching, but it does take care and work on the part of the manager.

## Assessment

The expert coach and the coaching manager use very different tools for assessment, and they assess in different ways. The coaching manager relies largely on observation and data from customers, peers, and others who have occasion to work with the coachee. The focus of such observation and data gathering is the coachee in his or her role. The coaching manager may also have access to previous performance appraisals and employee survey data if the organization makes use of such tools. Without question, though, the coaching manager's most important tools are observations and reports from the coachee and from others in the coachee's world. This is a rich source of data to which the expert coach, particularly the external coach, may have limited access.

The expert coach who is more removed from the coachee can with the coachee's consent ask others regarding the coachee's performance. The expert coach may be able to sit in on some meetings and observe the coachee in action, though this is typically on a more limited basis. The expert coach frequently does have access to personality assessment tools and instrumented multi-rater feedback. In fact, some external coaches, and occasionally internal coaches, have significant expertise in the area of personnel assessment and selection and are able to bring these skills to the aid of the coachee. Thus, the expert coach is able to conduct an expert assessment of the person in many instances as well as the person's fit with the work role.

## The Ongoing Coaching Process

Ongoing coaching for the coachee and the expert coach typically takes place in a scheduled meeting of 1-to-2 hours on a weekly, twice-weekly, or monthly basis. The meeting may have an agenda. There are likely homework assignments to be done in-between sessions and to be discussed in the coaching sessions themselves. The formal scheduled nature of the coaching sessions with the expert coach does lend itself well to creating a quiet, reflective space that supports the coachee's ability to step back from the issues at hand and more comfortably look at his or her own role in those issues.

Ongoing coaching with coaching managers may be quite formal or informal, depending on the organization's culture, the style of the individuals involved in the coaching relationship, and the nature of their working climate. In formal sessions, if the coaching-friendly context has been managed effectively, there may be a significant degree of support for reflection, not dissimilar to that found in expert coaching sessions. The great strength of the developmental coaching with one's manager, however, is the potential for less formal, more spontaneous, and more time-effective coaching sessions, occurring soon after the coachee's actions. Coaching and problem solving blend in together. Both the coaching manager and the coachee learn about the problems at hand and have a vested interest in addressing the challenges faced by the coachee.

## Accountability for Results

Without question, coaching managers are able to hold coachees accountable for coaching results. Not that they always choose to do so, but the ability of the coaching manager to evaluate the coachee can represent a push that some coachees may find helpful. It gives the developmental task a sense of urgency.

At the same time, an expert coach can also use various influence strategies to hold the coachee accountable. Just by staying on task and on goals and checking in on homework assignments between sessions, the expert coach sends a strong signal to the coachee that the work is important and progress should at least be attempted. This, of course, can be done quite directly, as the coachee in reality has no reason to fear the coach's ultimate evaluation.

## Expert Coaching Versus the Coaching Manager: An Assessment

As one can see from this brief overview, the coaching manager can bring some important strengths to the task of developmental coaching. The expert coach can leverage sophisticated assessment tools and the need for scheduled coaching sessions. The coaching manager can leverage the richness of work-related data available and ease of access to the coachee. However, the coaching manager has two specific challenges.

First, he or she must have the appropriate skill set and personal style. In Appendix A, we articulate one hypothesized set of competencies and attributes required for effective expert coaching. In Appendix B, we present a self-assessment tool that we have used to help managers assess their own skill sets and styles in relation to the tasks of developmental coaching as outlined in Chapter 2. (This self-assessment also serves at the core of a Coaching Manager Multi-Rater Feedback tool designed to give an even more robust assessment of the coaching manager's skill and attribute set.) We return to this topic in the next section.

In addition, the coaching manager must be able to successfully manage the role conflicts noted in the previous analysis. This is a function of the coaching manager's awareness of these potential conflicts. It is also, however, a function of the coaching manager's context. The organization has a significant impact on the coaching manager's ability to be an effective developmental coach.

# The Competencies of the Coaching Manager

In Appendix A, we propose that the following competencies or attributes are associated with being an effective coaching manager. This work draws heavily on the research we conducted for a previous volume (Hunt & Weintraub, 2002a) as well as numerous training and consultative activities that have taken place since.

## Self-Awareness

This competency points to an ability to seek out and make use of knowledge about the self and one's strengths and weaknesses in any given situation. Self-awareness requires both reflection and seeking out feedback from others. It also requires a certain ability to tolerate stressful circumstances so that one can think things through. Note that this is a requirement for the coaching manager, but it also provides an important modeling function for others, as will be the case for the remaining competencies as well.

## Promotes Learning

This reflects the coaching manager's ability to help others learn by demonstrating a positive attitude toward learning for the self as well as others, working on continuous improvement of his or her skill set, offering feedback, holding a positive attitude toward learning from errors, and asking questions that provoke thought.

## Communications

This competency refers to the coaching manager's sharing of information that creates a context for learning. Included here is the sharing of information about the business strategy, expectations, opportunities for action, and roles and responsibilities. Coaching managers tend to believe that sharing information empowers others to make good use of that information.

## Accessibility

One of the toughest behaviors associated with being an effective coaching manager, accessibility requires making oneself available to coach. If the other factors are in place, direct reports will for the most part want to seek out coaching. Being accessible, at least to a degree, implies that one is there to help.

## Listening

Obviously, listening to direct reports is a key behavior for the coaching manager. The coaching manager has to be able to listen without prejudice and without making assumptions about the correctness of the coachee's perspective. That is sorted out through feedback or dialogue.

## Creates a Trusting Environment

None of this works without trust. As we have already stated, there are significant role conflicts that can impact trust, but there are also stylistic issues. The judgmental manager may convey that he or she is always evaluating, looking for trouble. With such an attitude, the manager will not convey trust when delegating to a direct report the opportunity to take on a stretch assignment. At the same time, an effective coaching manager cannot be recklessly trusting. By seeking out good candidates to fill positions, individuals who have foundational skill sets, they can more readily exercise trust in the delegation process.

## The Perfect Manager?

We use this self-assessment tool in the skills training of coaching managers to help them assess their own strengths and developmental needs. It goes without saying that very few are perfect. We suggest that to be effective, the manager's style must be "good enough" such that on balance, he or she demonstrates these characteristics.

This does require that the manager take a different approach to management from that of the "command and control manager." The manager must learn to see the world in a more complex fashion and come to grips with the fact that influence, rather than control, is more likely to yield long-term results. Our research suggests that this is a developmental leap, not that different from the class challenge of "letting go" that all parents must face (Hunt & Weintraub, 2004).

## The Organizational Context and the Management of Role Conflicts

We have found that some managers are able to coach regardless of their contexts. They are just good at it and don't care a great deal about what others think, including their own bosses (Hunt & Weintraub, 2002a). However, this represents a tactical rather than a strategic view of coaching.

The individual, gifted manager may be a real asset to his or her organization, but the challenge the organization faces if it wants to build a coaching capability around its managers is to create many such individuals. It is necessary to make the assumption, then, that not everyone will demonstrate such talent at managing the complexities associated with the role.

We described in Chapter 3 an organizational assessment exercise that can be used to help assess the degree to which the organizational context supports a more adaptive management of these role conflicts. We draw your attention to two factors in this regard that we believe are essential to confront:

- *The behavior of senior managers:* In general, the senior managers of the unit need to be able to demonstrate that they can manage these role conflicts. They must be trustworthy. They must be capable of demonstrating trust in others. They should have a positive attitude toward learning. In other words, they should also be "good enough" as coaching managers, such that the average employee believes that taking the time necessary for coaching is appropriate and even valued.

- *The reward system:* The reward system is a powerful communications tool. Are people rewarded for being good at developing their direct reports? Or are they punished?

We are sufficiently impressed by the power of these two factors to suggest that misalignment between these and an effort to build a coaching capability around the organization's managers is an indicator that the effort is likely to fail. That is not to suggest that such skills-building activities are necessarily a waste of time, though they might be. It is, however, unlikely that the average manager will make use of those skills in the workplace; or if they do, they may not manage the conflicts inherent in the coaching manager role appropriately.

Let us offer one brief example from our research. A manager is meeting with her boss to discuss recent problems in her group. She is new to the position and is having difficulty dealing with an underperforming report, who is having trouble with a new assignment. The manager's boss says, "You're wasting too much time on that one, let him go." If she really believes that she will be penalized for not following her boss's advice, the manager will have a great deal of difficulty effectively coaching the underperformer. She will feel the push toward an evaluative stance even when it is not appropriate. The manager needs to feel that it is acceptable to "let go" within reason and that, as with launching a new project, she will win some even though she may lose a few.

## Organizational Readiness

Although the training of managers in the skills of coaching has represented a major portion of our professional lives over the past decade, we strongly suggest that organizational decision makers carefully consider the level of support for such an effort from senior managers. Likewise, decision makers should ask whether or not the culture and the reward systems support such work. Finally, decision makers should ask themselves, "What job would we like this capability to do for the organization? How can it help?"

In the next chapter, we present the case of Children's Hospital Boston, which took on such an initiative. We use this case to illustrate the points made in this chapter, as well as to illustrate the actual tactics of the coaching initiative intervention itself. Chapter 10 will also give the reader a sense of how the skills-training component of the intervention can be managed in a fashion that will facilitate the "letting-go" process. Those in charge of the intervention have to let go a bit themselves.

# 10

# The Coaching Manager in Nursing

*James M. Hunt, Joseph R. Weintraub,*
*Suzanne Levin, Laura Bobotas, Susan Shaw,*
*Herminia Shermont, and Patricia Hickey*

In this chapter, we describe the following:

- An initiative to build and enhance developmental coaching in the Department of Nursing at Children's Hospital Boston
- The skills-building component of the initiative in some detail and the importance of peer-to-peer learning in the transfer of skills learning back to the workplace
- Lessons learned from the effort to enhance the use of developmental coaching at Children's Hospital and their implications for other organizations

## Children's Hospital Boston and the Department of Nursing

Children's Hospital Boston is known worldwide for its leadership in pediatric patient care, teaching, and research. With 342 inpatient beds, it is one of the largest pediatric medical centers in the United States. It is the primary pediatric teaching hospital of Harvard Medical School.

The Department of Nursing at Children's Hospital Boston includes over 1,200 professional registered nurses, who practice in a variety of settings, including inpatient medicine, intensive care, perioperative units, surgical and ambulatory surgical clinics, psychiatry, ambulatory medical clinics, oncology/bone marrow transplant units, and an emergency department. Novice-through-experienced nurses provide direct patient care, interface with families, collaborate closely with physicians, coordinate interdisciplinary teams, train new nurses, mentor experienced nurses, and formally administer/lead multiple organizational units within the Department of Nursing.

## A More Realistic View of Nursing Leadership

A typical definition of *leadership* reads something like this: Leaders mobilize others to want to work toward shared aspirations (Kouzes & Posner, 1995). According to such a definition, nurses at all levels qualify as leaders—and this statement is not offered gratuitously. Nurses in the 21st century, in addition to carrying out direct care for patients, coordinate the work of physicians, other health care providers, and other nonclinical departments within the hospital as well as coordinating the actions of patients and their families. However, the notion of coordination is not adequate to describe the extra technical work that they do. An effective nurse is constantly scanning the environment for threats and opportunities, trying to communicate these to others who already are stretched, prioritizing a long list of "to-do's" every day, and keeping others focused on what is truly important. Inevitably, effective nurses have to manage conflicts and defuse very difficult situations. They must motivate others, help their colleagues deal with difficult times and personal stress, and help patients and families confront illnesses and take the difficult steps often required of treatment. And they must do this all proactively. Nurses do not learn these extra technical skills in nursing school, but on the job. The good and great nurses we've encountered are among the best leaders we have ever known at the effective and constructive use of influence tactics.

In general, nurses are also among the least, if not *the* least, supported in learning this highly complex form of human relatedness. The popularly held image of nursing probably does not evoke an image of leadership, but rather one of care, support, and/or perhaps technical expertise. Indeed, the notion that all registered nurses are leaders, not just the charge nurse and the formal nursing leadership, may be counterintuitive for many nurses. Historically, the nursing role required that nurses subordinate their actions under the direction of physicians. Ultimately, though, at this point in time, as one of the leaders of the Department of Nursing described, "If I'm to get any sleep at night, I have to trust that those who are in charge on each unit will make sure that what needs to be done is done." That requires leadership.

Command and control approaches to leadership, however, are not adequate to meet the challenge of making sure what needs to be done is done. Nursing is experiencing a significant labor shortage. Recruitment and retention are critically important to all health care professions, including nursing. If a nurse feels disrespected or misunderstood by his or her boss, he or she can usually find another job in short order. Staff nurses must be mobilized as much as directed. We know that an effective coaching-oriented manager is also an effective retention tool (Buckingham & Coffman, 1999). The tight labor situation within the profession also means that it is more difficult for even the best hospitals to bring in leadership from the outside. Whenever possible, it is much more economical and feasible to grow leadership from within.

The coaching initiative at the Department of Nursing at Children's Hospital Boston emerged as one aspect of a larger strategy to address these concerns, to help a large number of nurses, the entire department, identify and grow the "talented" next generation of nursing leaders. Unlike the leadership development activities that we have discussed in other chapters, this initiative was not aimed at a few high-potential candidates. Indeed, many of those who might benefit from developmental coaching might also never take on formal leadership positions. Regardless, the hope was that more nurses would enhance their abilities to influence others, to prioritize, and to support the development of others. The target beneficiary group was the Department of Nursing itself, all 1,200 individuals. As such, expert coaching, whether provided by internal or external coaches, would not be a cost-effective approach to the task.

Fortunately, certain aspects of the culture of Children's Hospital Boston made such efforts appropriate. Although they had not made great use of expert coaching in the past, practices in support of employee development, such as mentoring and peer reviews, had a long and positive history at the hospital. As a teaching hospital, learning was valued. Perhaps more importantly, at Children's Hospital, nurses are valued. Status differences among health care professionals were minimal, in contrast to some other teaching hospitals. Doctors and nurses work together on a first-name basis, for instance. It is expected that nurses will have the opportunity to participate in research and to publish, just as other health care professionals do.

An initial organizational assessment conducted in preparation for the coaching initiative suggested that the skills-building component of the initiative would provide many nurses with a language for what they were already doing and validate the on-the-job coaching that was already taking place. At the same time, it would send a message to others, encouraging them to change their behavior and consider how they might support one another's development through, for instance, greater attention to both giving and receiving useful feedback.

At the same time, the coaching initiative did have to deal with significant challenges. The sheer numbers of those for whom training was indicated represented a major issue. In addition, all of those involved were aware that Children's Hospital is a unique institution and that similar porting of skills-building training conducted elsewhere would not resonate with those targeted for further skill development. The sheer stress and time constraints experienced by the nurses make coaching of any sort difficult. And historically, as previously discussed, some more experienced nurses tended to look to the physician as the leader rather than to another nurse. It was critically important, therefore, to realistically assess the overall coaching context for the initiative rather than to impose our own enthusiasm on the process.

Organizational readiness is important in determining the impact of any effort to build or enhance a coaching capability. One critically important factor in the readiness of the Children's Hospital Boston coaching initiative was the support of senior leadership within the Department of Nursing. The senior vice president of patient care services and nursing vice presidents demonstrated their support by spending considerable time and devoting much energy to the planning and implementation of the initiative. That is not to say that they were all able to demonstrate the highest level of competence in developmental coaching. As discussed in the previous chapter, enough leaders must be "good enough," not necessarily perfect, at developmental coaching for the initiative to move ahead. The average manager and professional in any organization must be able to look up the chain of command several levels and believe that the managers he or she sees really do care about employee and leadership development. In this case, senior managers were able as a group to send this signal to the larger population of nurses.

# Building Leadership Through Coaching: The Coaching Initiative

The coaching initiative at Children's Hospital involved three basic steps: assessment and planning, a top-down rollout of the skills-training component of the initiative, and the follow-up conducted by nursing vice presidents and unit directors. The initial organizational assessment (see Chapter 3 for details) involved a number of meetings with the outside consultant/researchers (authors of this volume) and senior managers of the Department of Nursing to establish a vision for the initiative and consider how it would relate to other human resource practices. In addition, focus groups were held with nurses who represented differing career levels, to ascertain their developmental needs and the potential for building or enhancing a coaching manager capability in the department. The final activities in the initial stages of the initiative involved an announcement to the department from the senior vice president of Patient Care Services and a follow-up communications campaign.

The skills-building component of the intervention was based on the coaching manager model of developmental coaching (Hunt & Weintraub, 2002a). However, based on our initial assessment work, we realized that the model would need to be elaborated to deal with the uniqueness of the culture of the Department of Nursing at Children's Hospital Boston and the nature of the nursing role and the reality of the working conditions. Before presenting the customized aspects of our work at Children's Hospital, a basic outline of the skills-building training is presented in Box 10.1.

---

**Box 10.1**    Coaching-Skills-Building Curriculum at Children's Hospital Boston

| | |
|---|---|
| Participants: | All nurses in leadership roles as well as those in Levels 3 and 2 (those with approximately 5 or more years of service, who are expected to take on informal leadership responsibilities). Approximately 500 nurse leaders participated in the training in groups of 15 to 20 over a 1-year period. The senior management group of the department was the first group to participate in the training. They took responsibility for making sure that those targeted for the training attended subsequent sessions. |
| Training Structure: | One-and-one-half days of training. Days 1 and 2 were separated by approximately 6 weeks to facilitate transfer of learning through homework assignments. |
| Day 1 Content: | Developmental coaching<br>Coaching video role-plays (custom-made for Children's Hospital)<br>The leadership and teamwork competency model<br>Extended peer coaching activities with custom cases<br>Applications and homework assignment |

| | |
|---|---|
| Intersession: | Use the developmental coaching model. Complete a coaching "exemplar" or story about your inter-vention. Complete the Coaching Manager Multi-Rater Feedback (based on the competencies described in Appendix B) |
| Day 2 Content: | Review of coaching exemplars<br>Presentation of Coaching Manager Multi-Rater Feedback reports<br>Peer coaching and development planning |

# Nurses' Evaluation of the Coaching-Skills-Training Components

Though taking 1 1/2 days out of their schedules was without question a burden for the extremely busy participants, evaluations indicated that they found the sessions useful and relevant. One important finding that emerged from the evaluations, however, was that they found the review of coaching exemplars in Day 2 to be among the most valuable.

The coaching exemplars are brief stories, descriptions, or coaching conversations that participants held in the intersession period, the context within which the conversations took place. They were presented in the class-room setting, typically to 15 colleagues. The instructors encouraged partici-pants to use a developmental model when responding to the exemplars, in other words, to create a dialogue rather than jumping in with advice. How-ever, we also encouraged the participants to consider the relevance of each exemplar for their own practice.

The dialogues that followed raised a number of important issues that the participants needed to address if they were to really change their behavior, to coach, or to coach more:

- *The recognition of what a coaching dialogue really looked like in practice:* Though we had shown them and they had shown each other, they needed repeated exposure to the use of dialogue encouraging questions to help them really see the concept in action and to understand the difference between "coaching" and "jumping in," which we discuss further below.

- *How to recognize coaching opportunities:* Over the course of the day, nursing leaders are confronted with a variety of challenges. Developing others isn't necessarily at the top of their priority lists. The coaching exem-plar discussion helped them to talk with each other about what those coaching opportunities look like at Children's Hospital Boston.

- *How to give difficult feedback:* This aspect of coaching is challenging for most people. Examples *with which they could identify* gave them courage—in our view, the courage it takes to talk openly and effectively with others when critical feedback is required.

- *The impact of their own attitudes and behavior on their ability to coach and on each other:* In the exemplars, the emotional aspect of coaching challenges can emerge. The way nurses feel when engaged in coaching and the way their feelings influence their behavior are critically important factors of which the nurse should be aware. The relative safety of the exemplar discussions allows them to confront themselves and their attitudes.

The exemplar sessions coupled with the Coaching Manager Multi-Rater Feedback made it possible for the nurse leaders to consider how relatively minor adjustments in their own personal styles at work might make it possible for them to coach more, without spending more time coaching.

## Customizing the Coaching-Skills Training

As already mentioned, it was not appropriate to take standardized coaching-skills training and introduce it into the context of the skills-training sessions at Children's Hospital. Customization was required every step of the way and, in fact, continued after the skills training was under way and as we learned more about the issues facing the nurse leadership. Luckily, however, we had help in this process. *In each and every issue listed below, the appropriate intervention was to create a context in which the participants could talk together about that issue and problem solve with regard to how they could address it given the realities they faced.* In essence, a coaching approach was used to explore the issues and help participants generate solutions. This, of course, also gave us an opportunity to model coaching behavior in the sessions themselves. (Like the value of the coaching exemplars discussed above, this experience offered us insight into the incredible potential of guided peer coaching, the topic of Chapter 11.)

### Hiring the Right People

The issue of hiring the right people was discussed repeatedly throughout the sessions. In the midst of a labor shortage, can an organization be picky when it comes to hiring? There was strong support among the participants for continued vigilance in looking for future leaders, even though they acknowledged that younger nurses, particularly those right out of an undergraduate nursing program, might represent "unknowns" for a number of years. A "coaching mind-set" helped participants become students of talent as they discussed the characteristics of "good hires." They also began to grapple with how coaching, as opposed to a more directive management style, could (a) help them get a clearer sense of who would rise to the challenge of nurse leadership and (b) not penalize those "hidden" leaders who had potential but needed some freedom to express that potential.

## Defining Success

As we have discussed throughout, the use of a basic competency model, one that helps managers understand what to look for when coaching, was of enormous help. While nursing in general, and at Children's Hospital in particular, has a very advanced competency model, the coach training helped to explore specific behavioral indicators of leadership and teamwork. We were reminded again of the basic fact that most people have undeveloped "process observation" skills. Managers tend to focus on technical content or outcomes. Strengthened skills in this area meant that participants could both observe and describe process-related behaviors more effectively. In this case, the participants found it most useful to talk with one another about what a specific competency looks like, in practice, in their context. What does a good listener do in an emergency department, for instance?

## Establishing a Coaching-Friendly Context

Hospitals and health care professionals face unique challenges given the life-and-death nature of their work. Is it truly safe to admit that one has made a mistake? Many nurses have been exposed to environments that discourage explicit learning from experience, particularly learning from mistakes. As has been shown, punitive approaches toward all medication errors result in the suppression of reporting of those areas, with the resultant loss of both learning opportunities and trust (Edmundson, 1996). Yet many nurses have been exposed to environments in which punitive approaches to errors were the norm, and they bring with them the expectation that they should keep what they do not know to themselves. It was most useful for the participants to acknowledge the impact of the history of the profession and their own histories in this regard.

Similarly, an acknowledgment of these challenges helped participants explore the problems associated with career development within nursing. A very competent and experienced intensive-care nurse, for instance, might transfer to a very different type of unit to refresh her career and her motivation. In doing so, however, she may find that she is suddenly a novice.

Others, judging her by her age, may suddenly lose trust in her abilities as well, without realizing the amount of learning that needs to take place. It is critically important, then, that the coaching-friendly context support learning at all levels of individuals' careers when they are making significant transitions. Frank discussion of this issue helped raise awareness of just how unsupported nurses can feel during such transition points.

## Working With a Coachable Coachee

Nurses at Children's Hospital Boston in general appeared to be quite coachable and to expect that their colleagues would display a similar openness to coaching. They accepted the fact that continuing development is a part of the job. Newer and more ambitious nurses in particular seemed hungry for coaching. The more experienced nurses expressed the belief that coaching has always been part of their jobs but they have not been taught the skills to always coach effectively. Their past model had been to coach others either by being directive (i.e., by teaching) or by modeling successful behavior, rather than creating a coaching dialogue. Nevertheless, it was also helpful for them to discuss factors unique to their situations, such as career stage or recent trauma, that might impair coachability.

## Maintaining a Coaching Mind-Set

Stress and time represent constraints that work against a nurse's ability to attain a coaching mind-set. Yet times that are the most stressful may offer rich learning opportunities. Furthermore, times that are most stressful may require greater collaboration and the need to assess what happened, and why. The participants were able to acknowledge this tension and to consider how to best deal with it. The question of timing for discussions emerged as important to them in this regard: When is it best to sit down with someone who has been through a very difficult experience and try to help him or her learn from what has transpired?

## Stopping the Action and Starting a Coaching Dialogue

As with the need to maintain a coaching mind-set, this component of the developmental coaching model presented two major challenges. First, the action doesn't stop on an inpatient intensive-care unit. Yet the health care professionals who work there have to find times to confer. When is it possible for both a nurse leader and a nurse to step back and reflect on what is happening? Of course, under such circumstances, it is terribly easy for the coaching nurse to provide the right answer or offer critical feedback, neither of which may address the learning need in question. This second challenge for the nurse leader, to "shift gears" and encourage the "coachee" to engage more, is more a mental than a time management issue. The nursing leaders participating in the coaching-skills workshop had to address an underlying mind-set that influenced their ability to respond to both of these challenges.

While expected to lead (i.e., to mobilize others), nurses are also expected to act. As is the case for many professionals, there is an inherent contradiction that must be addressed if one is to be a successful coach. Note that this tension is similar to that experienced by human resource professionals, who must shift from being expert consultants to process consultants if they are to coach. For nurses, however, this challenge is even more intense. The risks associated with the context within which on-the-job learning takes place for nurses heightens the tension associated with managing this contradiction. The senior nurse has to sort out, in very short order, whether or not the most appropriate thing to do is to jump in to fix the problem or to help a younger colleague learn how to fix the problem.

In our experience, most savvy nurses are quite aware of the dangers of always jumping in rather than helping others learn. They know that they have to bring newer nurses up to speed or else there won't be sufficient trained staff to meet the demands facing the unit. At the same time, though, we also note the powerful urge to act that many nurses bring to the task of coaching. Even when they try to coach, many "tell," rather than engage the coachee in a coaching dialogue. The challenge for coaching nurses is to engage coachees in a fashion that encourages coachees to think for themselves. An opportunity to stop and reflect on a particular problem seems like a real luxury, one that nurses often feel they do not have time for.

We found it most important to help the participants experience firsthand their own tendencies to jump to action before dialogue, and we used a variety of exercises to help them build this self-awareness. These involved role-playing scenarios in which participants had to coach someone but had no opportunity to offer an opinion or, indeed, do anything other than ask questions. The intent of this was to help them help coachees achieve a greater sense of engagement in learning. We also reality tested the possibilities for using dialogue rather than instruction in a variety of coaching situations that they would actually confront. Ultimately, though, as we have found repeatedly, this step requires practice. Professionals have to suspend their own confidence in their ability to solve problems through independent action. They must "park their agendas at the door," the phrase we heard repeatedly, if they are to be successful at fully engaging coachees.

We should also report one complicating factor that emerged from the training. How does one "stop the action" in an action-filled environment?

How does one get the attention of a direct report or a peer to instigate a coaching discussion without creating undue anxiety? We heard about the "tap on the shoulder" from the boss who wanted to talk. Many can mistake that for a preamble to criticism. It became clear that it was important to make sure that coaching was seen as a developmental rather than a critical intervention. The only way to achieve this goal was to talk about it.

## Observing Effectively and Providing Balanced Feedback

Working in close quarters, nurses seem to have ample opportunity to observe one another in action. Yes and no. They may be working side by side, but may miss important parts of the action as they are called away to other duties. The tasks of getting good performance data are, ultimately, just as challenging for nurses as for those who work in much more dispersed environments. There were many horror stories of experiences in which participants' own supervisors walked in on the middle of a problem that was actually quite under control: The situation may have looked bad, but only because of the stage in the particular process of recovery. As such, participants cautioned one another with regard to the need to sometimes be tentative when providing feedback and, again, to fully engage the coachee in the conversation.

## Defining Next Steps and Following Up

What most coaching interventions have in common is that they end with the "next step." The coaching ends with a plan, as specific as possible, for what the coachee is going to try to do when he or she goes back into what could still be a very challenging situation. This is a critical part of the cycle of experiential learning. The next step could be that the coachee tries something differently and subsequently meets with the coach again to discuss what worked and what did not work. It could be that the coachee finds that he or she needs to get more objective data about his or her performance or a particular issue. In health care, as in many professional contexts, this is one of the most challenging aspects of coaching as a manager. Nurses rotate through shifts, and a nurse manager may not be working on the same day the coachee returns to try out a recently discussed skill. The participants found it important to consider how they could plug information gaps and how they could maintain a coaching flow for an individual over time.

## Follow-Up, Post–Skills Training

This step is critically important, one that is often ignored in coach training. Two of us (Hunt and Weintraub) have trained thousands of individuals to provide developmental coaching. We have been told repeatedly that one training session is insufficient if the goal is real skill development. One must coach repeatedly or use the concepts in closely related activities if one is to really internalize the skill set.

Children's Hospital Boston presents significant challenges in this regard because it is a highly decentralized organization. The units staffed by nurses vary tremendously with regard to their structure, pacing, and developmental issues. As such, it is more appropriate for each senior manager from the nursing unit to develop a plan specific to his or her unit to support continued use of concepts from the skills-building component of the training.

As such, developmental coaching, or various components of the developmental coaching model, were used in a variety of ways, depending upon unit need. On one unit, the director identified critical career points at which nurses were more likely to plateau in their careers or leave the hospital. She and her nurse educator developed a coaching-based intervention to reach out to this population to assess their needs, identify those who were interested in further development, and institute a plan to support them accordingly.

Process-oriented competencies related to leadership and teamwork behaviors were used in a variety of settings and included in a Children's Hospital Department of Nursing multi-rater feedback. Several units experimented with including developmental coaching in new-hire onboarding programs. In general, the senior leaders took existing processes and considered how a coaching component could be included or strengthened. Similarly, they looked at important unit needs or problems and considered how a coaching component might represent part of the solution.

These efforts had several important implications. First, they helped to keep the concepts and language alive. Just as importantly, they provided an opportunity for people to continue to practice aspects of developmental coaching. It is ultimately up to individual nursing leaders, formal and informal, to decide whether or not and how to create a coaching dialogue in any given situation. Only when the tool becomes second nature to a number of those involved will the behavior of large numbers of individuals change.

## Some Additional Lessons

Not surprisingly, the large-scale effort to build a coaching capability at Children's Hospital Boston resulted in some important insights regarding how coaching relates to other aspects of work and life. The following are offered as lessons learned that might be applicable to other organizations in other contexts.

## Developmental Coaching Must Leverage the Work

We found that nursing leaders, if they are to coach colleagues developmentally, need to consider how learning and the immediate work challenge relate to one another. Coaching is uniquely helpful in extracting learning from impromptu learning opportunities and events. Coaching requires little planning and can literally be done "on the fly." When we ask participants at the start of each program to remember and describe the nurses who have had the most positive impact on their own growth as nurses, we almost never hear about the nurse leaders who held long, individual coaching sessions behind closed doors. Most participants remember coaching interactions that occurred at the bedside. They remember learning a great deal about leadership and nursing in short conversations during which there was a focus on dealing with the immediate challenge, whatever it might be. They learned that their supervisors or charge nurses had confidence in them, held them accountable for thinking through a problem, wanted their input and ideas, encouraged them to take on difficult tasks, listened to them, asked them provocative questions, and so on. It appears that those coaching leaders simply knew that by learning something from the immediate work challenge, longer-term growth would likely take place, and it did.

## Developmental Coaching Shouldn't Create More Work

This may not sound realistic, but consider the following. Through linking coaching and the work, for the most part, those involved in coaching will be holding conversations that they would have been holding anyway; however, the conversations create a different outcome. As one participant said, "I had my performance appraisal with someone who had been through the coach training. It was amazing. We had a great discussion for the first time in 15 years. I even forgot to ask her about the money!" The ability to include a coaching dialogue in one's leadership activities in a rather seamless way, however, does require practice, as we have stressed.

## Developmental Coaching Ultimately
## Involves a New Way of Relating to Old Problems

This is a comment from an intensive-care-unit nurse:

> The new nurse here might go home and cry every night, that's the nature of the work. . . . When my husband has a bad day, it's because the FedEx package didn't get out on time. Would you like to know what my bad days are like?

Work is becoming more complex and stressful for many of us, and there is a real need for help in sorting things out. This aspect of leadership development receives little attention in formal training and development programs, with the exception of those that address issues related to loss or grief and perhaps to stress management. Competencies that build on emotional intelligence (Goleman, 1995) can't really be learned in the classroom. Developmental coaching, though rooted in learning from work, creates an opportunity for people to talk with one another in a different way. Coaching managers who learn to ask questions, seek out the perspectives of direct reports, and listen to their points of view will find that in at least some cases, their "coachees" will raise these more problematic concerns.

This is a double-edged sword. Developmental coaching often does result in a deeper relationship, and managers do get a clearer sense of their direct reports' concerns and issues. But this can be uncomfortable for some managers, challenging them in particular to manage their feelings. "I don't want to be someone's counselor" is the concern we have heard on a number of occasions. Again, we find it critically important to support managers through this process so that they have a better sense of how to engage in deeper relationships in an appropriate and comfortable fashion. This is what building emotional intelligence (Goleman, 1995) is all about.

## Developmental Coaching Can Represent a Means of Reaching Groups of Previously Ignored but Talented Individuals

Nurses and nurse leaders, like so many leaders everywhere, often invest incredibly valuable coaching time on those with performance problems (time often not well spent) while ignoring those who could make the best use of coaching—those who want to be coached. Focusing on good-to-great performers, however, is the vehicle to creating a coaching-friendly context. The great majority of midcareer nurses do their jobs effectively, often superbly, and yet they have their own developmental aspirations that they do not feel are being addressed. When coached and when provided developmental opportunities, they often are very happy to rise to the occasion. They often want to be leaders but need additional support to effectively express that desire.

## Developmental Coaching Skills Can Be Useful in Dealing With a Variety of Relationship Challenges

Coaching has much in common with a variety of other useful influence tactics, including negotiations and conflict management. To be able to coach, the coach has to understand the coachee. Understanding requires maintaining a positive attitude, asking questions that help build understanding of the point of view of the other party, listening carefully, trying not to prejudge, and using feedback effectively, not punitively. Nurses have told us that they use coaching to help them deal with physicians, families, and even hospital administrators. A coaching approach tends to result in a productive and even surprising discussion, as its nonconfrontational approach discourages defensiveness. This, of course, is critical when nurse leaders have to coach physicians and peers over whom they have no authority. A coaching dialogue creates a different kind of conversation that both parties tend to find at least nonoffensive and often satisfying.

## Conclusion

The coaching initiative at Children's Hospital Boston represented one of many efforts under way to ensure that the organization would continue to demonstrate a world-class ability to fulfill its mission. As with many organizational interventions, it was difficult to tease out which components were responsible for certain outcomes, such as a more aware and capable group of leaders. Overall, there was a significant level of satisfaction that it contributed to the strategic efforts for most participants on most units.

As we have seen throughout our explorations in building a coaching capability, one size does not fit all. Experience with the Children's Hospital Boston coaching initiative suggests that we keep in mind the following success factors:

1. There needs to be a clear rationale for training large numbers of professionals and managers in the skills of developmental coaching. In this case, the rationale was that of enhancing patient care through more assertive and proactive leadership throughout the institution. Of note, Children's Hospital Boston is very proud of being ranked as one of the best hospitals in the world. Such a ranking can be maintained only by continuous improvement of all capabilities. Developmental coaching was a relatively easy sell given that context.

2. With the rationale in place, top-management support on an ongoing basis is critical. Note that in this instance, the organization had not learned about coaching through their experiences with expert coaches. Rather, they had already instituted many related practices that gave them a foundation from which to build a coaching capability. Top-management support was critical to creating an articulated vision for this process and promoting that

vision through education and through the decisions they made, particularly with regard to follow-up.

3. The challenge of engaging large numbers of managers and others in leadership roles in the routine provision of developmental coaching for their direct reports requires careful attention to the alignment between every aspect of the coaching model and the organization's culture, reward system, and work flow. Customization is an absolute must if participants in the target population are to really embrace and make use of the skills being taught.

4. Opportunities to build developmental coaching into ongoing work are key to the transfer of learning. Senior managers have to be in a position to see opportunities for doing so and for capitalizing on those opportunities.

# 11

# Peer Coaching at Citizen's Financial Group (CFG)

*Paul A. Carroll, James M. Hunt,*
*and Joseph R. Weintraub*

In this chapter, we describe the following:

- The development of a peer coaching program in a large financial services firm
- The components of the program and the results of an internal study to examine the impact of peer coaching on the individuals and the organization
- The value proposition in using a peer coaching system
- Recommendations in developing an effective peer coaching program
- The use of peer coaching as an important component of executive education programs

*None of us are perfect by ourselves, and all of us need the help and correcting influence of close colleagues. . . . Even the frankest and bravest of subordinates do not talk with their boss in the same way that they talk with their colleagues who are equals.*

—Robert Greenleaf, *Servant Leadership* (1977)

T*he Coaching Organization* might have ended after the last chapter as we reviewed the basic coaching capabilities of expert internal or external coaching and developmental coaching by managers. If one is to take seriously the notion of a learning-oriented organizational culture, it is critical to unlink learning from "expertise" as well as from the hierarchy. Can learning take place in the absence of both? Of course. Informal peer coaching has probably been the single most important source of learning through the ages. In a study of new managers, for example, the relationship established with peers, not with superiors, was found to be the most important developmental experience (Harvard Business Essentials, 2004). Peer coaching has also been shown to be useful in helping individuals learn various technical skills, new technology, or even the elements of an existing business plan (e.g., Ike, 1997; Krewson, 2004; Miller, 1998).

Peer coaching has been defined as "a confidential process through which two or more professional colleagues work together to reflect on current practices; expand, refine, and build new skills; share ideas; teach one another . . . or solve problems in the workplace" (Robbins, 1991, p. 1). In addition, our work with peer coaching agrees with an earlier finding that peer coaching improves learning by offering "a simple, nonthreatening structure designed for peers to help each other" (Gottesman, 2000, p. 5).

Most of the early work on peer coaching comes from work with teachers and principals in educational settings. Studies in this area have consistently found that learning can be enhanced through the use of peer coaching (e.g., Gottesman, 2000; Robbins, 1991; Weimer, 1993). The use of formal peer coaching programs in business settings, however, has not received as much research attention in the literature. Furthermore, peer coaching as a methodology for leadership development is a relatively untapped resource in most organizations.

This chapter focuses on the use of peer coaching at Citizens Financial Group (CFG). CFG is a $148 billion commercial bank headquartered in Providence, Rhode Island, owned by the Royal Bank of Scotland. CFG is also the parent of Citizens Bank and Charter One, with more than 27,000 employees and 1,600 bank branches in 13 U.S. states in the Northeast and the Midwest.

## The Advanced Leadership Development Program at Citizens

In February 2004, CFG launched an executive leadership program at Babson College, in Wellesley, Massachusetts, titled the Advanced Leadership

Development Program, or ALDP, as it came to be known internally at CFG. The 6-day executive development program, delivered in two 3-day segments over a 4- to 6-week period, brought in vice presidents and senior vice presidents from across the company to discuss topics in strategic leadership. Coaching was one of the key leadership competencies taught in the program.

To reinforce the coaching and learning taught in the classroom, each participant was provided an external executive coach on the second day of the leadership program. All of the external coaches had prior experience working with financial services firms. The initial focus of the coaches was to provide an opportunity for the participants to discuss their individual results on a 360-degree-feedback survey. However, many of the participants found that the coaches, while skilled in what they did, lacked the intimate organizational knowledge about the CFG culture. As an alternative, the participants suggested that they partner with one another as coaches. The proposed benefits of creating a peer coaching process would be twofold: (1) Participants would see value in having a coach who would understand the business and unique culture of CFG; and (2) the participants could practice the theoretical principles of coaching with a colleague and thus apply the coaching knowledge that they gained in the classroom back to their jobs.

In ALDP, participants learned the *developmental model of coaching* (Hunt & Weintraub, 2002a). In this approach, coaches engage in a dialogue with their coachees by asking open-ended questions to get the coachees to reflect on issues that are important to the coachees. Peers in this coaching role at CFG are asked to avoid telling their coachees what to do. Rather, this developmental approach to coaching invites the coachees to participate in their own learning through reflection and the coach's use of questioning.

During ALDP, participants were asked to consider a number of factors in selecting a peer coaching partner, with the assumption that "one size didn't fit all." In other words, the decision of who was selected was made by the participants and was to be based primarily on working with a peer whom they trusted and who would offer a dimension to the relationship that they found useful to them individually. These factors included personal comfort with the individual (i.e., chemistry); personal philosophy of leadership as well as several geographical considerations, such as peers who shared geographical proximity who could meet face-to-face when needed; peers from the same organization who were separated geographically (i.e., different cities or states); peers from different functional areas who could offer different perspectives on issues; and peers who reported to the same boss.

Like other successful and results-oriented companies, CFG was also interested in determining whether the process of peer coaching actually impacted performance on the job. One of the authors, Paul Carroll, an instructional designer and program director for ALDP, wanted to determine whether there was a business case for peer coaching at CFG—did peer coaching actually provide the participants and the organization with real benefits? In consultation with one of the authors from Babson, Carroll conducted a study of the learning impact of the peer coaching process through the use of one-on-one interviews and telephone conferences in which past participants shared their experiences about the peer coaching process during and after ALDP.

Overall, the results of the impact of the peer coaching process at CFG were very positive. In describing the benefits of an internal coach versus an external coach, many participants stated that an internal coach made the learning more applicable and "real world." For example, one Citizens participant said, "There's nothing theoretical about your feedback partner. In practical terms, we have an appreciation of the pressures on Citizens managers, and the speed at which we have to work." Furthermore, having an internal coach fostered camaraderie and made the relationship more intimate. One participant said, "My [coaching] relationship is a personal relationship, not a sterile transaction . . . not a business transaction." Indeed, since the coaching partner was an internal colleague, many CFG employees felt a higher degree of commitment to the relationship. Another participant said, "I don't want to let her [my feedback partner] down." In addition, a participant said, "There is a finite amount of time I could spend with an external coach. I will work with [my feedback partner] on an ongoing basis." She then added, "I'm also building a great friendship."

The data also showed that there was more understanding and sympathy afforded to peer coaches if meetings had to be canceled or postponed. ALDP participants didn't think they would have this level of flexibility with an external coach. One participant explained, "There are realities to working at Citizens. There's an understanding of work schedules. It would be frustrating to have an outside coach."

Peer coaching partners met with varying degrees of frequency. Many met either biweekly or monthly. Some met in person; many used the phone as their coaching medium. Of interest in these relationships is that many coaching pairs worked for completely different business areas within CFG. As a side benefit, many colleagues were able to learn more about separate departments and develop new internal networking contacts. Some participants deliberately chose coaches outside their departments. For example, one CFG executive who worked in an operations unit actively sought out a partner from human resources, as he saw this as an opportunity to develop his interpersonal skills. One feedback partnership proved to be so successful that the feedback partners even toured each other's business areas. According to Carroll's results, "Every program participant found value in being coached by an internal business partner." However, the coaching relationship was created so that graduates of the leadership program would also receive practice in playing the role of coach. These skills were particularly put to the test in those partnerships that cut across business areas. One participant indicated, "I get to try out more coaching skills because I don't know her world." Another participant indicated that the partnership added to her classroom learning, as "the coaching part was the most difficult part of the program." Some participants confessed that they had fallen into a routine in coaching their employees, relying on their subject matter expertise to assist their employees. One CFG colleague admitted, "You can begin to think you've heard it all. It helps to open your eyes and helps with your listening skills."

As for the duration of the coaching relationships, some continued well after the leadership program's completion. Others came to an end for several reasons: the separation in geography, the need to focus on one's own business area, and even some apathy. Many found the coaching relationship sustainable immediately after the program yet found difficulty in maintaining it if the partners worked in different business areas of the bank. One participant said, "Her issues are not the same as mine," and "[she] and I have nothing in common." As a result, some of these colleagues "switched" partners to people who worked more closely in their own business areas. Overall, the data suggest that while peers need to consider the various factors in selecting a peer coaching partner, the selection of peers from the same business area who are also geographically close enough to have occasional face-to-face meetings produces the best peer coaching results.

Some of the principles useful in peer mentoring would also apply to the success of peer coaching at CFG: Peers agree that each has something to learn from each other; confidentiality can be maintained; and each partner is willing to reciprocate (Harvard Business Essentials, 2004). In addition, peer coaching at CFG was done in the context of a leadership development program and enjoyed the support and reinforcement of learning by senior-level executives throughout the company.

The peer coaching process at CFG proved to be so successful that it was continued throughout the remaining ALDP programs in 2004 and all of the programs taught in 2005 and into 2006. Although not all of the peer coaching relationships flourished, the results of the CFG analysis showed that many of the peer coaching partnerships that were cultivated in ALDP continued well after the close of the program. The positive, psychological support that participants experienced from their partners is consistent with an earlier study (Joyce & Showers, 1982). The positive impact of these continuing relationships was seen as a major contributor to both individual and organizational learning at CFG.

One of the contributing factors in the use of peer coaching at CFG was a highly regarded corporate credo that included the value of "Colleagues." The CFG definition of "Colleagues" includes providing an environment that "will be extraordinarily caring, like an extension of your own family" and creating "opportunities for professional growth," and always making "an effort to listen and act on your ideas." The acceptance of the credo at CFG appeared to make the peer coaching process feel "safer" for participants, resulting in a greater tendency to share personal and professional information with other ALDP participants.

## The Value Proposition for a Successful Peer Feedback System

One of the most appealing aspects of peer coaching is that it removes evaluation from the process and instead provides a system of learning that is driven by the needs of the coachee. The coachee, in most cases, provides the basis for feedback and dialogue for the coach. The coachee tells the coach, "This is what I want to work on," and the coach then follows the lead by the coachee and provides the mirror for the coachee to see himself or herself through observations or other data that might be available. Peer coaching also "sells" well to senior management, since the process is a low-cost/no-cost operation once an initial training process is provided.

Because participation is generally voluntary in peer coaching programs, especially after a formal leadership program ends, as in the case of CFG, employees who experience successful peer coaching are more likely to continue in its use and thrive. They are also more likely to expand their spheres of influence and start to use coaching in their interactions with their own direct reports.

---

**Box 11.1   Peer Coaching at Millennium Pharmaceuticals**

Most organizations have failed to take advantage of the talent already in place in their organizations. With skilled hiring, the potential to leverage the strengths and talent of employees in peer coaching remains high. At Millennium Pharmaceuticals, in Cambridge, Massachusetts, for example, Dr. Fabio Sala and his colleagues from the Learning and Development Department have successfully introduced a peer coaching process in which a committed group of peers (e.g., supervisors, directors) from across functions meet regularly to address real work challenges/opportunities that each member is currently experiencing. When given a choice between being part of group of peers from their own division or a group of cross-functional peers, participants have always chosen the latter. Participants bring real work initiatives, issues, or challenges, and the group works together to provide assistance or direction.

Participants go through a training orientation to learn how the peer coaching process works and some simple coaching strategies. Dr. Sala and his colleagues have found that the peer coaching program at Millennium has resulted in four important benefits: (1) It provides new perspectives, challenges assumptions, and helps reframe issues, thereby increasing strategic thinking; (2) it helps participants with their most difficult issues/problems/challenges and translates new perspectives into real actions that lead to results; (3) it improves general coaching and leadership skills; and (4) it builds a network of peers. In fact, participants often cite networking as an important benefit. They know that networking is a high-level skill with several benefits (e.g., cross-boundary collaboration, improved horizontal/strategic thinking, gaining of buy-in). Dr. Sala believes that people who are more successful in their work lives also tend to have wider and deeper networks.

According to Dr. Sala, the results of this effort have been positive, with new peer coaching teams continuing to form. The peer coaching program achieves the highest levels of satisfaction among all the training and development programs offered at Millennium.

Peer coaching also has some potential issues that need to be considered. The need to be geographically close seems to be important overall to many peer coaching partners. Distance makes it more difficult to stay in contact, and coaching does not work as well when face-to-face meetings are not as prevalent. Also, the tendency among peer coaches to not "push back" is more likely with peers than if one has an outside executive coach. Peer coaches often don't want to appear too direct or challenging, a tendency not as likely when dealing with an outside coach. The way that peers will interact with each other is difficult to predict, but it is essential that there is discussion about how to move each other outside of a person's comfort zone if coaching is to be effective. With peers, however, the amount and extent of "pushing" must be weighed very carefully so that the overall relationship is preserved. Our work has found, however, that the benefits of peer coaching seem to outweigh its disadvantages.

Peer coaching is a relatively simple, powerful tool that, if implemented well, in the right culture, with the right support system, can produce increases in both individual and organizational learning. In addition, the impact of improved relationships between individuals and departments and the transfer of knowledge are important outcomes.

## The Formula for a Successful Peer Coaching Program

As seen in the CFG case, creating a peer coaching program can be a very powerful way to create an ongoing culture of learning and development. The implementation of such a program often works best when combined with a leadership development initiative. The payoffs can be enormous, and the cost of implementation is low, especially after the initial creation of the peer coaching program.

To implement an effective peer coaching program, we offer several success factors to consider:

• Build your business case for peer coaching: Show how individual and organizational performance can be improved through the use of peer coaching (whether in good times or bad).

• Trust is key: Peer coaching works best in a culture in which trust and colleagueship are highly valued. If this culture doesn't exist in the overall organization, make sure your department has a strong commitment to the development of trust and collegiality.

• Training in developmental coaching: A common language and methodology are important—don't throw people together in a room and say, "Go coach each other." Give them a coaching framework (see Hunt & Weintraub, 2002a) that can be learned easily and applied immediately.

• Allow people to select their own peer coaching partners.

• Encourage a willingness on the part of both peer coaches to share, to help, to learn, to implement, and to improve.

• Strive to keep the peer coaching process simple and low maintenance. You will need a "champion" to keep it all organized, but the best peer coaching processes are driven by the employees themselves.

- Get peer coaches together periodically (in person or by phone) for the sharing of stories. Have people discuss successes and ways they are using peer coaching throughout the organization.

- Periodically evaluate the effect of peer coaching and look for ways to energize the process using recommendations from the peer coaches.

## Peer Coaching as a Follow-Up Strategy to Executive Education

As we have discussed in previous chapters, coaching can play a significant role in enhancing learning. The experience for most companies involved in executive education is that the program "ends" on the final day of a scheduled program. Unfortunately, so does much of the learning and development that was so prominent during the program itself. With a systematic plan of integrating and reinforcing the learning gained in an executive program, however, executive education programs can yield significant learning benefits back on the job. Peer coaching represents one important method of maximizing the probability that learning will be used by participants after completing an executive education program. Our experience at Babson Executive Education has shown that peer coaching works particularly well with leadership programs, since personal development, emotional intelligence, and coaching are themes often included within these types of programs.

Peer coaching is often introduced early in an executive education program's agenda, and peer coaching partners are chosen by the second day of a typical 5- to 10-day program. In executive programs that are taught in modules separated by weeks or months, the peer coaches are given assignments in which their interaction is strongly encouraged before they return to complete the program in the next module. In this way, we "jump-start" the peer coaching process and use the debriefing of the peer coaching experience to reinforce learning within the entire executive education class. The integration of follow-up systems in executive education is often ignored but is absolutely critical to learning. Our findings in executive education suggest that peer coaching enhances learning during, in-between, and after an executive program has formally ended. In one sense, it is important that executive education and learning do not end, but rather begin with the real work to be done as participants and their peers bring their learning back to the workplace and apply what they have learned to their own jobs. Box 11.2 presents a sample of the phases of the use of peer coaching in an executive education program that focused on developing senior leaders in leadership and personal change.

---

**Box 11.2   Phases of Peer Coaching in Executive Education Programs**

- Introduction to peer coaching.
- Preparing for the peer coaching relationship.
- Selecting your own peer coaching partner.
- Training in developmental coaching.
- Peer coaching practice and video case studies.
- Observation and the use of 360-degree feedback.
- Contracting on what's important with your coaching partner.
- Ongoing exercises: creating vision.
- Ongoing feedback, as appropriate.
- Preparing your partner for going back home: dealing with your boss, peers, and colleagues.
- Creating a mechanism for follow-up and staying in contact.
- Organizational/team support and follow-up.
- Check-in periods for review: Does peer coaching make a difference? How have we used peer coaching? Use of stories as a way to keep coaching and learning alive.

---

## Feedback Is Not Always Easy, Even From a Peer

Receiving feedback from a peer can be difficult. During an initial rehearsal for the television series *The Odd Couple*, actor Jack Klugman received feedback from costar Tony Randall that Klugman perceived as being overly critical. After the rehearsal, Klugman threatened to leave the show and told Randall, "I just can't work this way . . . with you telling me how to act." Klugman didn't leave the show, and several weeks later, after working together, Randall said to Klugman, "Why can't I tell you what to do when I think you've made the wrong choice?" "Now," Klugman said, "you can tell me anything you want." Randall then asked Klugman, "Why? What's different now? What's changed?" Klugman responded, "Now it's a suggestion, not an order." Klugman stated that Randall could offer him any suggestion he wanted as long as he understood that "I didn't have to take it" (Klugman, 2005, pp. 5–6).

When people are given input by peers, they don't "have to take it," which is one of the great advantages of receiving coaching and feedback from peers.

# Concluding Remarks

## *The Frontiers of the Coaching Organization*

I n *The Coaching Organization*, we have tried to offer some best-practices examples of strategy and execution in the use of developmental coaching to promote employee and particularly leadership development. The study of coaching is young. This should not be considered the last word on the subject, but rather some pioneering words from individuals and organizations that have shown up relatively early on the scene. We had several major goals in this effort. First, and perhaps foremost, we would like to encourage decision makers in organizations to think carefully about developmental coaching as an organizational capacity. Developmental coaching, when properly managed, is a tool—a very powerful tool, if the research is to be believed (Buckingham & Coffman, 1999, for instance).

When conditions are right, developmental coaching is a tool that can be built up and can ultimately represent a real competitive advantage for a business. Likewise, developmental coaching can give a not-for-profit organization the opportunity to more assertively fulfill its mission through strengthening employee engagement and enhancing employee performance, short- and long term.

We are painfully aware, however, that we have stumbled into the larger morass of human resource and talent management. We say "morass" because of the somewhat discouraging finding that relatively few organizations actually practice human resource management in a fashion that can offer them sustained competitive advantage (Pfeffer, 1998). There is a tremendous gap between what people know and what they do in this area.

The effective management of human resources, human capital really, can help a business fulfill its mission, but for the most part, we don't follow through on that knowledge. This leaves lots of running room for the Southwest Airlines's of the world, companies that have integrated a strategic view of their talent into the very heart and soul of their business models. What does this mean for the practice of developmental coaching?

It likely means that too many organizations will continue to view coaching as a fad, something to be taken to heart in an ad hoc way and ultimately discarded when it disappoints. The failure to view coaching as a capability to be managed, as we have stressed, harms the entire enterprise. An old mentor to one of the authors once made the point that "bad competition is worse than no competition at all." We hope that that he was wrong. Additional research may help.

Recent trends in the measurement of human capital are promising. There is a need to tease out and document what works. However, this effort will likely require much more sophisticated analyses than that found in simple return-on-investment (ROI) studies. When a good organization manages the inputs to coaching (i.e., the coachees), they are likely to choose individuals who can have a significant impact on their business units or the organization as a whole. Some of the ROI studies on coaching that have been done to date report massive returns (see Anderson, 2003, for example). Stratospheric ROI can be delivered by just one individual who uses coaching in a way that helps the individual do great things.

Such an analysis certainly argues for being careful about who receives expert coaching. However, it does not address some of the broader and perhaps more important issues that we face. We have seen institutions such as Whirlpool, Wachovia, and Children's Hospital Boston make efforts to greatly expand the impact of coaching in their organizations through a variety of means. We need research that can help us sort out the impact of those interventions on middle management or, when leadership is required across the organization, on everyone. We challenge more academic researchers to explore the field of coaching and address some of the questions raised through these case studies and accompanying analyses. There is much work to be done.

# References

Anderson, M. (2003). *Bottom-line organization development: Implementing and evaluating strategic change for lasting value.* Amsterdam, Netherlands: Elsevier.

Benner, P. (2001). *From novice to expert: Excellence and power in clinical nursing practice.* Upper Saddle River, NJ: Prentice Hall.

Berglas, S. (2002, June). The very real dangers of executive coaching. *Harvard Business Review,* pp. 86–92.

Boyatzis, R. (1982). *The competent manager.* New York: Wiley-Interscience.

Buckingham, M., & Coffman, C. (1999). *First break all the rules.* New York: Simon & Schuster.

Chappelow, C. (2004). 360-degree feedback. In C. McCauley & E. Van Velsor (Eds.), *Handbook of leadership development* (2nd ed., pp. 58–84). San Francisco: Jossey-Bass.

Charan, R., Drotter, S., & Noel, J. (2001). *The leadership pipeline.* San Francisco: Jossey-Bass.

Conger, J., & Benjamin, B. (1999). *Building leadership: How successful companies develop the next generation.* San Francisco: Jossey-Bass.

Davenport, T. (1999). *Human capital.* San Francisco: Jossey-Bass.

Davenport, T., & Prusak, L. (2002). *Working knowledge.* Boston: Harvard Business School.

De Long, D. (2004). *Lost knowledge: Confronting the threat of an aging workforce.* New York: Oxford University Press.

Dreyfus, H. L., & Dreyfus, S. E. (1986). *Mind over machine: The power of human intuition and expertise in the era of the computer.* New York: Free Press.

Edmondson, A. (1996). Learning from mistakes is easier said than done: Group and organizational influences on the detection and correction of human error. *Journal of Applied Behavioral Sciences, 32*(1), 5–28.

Eichinger, R., & Lombardo, M. (2003). Knowledge summary series: 360-degree assessment. *Human Resource Planning, 26*(4), 34–45.

Eichinger, R., Lombardo, M., & Stibler, A. (2005). *Broadband talent management: Paths to improvement.* Minneapolis, MN: Lominger Ltd.

Ennis, S. (2002). Initiating executive coaching in your organization. In C. Fitzgerald & J. Berger (Eds.), *Executive coaching: Practices and perspectives* (pp. 157–184). Palo Alto, CA: Davies-Black.

Ennis, S., Goodman, R., Hodgetts, W., Hunt, J., Mansfield, R., Otto, J., & Stern, L. (2005). *Core competencies of the executive coach*. Boston: The Executive Coaching Forum. (See http://www.TheExecutive CoachingForum.com_)

Ennis, S., Otto, J., Stern, L., Goodman, R., Hodgetts, W., & Hunt, J. (2004). *The executive coaching handbook: Principles and guidelines for a successful coaching partnership* (3rd ed.). Boston: The Executive Coaching Forum. (See http://www.The ExecutiveCoachingForum.com)

Fitzgerald, J., & Berger, J. (Eds.). (2002). *Executive coaching: Practices and perspectives* (pp. 225–242). Palo Alto, CA: Davies-Black.

Frisch, M. (2001). The emerging role of the internal coach. *Consulting Psychology Journal, 53*(4), 240–250.

Frisch, M. (2005). Extending the reach of executive coaching: The internal coach. *Human Resource Planning, 28*(1), 23.

Fritts, P. (1998). *The new managerial mentor*. Palo Alto, CA: Davies-Black.

Gittell, J. H. (2003). *The Southwest Airlines way*. New York: McGraw-Hill.

Goleman, D. (1995). *Emotional intelligence*. New York: Bantam Books.

Goleman, D. (2000, March–April). Leadership that gets results. *Harvard Business Review*, pp. 78–90.

Goleman, D., Boyatzis, R., & McKee, A. (2002). *Primal leadership*. Cambridge, MA: Harvard Business School.

Gottesman, B. (2000). *Peer coaching for educators*. Lanham, MD: Scarecrow Press.

Greenleaf, R. K. (1977). *Servant leadership: A journey into the nature of legitimate power and greatness*. New York: Paulist Press.

Guthrie, V. (1999). *Coaching for action: A report on long-term advising in a program context*. Greensboro, NC: Center for Creative Leadership.

Hall, D. T. (2002). *Careers in and out of organizations*. Thousand Oaks, CA: Sage.

Hall, D. T., & Otazo, K. (1995). *Executive coaching study: A progress report* (Executive Development Roundtable at Boston University Working Paper). Boston: Boston University School of Management.

Hall, D. T., Otazo, K., & Hollenbeck, G. (1999). Behind closed doors: What really happens in executive coaching. *Organizational Dynamics, 27*(3), 39–53.

Harvard Business Essentials. (2004). *Coaching and mentoring*. Boston: Harvard Business School Press.

Hernez-Broome, G. (2002). In it for the long haul: Coaching is key to continued development. *Leadership in Action, 22*(1), 14–16.

Hodgetts, W. (2003, January). *The deeper work of executive coaching*. Paper presented at the Conference Board Conference on Executive Coaching, New York.

Hollenbeck, G. (1996). An essay on issues in executive coaching. In G. Hollenbeck (Ed.), *Current practices in 360-degree feedback and coaching for executive evaluation and development: Reference materials* (pp. 1–19). (Executive Development Roundtable at Boston University Working Paper). Boston: Boston University School of Management.

Hollenbeck, G. (2004). This ain't your momma's doublewide! Or executive coaching at the crossroads. *Industrial-Organizational Psychologist, 42*(1), 16–23.

Hudson, F. (1999). *The handbook of coaching*. San Francisco: Jossey-Bass.

Hunt, J. (2004). Successful executive coaching from the consumer's perspective: Adaptive and developmental learning. In A. Buono (Ed.), *Creating consulting, innovative perspectives on management consulting* (pp. 165–200). Greenwich, CT: IAP Press.

Hunt, J., Strei, K., & Weintraub, J. (2002, January 29). *Coaching from the inside: Lessons from experience.* Paper presented at the Conference Board Executive Coaching Conference, Coaching for Business Results, New York.

Hunt, J., & Weintraub, J. (2002a). *The coaching manager: Developing top talent in business.* Thousand Oaks, CA: Sage.

Hunt, J., & Weintraub, J. (2002b). Executive coaching as the intervention of choice for the derailing executive: Some unanswered questions. In A. F. Buono (Ed.), *Developing knowledge and value in management consulting* (pp. 83–112). Greenwich, CT: IAP Press.

Hunt, J., & Weintraub, J. (2004). Learning developmental coaching. *Journal of Management Education, 28*(1), 39–61.

Ike, C. A. (1997). Development through educational technology: Implications for teacher personality and peer coaching. *Journal of Instructional Psychology, 24,* 42–49.

International Coach Federation (ICF). (2005). *Coaching core competencies.* Retrieved February 9, 2006, from http://www.coachfederation.org/eweb/DynamicPage .aspx?Site=ICF&WebKey=7d8d0474–9f62–4b16-bd42-b39ef128537b

Joyce, B., & Showers, B. (1982). The coaching of teaching. *Educational Leadership, 40*(1), 4–10.

Kegan, R. (1994). *In over our heads: The mental demands of modern life.* Cambridge, MA: Harvard University Press.

Kirsner, S. (2003, July). Are you Insperienced? *Fast Company,* p. 32.

Klugman, J. (2005). *Tony and me: A story of friendship.* West Linn, OR: Goodhill Press.

Kouzes, J., & Posner, B. (1995). *The leadership challenge.* San Francisco: Jossey-Bass.

Kram, K. (1988). *Mentoring at work.* New York: University Press of America.

Kram, K., & Bragar, M. (1992). Development through mentoring: A strategic approach. In D. Montrose & C. Shinkman (Eds.), *Career development: Theory and practice* (pp. 221–254). Springfield, IL: Charles C Thomas.

Krewson, H. (2004). Integrating coaching, training, and development with talent management. In L. Berger & D. Berger (Eds.), *The talent management handbook* (chap. 27). New York: McGraw-Hill.

Lawler, E. (2003). Reward practices and performance management system effectiveness. *Organizational Dynamics, 32*(4), 294–404.

Levin, S., Hunt, J., & Weintraub, J. (2003). *The coaching manager assessment.* Westborough, MA: Hunt Associates.

Lombardo, M., & Eichinger, R. (2001). *The leadership machine.* Minneapolis: Lominger Ltd.

McCall, J., Lombardo, M., & Morrison, A. (1988). *The lessons of experience.* New York: Lexington Books.

McCullough, D. (2004). *John Adams and the good life of the mind* (Boston Atheneaeum Occasional Papers, No. 4). Boston: Ascensius Press.

McDermott, M., Levenson, A., & Clarke, S. (2005). *What coaching can and cannot do for your organization* (Capital One Corporation report). McLean, VA: Capital One Corporation. (Used by permission of the authors)

Miller, N. N. (1998). The technology float in education today. *Science Activities, 35*(2), 3–4.

National Aeronautics and Space Administration (NASA). (2005). *NASA business coaching handbook: A guide for human resource professionals.* Retrieved February 10, 2006, from http://www.nasapeople.nasa.gov/training/coachmentor/business coaching HR.pdf

Olivero, G., Bane, D., & Kopelman, R. (1997). Executive coaching as a transfer of training tool: Effects on productivity in a public agency. *Public Personnel Management, 26*(4), 461–469.

Pfeffer, J. (1998). *The human equation.* Cambridge, MA: Harvard Business School.

Ready, D., & Conger, J. (2003, Spring). Why leadership development efforts fail. *MIT Sloan Management Review,* pp. 83–88.

Robbins, P. (1991). *How to plan and implement a peer coaching program.* Alexandria, VA: Association for Supervision & Curriculum Development.

Robertson, R., Higuchi, P., & Huff, K. (2004, November). *Dynamics of internal corporate coaching survey report.* Paper presented at the International Coach Federation Conference, Quebec, Canada.

Rothwell, R. (2001). *Effective succession planning.* New York: AMACOM.

Schein, E. (1985). *Organizational culture and leadership.* San Francisco: Jossey-Bass.

Sellers, P. (2002, June 24). Something to prove. *Fortune,* pp. 85–98.

Smart, B. (1999). Topgrading. Paramus, NJ: Prentice Hall.

Smith, J. (2005). Beware: Internal traps for internal coaches. *OD Practitioner, 37*(2), 8–13.

Smither, J., London, M., Flaut, R., Vargas, Y., & Kucine, I. (2003). Can working with an executive coach improve multisource feedback ratings over time? A quasi-experimental field study. *Personnel Psychology, 56*(1), 23–44.

Spencer, L., McClelland, D., & Spencer, S. (1994). *Competency assesssment methods.* Boston: Hay/McBer.

Strumpf, C. (2002). Coaching from the inside. In C. Fitzgerald & J. Berger (Eds.), *Executive coaching: Practices and perspectives* (pp. 225–242). Palo Alto, CA: Davies-Black.

Thalheimer, K. (2002). *A study of executive coaching.* Unpublished manuscript. Babson College, Babson Park, MA.

Ting, S., & Hart, E.W. (2004). Formal coaching. In C. McCauley & E. Van Velsor (Eds.), *Handbook of leadership development* (2nd ed., pp. 116–150). San Francisco: Jossey-Bass.

Valerio, A., & Lee, R. (2005). *Executive coaching: A guide for the HR professional.* San Francisco: Pfeiffer.

Van Velsor, E., & McCauley, C. (2004). Our view of leadership development. In C. McCauley & E. Van Velsor (Eds.), *Handbook of leadership development* (2nd ed., pp. 1–23). San Francisco: Jossey-Bass.

Weimer, M. (1993). *Improving your classroom teaching.* Newbury Park, CA: Sage.

Wolfe, D., & Kolb, D. (1984). Career development, personal growth, and experiential learning. In D. Kolb, I. Rubin, & J. MacIntyre (Eds.), *Organizational psychology: Readings on human behavior in organizations* (4th ed., pp. 124–152). Englewood Cliffs, NJ: Prentice Hall.

Wrich, J. (1982). *Guidelines for developing an employee assistance program* (AMA briefing). New York: American Management Associations.

# Appendix A

## The Competencies of the Expert Executive Coach

*Susan Ennis, Robert Goodman,*
*William Hodgetts, James Hunt,*
*Richard Mansfield, Judy Otto, and Lew Stern*

The model presents a hypothesized list of the competencies associated with effective executive coaching outcomes. It was developed through a reflective dialogue with a group of highly seasoned executive coaches. Two of those coaches had also served as practice managers within organizations, responsible for building and maintaining a coaching capability. This model is not meant to be exhaustive or final. However, it should be useful to those responsible for hiring or training expert coaches, to coaches interested in rounding out their skill sets, and to those responsible for educating future expert coaches. Obviously, it may need to be modified to fit specific organizational, business, or cultural requirements.

Competencies that involve knowledge, skills, and personal attributes are described in the model. Areas of knowledge associated with effective expert coaching include the following:

- Psychological knowledge
- Business acumen
- Organizational behavior and development knowledge
- Knowledge of coaching theory

Skills required by coaches include those related to the following:

- Building and maintaining coaching relationships
- Contracting
- Assessment
- Development planning
- Facilitating development and change
- Ending formal coaching and transitioning to long-term development

Attributes required for coaching include the following:

- Mature self-confidence
- Positive energy
- Assertiveness
- Interpersonal sensitivity
- Openness and flexibility
- Demonstrating a goal orientation
- Partnering and influence
- Continuous learning and development
- Integrity

We now present the model with appropriate anchors in more detail:

# Knowledge Areas

## Psychological Knowledge

- Personality theories
- Models of human motivation
- Adult development theories, including moral, intellectual, emotional, relational, and spiritual development
- Models of adult learning
- Models of career development
- Models of personal and behavioral change
- Work-life balance
- Stress management knowledge
- Social psychology and how social factors impact individual and group behavior
- How to identify individuals in need of psychological or medical referral
- Models of emotional intelligence
- The role of gender differences in adulthood
- Models and methods of 360-degree feedback
- Models of personal and leadership style (e.g., MBTI, DISC)

## Business Acumen

- Business practices and concepts
- Basic financial concepts (e.g., income and balance sheets)
- Business functions and their interdependencies
- The strategic-planning process and its relationship with team and individual goal setting
- Basic information technologies and the role of information technology in business (e.g., Enterprise Resource Planning software)
- Process improvement technologies
- Global capitalism and global firms
- The differences between regulated and nonregulated businesses
- The differences between for-profit and not-for-profit businesses
- The key leadership roles of organizations (e.g., COO, CFO, CTO, CEO, executive director, board chair, etc.)
- Knowledge of current business events, issues, and trends
- Management principles and processes
- Human resource management programs and processes
- The appropriate use of communication technologies

## Organizational Knowledge

- Basic organizational structures, systems, and processes, including functional, divisional, and matrix organizational forms as well as the behavioral patterns associated with each
- Organizational assessment and diagnosis
- Organizational design and development principles and practices
- The impact and role of organizational cultures and subcultures
- The phases of team development and the characteristics of effective team leadership
- Models of leadership
- Leadership development programs and processes
- Organization development methodologies
- Organizational systems theory
- The nature and role of organizational politics, power, and influence
- Organizational change management theories and practices
- Consulting theory and practices
- The role of ethics in business and in organizational consulting
- Models of the learning organization
- Models of succession and leadership transition

## Coaching Knowledge

- The history of executive coaching
- Executive coaching models and theories

- The definitions of coaching and executive coaching as a specialty practice
- Seven overarching principles for executive coaching: systems perspective, results orientation, business focus, partnership, competence, integrity, and judgment
- Seven guidelines for practicing the different phases of executive coaching by the coach, the executive, and the executive's organization: managing confidentiality, precoaching activities, contracting, assessment, goal setting, coaching, and transitioning to long-term development
- The underlying principles and approaches of the different types of coaching and how they differ from and/or can be incorporated into executive coaching
- The distinction between executive coaching and other models of coaching
- The role of manager as coach and the impact of executive coaching on the development of that capability
- The roles coaches can play and when and how to effectively apply them (e.g., trainer, mentor, advisor, etc.)
- The differences between executive coaching and other helping methods for executives (e.g., counseling, consulting, therapy, mentoring, etc.)
- How coaching theories and methods apply to various situations of individual coaching clients
- How to tailor the coaching process to adapt it to the unique needs and circumstances of the coachee and the organization
- Measurement of coaching outcomes and processes
- Research findings on executive coaching (past and emerging)
- The core competencies of executive coaches
- The wide variety of available coaching resources (e.g., books, articles, Internet sites, tools, etc.)
- How to maintain and implement a continuous plan for one's own professional development

# Coaching Skills

## Building and Maintaining Coaching Relationships

- Build and sustain trust
- Hold the coachee, his or her boss, and human resources accountable
- Identify and manage resistance and conflict
- Influence with and without authority
- Maintain confidentiality on sensitive organizational and individual issues
- Hold multiple perspectives
- Solicit feedback on one's own performance as coach
- Use the coaching relationship as a tool to help the coachee
- Maintain the balance of the close coaching relationship and professional boundaries
- Make and explain observations about what goes on in the coaching relationship and its similarities and differences to the coachee's other relationships
- Appropriately challenge the coachee and deal with his or her defensiveness without impairing the coaching relationship

## Contracting

- Evaluate the readiness of the coachee for coaching
- Engage all appropriate constituents in goal setting and agenda setting for the coaching (e.g., coachee, boss, human resources, others)
- Obtain commitment and support from all appropriate constituents
- Establish guidelines for confidentiality
- Establish the role in the coaching of the boss and human resources
- Facilitate agenda-setting and goal-setting meetings between the coachee, his or her boss, and the human resource professional
- Develop realistic and challenging coaching goals
- Set realistic time frames for accomplishing the coaching goals
- Recontract when appropriate
- Tailor the coaching process to the unique needs of the coachee and the organization

## Assessment

- Design assessment plans
- Administer and interpret 360-degree-feedback instruments and measures of personal and leadership style (e.g., MBTI, DISC)
- Interview the coachee and his or her key constituents
- Unobtrusively observe/shadow the coachee in his or her work environment
- Gather data from multiple sources, aggregate them, and present the results and implications in a useful format
- Use the results of assessment tools and instruments to evaluate the coachee's strengths, weaknesses, abilities, tendencies, preferences, behavior patterns, emotions, thinking styles, opportunities, constraints, and other factors important to coaching
- Use the results of assessment tools, instruments, and other methods to evaluate the coachee's organizational context (e.g., characteristics, strengths, weaknesses, opportunities, constraints, etc.)
- Refer when appropriate to employee assistance programs, career counselors, or other specialists for the administration, scoring, and interpreting of assessments
- Identify the coachee's learning style

## Development Planning

- Partner with human resources
- Conduct debriefing and feedback sessions with the coachee about the assessments and 360-degree results
- Establish specific coaching goals (e.g., behavioral, cognitive, skills, business, relationships, etc.)
- Help the coachee design and create action plans and a coaching time table
- Help the coachee, his or her boss, and human resources to review assessment results within agreed-upon guidelines for confidentiality and translate those results into actionable coaching strategies

- Establish qualitative and quantitative measures of results for the coaching goals
- Determine what can be achieved in coaching and recommend appropriate training and other methods to achieve other developmental goals
- Quickly identify the need for and make referrals to other helping professionals
- Gain commitment for the coachee's self-management of coaching action plans
- Help the boss to provide useful feedback and coach the coachee as his or her manager

## Facilitating Development and Change Through Coaching

- Take the coachee's point of view and offer alternative points of view
- Show accurate empathy
- Listen actively and respectfully
- Communicate clearly, concisely, and directly
- Provide constructive feedback
- Observe the coachee's behavior in coaching sessions and provide real-time feedback
- Offer specific strategies and suggest behavior changes
- Demonstrate and serve as a role model in the coaching for new work methods and ways of communicating
- Create and raise awareness
- Design assignments that encourage experimentation, reflection, and learning
- Ask powerful questions
- Support and confront appropriately
- Challenge assumptions
- Solicit solutions
- Swiftly translate ideas into action plans
- Develop management, executive, and leadership skills
- Provide learning resources as needed (e.g., reading, models, etc.)
- Involve the boss as the ongoing coach
- Measure and monitor the coaching process and results
- Address new issues and learning opportunities as they arise
- Be aware of and recognize one's own part in the coachee's problem or situation through various methods (e.g., peer supervision, consultation, etc.)
- Coach the boss to better support the coachee and his or her business and coaching objectives

## Ending Formal Coaching and Transitioning to Long-Term Development

- Identify the appropriate ending point in the formal coaching process
- Initiate discussion with the coachee, his or her manager, and others in the organization about bringing the formal coaching to an end

- Work with the coachee to identify ongoing developmental supports and resources in his or her environment and to establish a transition/ending plan
- Work with the coachee to establish postcoaching developmental goals and a plan for meeting those goals
- Work toward and encourage the coachee's independence
- Encourage the coachee to continue learning on his or her own
- Conduct formal ending meeting with the coachee, his or her manager, and human resources
- Leave open the possibility for future coaching as the need arises and within the guidelines of the coaching contract

# Coaching Attributes

## Mature Self-Confidence

- Appears comfortable with himself or herself
- Shows maturity; demonstrates that he or she has gained wisdom from personal and professional experience
- Shows confidence; places an appropriate value on his or her own abilities and perspectives
- Shows humility; demonstrates awareness that success usually follows from the efforts of a group or team of other individuals, not solely from one's own efforts

## Positive Energy

- Shows energy, optimism, and enthusiasm
- Effectively manages his or her emotions
- Demonstrates resilience; bounces back after mistakes and failures
- Demonstrates an appropriate sense of humor
- Helps the coachee to appreciate his or her strengths and ability to overcome barriers
- Helps the coachee to imagine new possibilities
- Conveys hopefulness

## Assertiveness

- Asserts himself or herself and appropriately says "no" to set limits
- Confronts coachees and others who are not following through on commitments
- Speaks directly with others even when discussing difficult or sensitive issues
- Addresses conflict with others directly and constructively
- Communicates in ways that reflect respect for one's own worth and the worth of others

## Interpersonal Sensitivity

- Shows empathy with others
- Is sensitive to the way his or her style impacts others or fits with the needs of others
- Demonstrates an interest in people; shows curiosity about the lives, goals, experiences, and perspectives of others
- Shows compassion and demonstrates concern for the needs and emotional well-being of others
- Demonstrates tact; gives difficult or critical information to others in a respectful and supportive fashion
- Learns and remembers other people's most important concerns
- Uses active listening techniques (e.g., maintaining full attention, periodically summarizing, being nonjudgmental) to reflect and acknowledge the other person's feelings and concerns

## Openness and Flexibility

- Is able to understand and appreciate perspectives that differ from his or her own
- Tailors his or her own approach to fit the preferences and needs of the coachee
- Demonstrates flexibility; changes course or approach when the situation demands it
- Understands and relates to individuals and groups from a variety of cultures with values different from his or her own culture
- Seeks out and uses feedback to enhance the coaching engagement

## Goal Orientation

- Sets challenging but achievable goals for himself or herself
- Helps coachees to identify and set realistic and challenging goals
- Is highly motivated toward the pursuit of his or her goals
- Shows resourcefulness; seeks out or helps others seek out solutions under difficult or challenging conditions
- Demonstrates stability; stays on tasks for extended periods of time
- Shows persistence; does not give up when faced with a challenge
- Demonstrates the ability to organize work; effectively plans and manages resources and time when pursuing a goal

## Partnering and Influence

- Carefully plans and tailors his or her own words in ways that achieve a desired impact
- Presents arguments that address others' most important concerns and issues
- Involves others as partners in a process, to gain their support and buy-in

- Shows interest in and comfort with the context in which the coaching is taking place (e.g., for-profits, not-for-profits, health care organizations, the public sector, marketing, finance, sales, research and development, etc.)
- Shares some of the values of those in the context in which the coaching is taking place and has a fundamental comfort with private enterprise and/or public endeavors
- Demonstrates inclusiveness by encouraging the participation of multiple stakeholders

## Continuous Learning and Development

- Seeks feedback to enhance overall coaching effectiveness
- Assesses and addresses gaps in his or her own knowledge and skills
- Undertakes study and learning to enhance skills that will contribute to his or her coaching

## Integrity

- Takes and holds an ethical stand regardless of financial or other pressures
- Carefully maintains appropriate confidentiality in all dealings
- Determines what is appropriate through careful contracting in his or her coaching and consulting relationships, with the goal of meeting the needs of all stakeholders
- Demonstrates personal integrity; "walks the talk"
- Appears genuine, honest, and straightforward regarding his or her agenda and needs
- Focuses on and puts the client's needs ahead of his or her own needs
- Makes and keeps commitments to others
- Avoids a coaching workload that compromises the quality of the coaching service
- Respects the established relationships between the client and other providers of coaching, consulting, and/or other services

# Appendix B

## The Coaching Manager
## Self-Assessment

The following self-assessment tool was designed to assist managers in identifying their strengths and developmental opportunities with regard to the provision of developmental coaching to their direct reports. The model underlying the assessment includes behaviors associated with the following:

- Self-awareness
- Promoting learning
- Communication
- Accessibility
- Listening
- Creating a trusting environment

The self-assessment in its entirety begins on the next page.

---

SOURCE: Adapted from Levin, Hunt, and Weintraub (2003).

# The Coaching Manager: Self-Assessment Form

This coaching manager assessment instrument includes 27 behavioral statements. To the right of each statement, you have a choice of the following:

| Hardly Ever I hardly ever demonstrate this behavior. | Sometimes I sometimes demonstrate this behavior. | Often I often demonstrate this behavior. | Usually I usually demonstrate this behavior. | Almost Always I almost always demonstrate this behavior. | Not Applicable I have not had the opportunity to display this behavior. |
|---|---|---|---|---|---|

Please indicate your response to each item by placing an "X" in the appropriate box:

| | Hardly Ever | Sometimes | Often | Usually | Almost Always | Not Applicable |
|---|---|---|---|---|---|---|
| **Self-Awareness** | | | | | | |
| 1. I encourage others to give me honest feedback. | | | | | | |
| 2. I take time to reflect upon the best course of action rather than jumping to conclusions. | | | | | | |
| 3. I encourage others I work with to reflect on their work. | | | | | | |
| 4. I handle myself in a calm manner when work becomes hectic. | | | | | | |
| **Promotes Learning** | | | | | | |
| 5. I encourage ongoing learning and development of others. | | | | | | |
| 6. I take time to develop my own skills and abilities through continuous learning. | | | | | | |
| 7. I give timely feedback that helps others understand their own work performance. | | | | | | |
| 8. I view mistakes as learning opportunities, when appropriate. | | | | | | |
| 9. I use questions to help others think through an issue or problem rather than immediately telling others what I think is the right solution. | | | | | | |

235

| Self-Awareness | Hardly Ever | Sometimes | Often | Usually | Almost Always | Not Applicable |
|---|---|---|---|---|---|---|
| **Communication** | | | | | | |
| 10. I share useful information with others in a timely manner. | | | | | | |
| 11. I communicate my management philosophy with those around me. | | | | | | |
| 12. I impart a clear vision to others of what successful work performance looks like. | | | | | | |
| 13. I communicate clearly to others regarding their roles and responsibilities. | | | | | | |
| **Accessibility** | | | | | | |
| 14. I have an "open-door policy": When others need assistance, they know I will set aside time to address their concerns. | | | | | | |
| 15. I respect the confidential nature of my discussions with others, when appropriate. | | | | | | |
| 16. I set up a future time to meet with others when I am not immediately available. | | | | | | |
| 17. I encourage others to share new ideas regarding work, even if they are contrary to my own. | | | | | | |

| | Hardly Ever | Sometimes | Often | Usually | Almost Always | Not Applicable |
|---|---|---|---|---|---|---|
| **Self-Awareness** | | | | | | |
| **Listener** | | | | | | |
| 18. I do not interrupt others when they are speaking. | | | | | | |
| 19. I pay attention to the manner in which others are speaking as well as their words (i.e., body language, tone of voice, etc.). | | | | | | |
| 20. I stop what I am doing and pay attention when someone is speaking. | | | | | | |
| 21. I restate others' conclusions to ensure that I have a proper understanding of what they are trying to say. | | | | | | |
| **Creates a Trusting Environment** | | | | | | |
| 22. I help people feel comfortable discussing issues with me by acting in a nonjudgmental manner. | | | | | | |
| 23. I recognize the people I interact with as unique individuals who have different needs and goals. | | | | | | |
| 24. I create an environment in which people want to make decisions related to their own development. | | | | | | |
| 25. I support people when they have dealings with others outside their individual units. | | | | | | |
| 26. When deciding whom to hire, I look for competent, self-motivated candidates who have a desire to grow with the organization. | | | | | | |
| 27. I follow through on commitments. | | | | | | |

# Index

Accountability, 62–63, 184
Action-based learning, 38, 105
Adaptation, role of learning in, 28
Anderson, M., 147–148, 216
Acquisition activity, 65–66
Assessment:
    coaching value of, 23,
        24 (box)–25 (box)
    coaching initiative and, 95–97
    defining, 4
    initial organizational assessment, 193
    manager vs. expert coach, 182–183
    self-assessment, 38, 42, 44–45,
        184–185, 233–237
    *See also* Organizational coaching
        initiative; 360-degree assessment
Athletic coaching *vs.* psychotherapy,
    128 (Box)
Attitude, 29–30

Bane, D., 101
Benjamin, B., 101
Benner, P., 40, 41
Berger, J., 37, 120
Berglas, S., 34, 129
BioTech coaching initiative, 81–83
    assessment, 80 (box)–81 (box)
    overview, 78–81
Boyatzis, R., 6, 69
Bragar, M., 72
Buckingham, M., 6, 16, 82, 180, 191, 215

Career identity, 32
Carroll, Paul, 207–209
Case study:
    attitude, 30
    career identity, 32
    change, 31
    choosing coach, 89

    choosing coachee, 90–91
    coaching practice manager, 132–137
    executive coaching intervention, 10
    ineffective coaching, 150
    management effectiveness business
        partner, 151
    management effectiveness, 151–153
Center for Creative Leadership, 4
Center point of contact, 160
"Champion," 121
Chappelow, C., 46
Charan, R., 28
Children's Hospital Boston coaching
    initiative:
    defining success in, 196
    Department of Nursing, 189–190
    initial organizational assessment, 193
    nursing leadership and, 190–192
    organizational readiness and, 192
    skills-building curriculum of, 193
        (box)–194 (box)
    success factors in, 203–204
    *See also* Children's Hospital Boston
        coaching initiative, training for
Children's Hospital Boston coaching
    initiative, training for, 195–200
    follow-up/post-skills training, 199–200
    hiring right people, 195–196
    maintaining coaching mind-set, 197
    next steps/following up, 199
    nurse evaluation of, 194–195
    observing/providing feedback, 199
    stopping action/starting coaching
        dialogue, 197–199
    working with coachable coachee, 197
Citizen's Financial Group. *See* Peer
    coaching, at Citizen's Financial
    Group (CFG)
Clarke, S., 154–155

Classroom learning, 68, 72, 100, 105, 110, 142, 162, 169–170
Coach certification, 18
    external, 157, 161–162
    internal, 109
Coachability, 142, 169, 197
Coaching:
    benefits of, 6, 7
    defining, 6
    missions of, 137–138
    as remedial intervention, 32–33, 73–74, 96, 107, 167
    as skill, 6–7, 11
    vs. evaluation, 94
Coaching assignment, appropriate, 149–151, 162
Coaching capacity:
    development of, 120–126
    See also Coaching practice manager (CPM) tasks
Coaching contract, 181–182
Coaching conversation/dialogue, 8, 40, 207
    at Children's Hospital Boston, 194, 197–199, 200, 201, 203
    destigmatizing, 9
    finding performance problem through, 75–76
    learning-oriented, 76–77
    peer network role in, 21
    reflection and, 44–45
    safety zone for, 86–87, 93–95
    senior manager roles in, 12
    at Whirlpool, 114, 115
Coaching-facilitated learning, 8
Coaching-friendly context, 7–9, 17
    at BioTech, 77–83, 80 (box)–81 (box)
    at Children's Hospital Boston, 196–197
    coaching manager role in creating, 43, 182
    executive coach role in creating, 19, 43, 182
    overview of, 42–43
    at Wachovia, 171
    at Whirlpool, 107–108
Coaching initiative:
    alternative initiative outcomes, 95 (box)
    comprehensive assessment of, 95–97
    factors shaping, 50–51
    See also Children's Hospital Boston coaching initiative; Organizational coaching initiative; Whirlpool, executive coaching at
Coaching manager, 5, 7–8, 16–17

    coaching-friendly context and, 43, 182
    continual learning and, 46
    feedback and, 45
    formal/informal coaching and, 36
    hiring issues for, 9, 40
    overview of, 16
    self-assessment tool for, 233–237
    time involved with coaching, 44
    See also Children's Hospital Boston coaching initiative; Coaching manager capability; Coaching practice manager (CPM) tasks
The Coaching Manager: Developing Top Talent in Business (Hunt & Weintraub), 7
Coaching manager capability:
    ability to coach developmentally, 180–181
    competencies, 185–186
    manager vs. expert coach, 181–184
    organizational context/role conflict, 186–187
    organizational readiness, 188
    See also Coaching practice manager (CPM) tasks
Coaching Manager Multi-Rater Feedback, 184, 195
Coaching mind-set, 11, 196, 197–198
Coaching organization:
    coaching capability, 15–22
    coaching manager, 16–17
    coaching value chain, 23, 24 (box)–25 (box)
    defining, 15
    external expert/executive coach, 17–19
    internal expert coach, 20–21
    overview of, 11–15
    peer coaching, 21–22
    zone of execution in, 11 (box)
Coaching practice manager (CPM) case study, 132–137
Coaching practice manager (CPM) tasks, 130 (box)–131 (box)
    assess need for expert coaching, 141–142
    before coaching, 137–138
    coach/coachee match, 142–143
    coordinate coaching/leadership development, 143–144
    educate/align key stakeholders, 138–139
    follow-up, 142
    measure results, 144
    orient coach, 141

qualify coach, 139–141
support ongoing coaching, 143
Coaching/psychotherapy connection,
    127–130, 128 (Box)
Coaching value chain, 23,
    24 (box)–25 (box)
Coffman, C., 6, 16, 82, 180, 191, 215
Community of practice, 175
Compensation systems, 71, 79
Competency models, 12, 69, 112, 141
Confidentiality, 42, 60, 121, 161
Conger, J., 101
Contextual factors. See Coaching-friendly
    context
Control issues, 7
Credibility, 157, 162, 171
Customer satisfaction, 6

Data gathering, 46, 169
Davenport, T., 14, 58
De Long, D., 14
Developmental coaching, 27–47
    applying to relationship challenges,
        202–203
    case study, 30, 31, 32
    core elements of. See Developmental
        coaching, core elements of
    defining, 15, 27
    development framework for,
        40–42, 40 (box)–41 (box)
    ethics and, 35
    formal/informal, 35–37
    goals of, 28–33
    as new way of relating to old
        problem, 201–202
    previously ignored/talented
        individual, 202
    vs. life coaching, 34–35
    vs. mentoring, 35
    vs. psychotherapy, 34
Developmental coaching, core
    elements of, 37–47
    coachee, 39
    coaching-friendly context, 42–43
    coaching relationship, 44
    feedback, 45–46
    opportunity to keep learning, 46–47
    opportunity to learn, 43–44
    self-assessment/reflection, 44–45
    skilled coach, 39–40
    summary of, 38 (box)
Diversity issues, 40, 63–64, 104, 109–110,
    115, 123, 124, 170–171, 175

Dreyfus, H. L., 40
Dreyfus, S. E., 40
Dreyfus model of skill acquisition,
    40 (box)–41 (box)
Drotter, S., 28

Edmondson, A., 196
Effectiveness. See Coachability
Eichinger, R., 7, 70, 157
Emotional intelligence, 202, 213
Employee assistance program (EAP),
    34–35, 160
Ennis, S., 130, 140
Evaluation:
    coaching manager as coach/evaluator,
        16–17
    coaching program, 176–177
    developmental activities, 14–15
    vs. coaching, 94
Executive coach, 12, 13
    benefits of using, 17–18, 111
    coaching attributes for, 140,
        229–231
    coaching skills for, 140, 226–229
    challenges to using, 18–19
    competencies of expert, 223–231
    continual learning and, 46
    creating coaching-friendly
        context, 19, 43
    defining executive coaching,
        139–140
    formal coaching and, 37
    internal coaching and, 162
    knowledge areas for, 140, 224–226
    length of meetings with, 44
    limited confidentiality and, 19
    reasons to use, 9, 14
    self-assessment and, 46
    See also Whirlpool, executive
        coaching at
Experiential learning, 37–38,
    44, 142, 173, 199
External certification, 157, 161–162
External coach. See Executive coach

Feedback, 5, 9, 39, 40, 42, 184
    as coaching core element, 38 (box),
        45–46
    at Children's Hospital Boston, 199
    giving difficult, 195
    multi-rater, 183, 200. See also
        360-degree assessment
    peer, 210–212

providing balanced, 199
   *See also* Self-assessment
Fetig, Jeff, 105
Fitzgerald, J., 37, 120
Flaut, R., 118
Follow-up, 157, 192–193, 199–200,
   213–214 (box)
   *See also* Goals
Formal *vs.* informal developmental
   coaching, 35–37
Frisch, M., 146, 147
Fritts, P., 72

Gittell, J. H., 8
Goals:
   of building coaching capability, 87
   of developmental coaching, 28–33
   of internal coaching program, 154, 163
Goleman, D., 6, 17, 88, 202
Goodman, R., 140
Gottesman, B., 206
Greenleaf, R. K., 205
Guthrie, V., 44

Hall, D. T., 6, 29, 30, 32,
   153, 163, 164, 180
"Hard" knowledge, 62
Hart, E. W., 36
Harvard Business Essentials, 206, 209
Hernez-Broome, G., 89
High potentials (HIPOs), 72
Higuchi, P., 154, 156, 157
Hiring, taking care in, 9, 40, 195–196
Hodgetts, W., 102, 140
Hollenbeck, G., 6, 125–126, 143, 163
Home Depot, 12
Hudson, F., 37, 127
Huff, K., 154, 156, 157
Human capital, 2–3, 11, 60, 155, 216
Human resource (HR) professional, xii
   confidentiality and, 75–76
   as executive coach, 18
   informal coaching by, 146–147,
      175–176
   internal coaching practice guidelines
      and, 160–161
   organizational failure and, 74–75
Human resource management, 215–216
Human resource organizational coaching
   initiative, 67–72
   high potential cadre for, 72
   management practices and, 50, 68–71
   mentor partnerships in, 72

succession planning in, 72
talent acquisition and, 67–68
talent review in, 71–72
Hunt, J., 6, 7, 9, 17, 18, 21, 36, 38, 39,
   44, 45, 58, 72, 74, 76, 93, 95, 96,
   101, 106, 111, 113, 139, 140, 142,
   143, 147, 151, 157, 160, 169, 180,
   182, 185, 186, 193, 199–200, 207,
   212, 233

Ike, C., 206
Impression management, 93
Informal coaching, 59, 146–147, 175–176
Informal *vs.* formal developmental
   coaching, 35–37
Internal coaching, 145–164
   advantages of, 147–148, 163
   case study, 151, 152
   characteristics of internal coach, 153
   coach selection, 156–160
   defining "expert" coach, 20–21,
      146–147
   disadvantages of expert internal
      coaching, 148–151
   ICF competencies, 158 (box)–159 (box)
   mission of, 155
   NASA competencies, 159 (box)
   ongoing development, 161–162
   practice guidelines, 160–161
   program purpose, 154–156
   reasons to develop, 3–4
   strategic *vs.* ad hoc approach to, 149
   *See also* Wachovia Corporation, ELP
      Internal coaching program at
International Coach Federation (ICF),
   139, 157, 158 (box)–159 (box),
   160, 161–162
Interpersonal skills, of coach, 9, 40

Joyce, B., 209

Kegan, R., 28
Kirsner, S., 100
Klugman, J., 214
Knowledge:
   hard/soft, 62
   organization-specific, 61–62
   tacit, 13, 14
Knowledge economy, 2
Knowledge management, 13–14
Kolb, D., 37
Kopelman, R., 101
Kouzes, J., 190

Kram, K., 21, 35, 72
Krewson, H., 206
Kucine, I., 118

Lawler, E., 70
Leadership:
  at all levels, 16
  defining, 190
  effect of coaching on style, 7
  need for, 120
  nursing, 190–192
Leading the Whirlpool Enterprise (LWE),
  105–107
  coaching practices, 110–111
  experience of coaching, 111–115
  external coaching support program
    flow, 107 (box)
  management of coaching, 108–110
  See also Whirlpool,
    executive coaching at
Learning:
  action-based, 38, 105
  case study, 10
  classroom, 68, 72, 100, 105,
    110, 142, 162, 169–170
  coaching and, 3, 5–6, 7–8
  coaching-facilitated, 8
  continual learning, 46
  cultural context of, 59–60
  experiential learning theory,
    37–38, 44, 142
  failure in, 8
  learner-driven, 8
  learning-oriented coaching conversation,
    76–77
  on-the-job, 4, 7, 9, 10, 13, 64, 67–68,
    71, 72
  opportunity to keep learning, 46–47
  opportunity to learn, 28, 43–44
  performance problem vs.
    learning/performance challenge,
    92–93
  role in personal growth, 28
  transformational, 17
Learning potential, 142
Lee, R., 120
Legacy First Union, 167
Leichtman, Steve, 151
Levenson, A., 154–155
Levin, S., 233
Life coaching, 34–35, 128
Lombardo, M., 7, 43, 70, 157
London, M., 118

Manager:
  learning to coach with
    executive coach, 18
  manager vs. expert coach assessment,
    182–183
  See also Coaching manager; Coaching
    practice manager (CPM) tasks
Mansfield, R., 140
McCall, J., 43
McCauley, C., 4, 161
McClelland, D., 69
McCullough, D., 1
McDermott, M., 154–155
McKee, A., 6
Mentoring, 5, 6, 12, 35, 59, 72
  See also Peer coaching
Mickelson, Nina, 138
Miller, N. N., 206
Morrison, A., 43
Motivation:
  of coach, 82, 90, 173, 177
  of coachee, 39, 169
Multi-rater feedback, 183, 200
  See also 360-degree assessment

Nardelli, Bob, 12
National Aeronautics and Space
    Administration (NASA), internal
    coaching at, 155–156
  coach competencies, 159 (box)
  guidelines for, 160
  ICF certification, 161–162
  partnering with external
    experts, 162
Natural coaches, 61
Noel, J., 28
Nursing. See Children's Hospital Boston
    coaching initiative

Olivero, G., 101
Omgeo LLC, 132–137, 138, 139,
    141–142, 144
On-the-job learning, 4, 7, 9, 10, 13, 64,
    67–68, 71, 72
Ongoing coaching, 143
Organic growth, 65, 66
Organization-specific knowledge, 61–62
Organizational coaching initiative:
  business context, 50, 64–67
  business strategy, 65–67
  coaching stigmatization, 73, 74–75
  factors shaping, 50–51
  high potential cadre, 72

human resource management context,
  67–72
human resource management practices,
  50, 68–71
member experiences with coaching, 50
mentor partnerships, 72
organizational experiences with
  coaching, 73–77
positive experience with internal
  coaching, 73, 75–77
senior leaders, 73–74
strategic development practices, 71–72
succession planning, 72
talent review, 71–72
talent acquisition, 67–68
See also Organizational coaching
  initiative, at BioTech;
  Organizational coaching initiative,
  cultural context of
Organizational coaching initiative, at
  BioTech:
  coaching initiative, 81–83
  company overview, 78–81
  coaching assessment, 80 (box)–81 (box)
Organizational coaching initiative, cultural
  context of, 50, 51, 57–64
  diversity, 63–64
  employee individuality, 58
  guidance seeking, 60–61
  innovation, 64
  learning, 59–60
  management, 62
  organization-specific knowledge, 61–62
  performance/performance management,
    62–63
  quality/continuous improvement, 64
  relationships, 59, 63
  trust level, 57–58
Organizational-level view of coaching, 33
Organizational readiness, 50, 77, 188, 192
Otazo, K., 6, 153, 163
Otto, J., 140
Outsourcing, 67

Peer coaching, 21–22, 70, 77
  defining, 206
  See also Peer coaching, at Citizen's
    Financial Group
Peer coaching, at Citizen's Financial Group
  (CFG), 205–216
  Advanced Leadership Development
    Program (ALDP), 206–210

developmental model, 207
duration of coaching
  relationships, 209
feedback from peer, difficulty of, 214
as follow-up intervention to executive
  education, 213–214 (box)
formula for successful program,
  212–213
frequency of meetings, 208–209
partner selection, 207
peer coaching at Millennium
  Pharmaceuticals and, 210
  (box)–211 (box)
value of "colleagues" and, 210
value proposition for success,
  210–212
Performance appraisal, 63, 69–70, 110
Performance gap, 38
Performance management, 70, 79–80
Performance ratings, 70
Personal growth, role of learning in, 28
Personal style, 143, 157, 184, 195
Pfeffer, J., 215
Posner, B., 190
Process check, 4–5
Productivity, 180
Profitability, 6, 78, 180
Promotion/promotion process, 14, 16, 51,
  67, 70, 72
Prusak, L., 14
Psychologist:
  as executive coach, 18
  skills of, as useful to coach, 140–141
Psychotherapy:
  connection with coaching, 127–128
  vs. athletic coaching, 128 (Box)
  vs. developmental coaching, 34

Qualitative evaluation, 138, 228

Ready, D., 101
Recruitment, 68, 81
Reflection, 44–45, 207
Relationships. See Interpersonal skills
Remedial coaching, 32–33, 73–74
Retention, 81, 191
Reward/reward system, 16, 17, 29, 70, 71,
  125, 171, 187, 188
Robbins, P., 206
Robertson, R., 154, 156, 157
ROI (return on investment), 66–67, 116,
  124, 147–148

Role model, 58, 70
Rothwell, R., 72

Schein, E., 51, 57
Self-assessment, 38, 42, 44–45, 184–185
Self-awareness, 185, 198
Self-development, 161–162
Sellers, P., 12
Showers, B., 209
"Sink-or-swim" culture, 60–61, 125
Smart, B., 70
Smith, J., 149
Smither, J., 118
Social capital, 21, 59
"Soft" knowledge, 62
Southwest Airlines, 8
Spencer, L., 69
Spencer, S., 69
Stern, L., 140
Stibler, A., 157
Stigmatization, of coaching, 101
Strategic approach to coaching, 85–97
    alternative coaching initiative
        outcomes, 95 (box)
    case study, 89, 90–91
    coaching skill building, 94–95
    coaching strategy need, 86–87
    comprehensive assessment of coaching
        initiative, 95–97
    outcomes, summary of desirable,
        88 (box)
    performance problem vs. learning/
        performance challenge, 92–93
    safe space for coaching conversation,
        93–94
    selecting coach, 89–90
    selecting coachee, 90–92
Strategic Human Capital Plan (NASA), 155
Strei, K., 21
Strumpf, C., 155, 160, 161, 162
Succession planning, 72

Tacit knowledge, 13, 14
Talent review, 71–72
Team leadership, 4–5
Technology, 14, 44
Thalheimer, K., 18
360-degree assessment, 45–46, 69, 70, 105,
    110, 111, 160
    at Wachovia, 166, 169, 170, 174 (box)
Ting, S., 36
Total quality management, 64

Transformational learning, 17
Trust issues, 43, 59, 149, 153, 157, 163,
    186, 196
Turner, Summer, 132–137, 140–142

Valerio, A., 120
Van Velsor, E., 4, 161
Vargas, Y., 118

Wachovia Corporation, ELP Internal
        coaching program at, 165–177
    choosing ELP participants, 169
    Coaches' coaches in, 174–175
    coaching practice leader in, 169–170
    decision to build internal coaching
        capability, 167–168
    Diversity Practitioner Development
        Program, 170
    ELP coach development process,
        172 (box)–173 (box)
    evaluation of program, 176–177
    Executive Leadership Program
        overview, 166–167
    HR comments on being internal coach,
        175–176
    internal coaches at, 170–172
    ongoing support/development of ELP
        coaches at, 174–175
    partnering with external coaches in, 162
    phases of 360-degree debrief coaching,
        174 (box)
    program design elements in, 168–170
    training/support for internal coaching
        cadre, 172–174
Wachovia Executive Leadership Model,
    168 (box)
Weimer, M., 206
Weintraub, J., 7, 17, 21, 36, 38, 39, 72,
    74, 93, 96, 101, 106, 111, 113, 142,
    169, 185, 186, 193, 199–200, 207,
    212, 233
Whirlpool, executive coaching at, 18,
    99–118, 123, 138, 141, 142, 143
    certification process, 109
    classroom learning, 110
    coaching/leadership development
        challenges, 101–102
    context for coaching, 107–108
    diversity of coaches, 109–110, 115
    driver-of-change competency, 111
    Leadership Model 360-degree
        assessment, 110, 111

MyPlan, 106, 111
organizational change strategy, 11
outcomes, 116–118
people-development issues, 115
Pulse-360 assessment, 111
*See also* Leading the Whirlpool
    Enterprise

Whirlpool Leadership Model, 102–107,
    103 (box)–104 (box), 112, 114
Whitman, Dave, 11
Whitwan, Dave, 107
Wolfe, D., 37
World Bank, 125, 138
Wrich, J., 35

# About the Authors

**Dr. James M. Hunt** is Associate Professor of Management, Chair of the Management Division, and Charles C. Barton Term Chair at Babson College, in Wellesley, Massachusetts. He teaches management, strategic human resource management, and leadership. James is also a faculty member of the Leadership and Influence Program at Babson's School of Executive Education. Previously, he served on the faculty of Clark University's Graduate School of Management. James is the coauthor, with Dr. Joseph Weintraub, of *The Coaching Manager: Developing Top Talent in Business* (Sage Publications, 2002).

James is faculty codirector of the Coaching for Leadership and Teamwork Program at Babson. The Babson coaching program provides developmental coaching for Babson students working toward enhancing their competencies in leadership and teamwork. Each year, the faculty trains over 600 Babson Alumni and MBA students in coaching techniques and development planning. He has conducted published research in executive coaching and leadership development and is a faculty member of the Professional Executive Coaches Program of the Massachusetts School of Professional Psychology. He is also a member of The Executive Coaching Forum, a group of executive coaches, coaching practice managers, and researchers devoted to improving the practice and standards of executive coaching.

James is also a founder of Hunt Associates, a career and leadership development firm that provides executive coaching, career counseling, employee assistance programs, and strategic human resource consulting (http://www.HuntAssociates.com). Since 1990, Hunt Associates has worked with companies such as the Bose Corporation, 3Com, Genzyme, and Stratus Computer. James graduated from the Massachusetts Institute of Technology with a bachelor of science degree and received the doctorate in business administration from Boston University's Graduate School of Management, where he studied career and leadership development and work-life balance. He can be reached at Huntj@babson.edu.

**Dr. Joseph R. Weintraub** is a Professor of Management and the Charles C. Barton Term Chair at Babson College, in Wellesley, Massachusetts. He is the founder and faculty codirector of the Coaching for Leadership and Teamwork Program, which has trained over 6,000 coaches since the program's inception. Dr. Weintraub is a faculty director at Babson Executive Education, where he develops and conducts executive development programs in leadership and coaching for both domestic and global companies. He is a member of the board of directors of the Graduate School Alliance for Executive Coaching, an organization of graduate-level schools dedicated to advancing the discipline of executive coaching. He is a past president of the Human Resources Council, a Boston-based association of human resources executives. His work has appeared in many publications, including *Fortune, Entrepreneur, The Wall Street Journal, The New York Times,* and *The Harvard Management Update.* His paper on coaching (with Dr. James Hunt) was awarded the "Best Management Development Paper" by the Academy of Management, the largest professional association of business school professors in the world. He is the coauthor (with Dr. James Hunt) of *The Coaching Manager: Developing Top Talent in Business* (Sage Publications, 2002), which is also published in India and China.

Dr. Weintraub is also the founder and president of Organizational Dimensions, a management consulting firm in Wellesley, Massachusetts, specializing in leadership training and development, assessment, team building, and executive coaching. Dr. Weintraub has consulted with many organizations, including General Electric, Duke Energy, Millennium Pharmaceuticals, Dunkin' Donuts, Children's Hospital Boston, P&O Ports, Fidelity Investments, Titleist Golf, Marriott, and the Los Angeles Dodgers. Much of his current work focuses on helping organizations develop leaders through the integration of assessment, feedback, and developmental coaching. He is also actively involved in the development of certification programs for internal organizational coaches.

Dr. Weintraub is one of the developers of Star-Teams Insights™, a Web-based assessment report providing developmental feedback in the areas of leadership, teamwork, communications, and work style (http://www.star-teams.com). He received his BS degree from the University of Pittsburgh and both his MA and PhD degrees in Industrial-Organizational Psychology from Bowling Green State University. Dr. Weintraub can be reached at Weintraub@babson.edu.

# About the Contributors

**Laura Bobotas,** RN, BSN, is the Nurse Manager of the Neonatal Intensive Care Unit (NICU) at Children's Hospital Boston. She is an outstanding leader who exemplifies the coaching manager in all that she does. The principles of coaching are embedded into the NICU program for new graduates. This has resulted in a 100% retention rate after 2 years. Laura has nationally presented successful strategies for fostering a coaching culture in health care.

**Paul Carroll** is an Instructional Designer and Program Manager at Citizens Financial Group in Providence, Rhode Island. He has 11 years of experience in the training and development field and has worked in several training positions at various financial institutions, including BankBoston, Boston Financial, and Citizens Bank. While offering leadership and organizational development solutions in his current position, Paul is studying to be a certified financial planner (CFP ®) to complement his training and development background.

**Susan Ennis,** founder of Susan Ennis Associates, is an executive development consultant with over 25 years of experience. She coaches senior executives and high potential managers from bio-tech, financial services, medical products, high tech, public safety, and non-profit think tanks. Susan specializes in executive level competency modeling and applications such as 360 assessment and development, selection, executive orientations and succession planning. Susan helps companies set up executive coaching systems, along with sourcing, qualifying and brokering executive coaches. As a founding member of *The Executive Coaching Forum*, Susan has been at the forefront of establishing guidelines and professional standards for the practice of executive coaching. Previously, Susan was the acting Vice President of Learning and Development for Millennium Pharmaceuticals.

**Joe Frodsham** is Vice President of Talent for Tenet Healthcare in Dallas, Texas. Before he joined Tenet, Joe was the Corporate Director of Leadership and Professional Development at Whirlpool Corporation. He is originally from western Canada and received his bachelor's and master's degrees from Brigham Young University. Joe has worked with some of the most successful companies in the world and has led groups and successful transformational changes in companies such as Compaq Computer Corporation and Anderson Consulting. He is seen as a thought leader on leadership and organizational development, is a sought-after speaker, and is the coauthor of the book, *Make It Work: Navigate Your Career Without Leaving Your Organization*.

**Colleen Gentry** is Senior Vice President, Executive Development for Wachovia Corporation, the nation's fourth-largest financial services firm. She leads Wachovia's Executive Coaching Practice, which is nationally recognized and benchmarked as a best practice in the arena of corporate coaching and executive development. Prior to her current role, she provided organizational development consulting for several Fortune 200 firms over the past 20 years. Her expertise includes culture integration, executive team development, succession planning, and high-potential development, as well as leading several leadership development functions throughout her career. Colleen is an active member of the Conference Board's Executive Coaching Council, the National OD Network, the New York Coaching Coalition, the International Enneagram Association, and the International Coach Federation. She lives with her partner and husband, and teenage son in Charlotte, North Carolina, but heads to the mountains whenever she can.

**Robert Goodman**, founder of RG Goodman Associates, has fifteen years experience helping organizations and individuals perform more effectively around critical business issues. He coaches executives at all levels, including Board Chairs, CEO's, managing partners and group and team leaders. His clients include Barker Steel, Pick 'n Pay, Inc., Omgeo, Pfizer, Citigroup, Fidelity Management Resources, Putnam Investments and Thompson Financial. Trained at Harvard in Human Development, Bob is a Clinical Associate at McLean Hospital and Clinical Instructor in the Department of Psychiatry, Harvard Medical School. He is a founding board member of The Executive Coaching Forum, a non-profit organization dedicated to advancing best practices and ethical guidelines worldwide in the field of executive coaching.

**Patricia A. Hickey**, RN, MS, MBA, CNAA, is Vice President of Cardiovascular and Critical Care Services at Children's Hospital Boston. Patty is a transformational leader who has a passion for cultivating talent. Her expertise in program and leadership development is internationally recognized. Her work is extensively published, and she presents regularly at national and international meetings. As a former student of Drs. Hunt and

Weintraub, Patty saw the potential for their work at Children's Hospital and co-led the implementation of the coaching leadership model at Children's Hospital Boston.

**William Hodgetts,** founder of Hodgetts Associates, is a senior executive coach who brings an extensive knowledge of leadership development, executive assessment, behavioral science and family business to his work with CEO's and other senior leaders. Bill is also currently Vice President of Leadership & Executive Development at Fidelity Investments, where his responsibilities include providing executive coaching, developmental assessments, and other learning resources to senior executives, overseeing executive coaching company wide, and maintaining an extensive referral network of coaching and other development resources. Bill is a founding Board member of *The Executive Coaching Forum,* an organization devoted to establishing and promoting the highest standards of professional and ethical practice for the field of executive coaching. Bill holds and EdD in human development and psychology from Harvard University, and a BA in government from Cornell University.

**Ellen Kumata** is a partner at Cambria Consulting. She led the development of Cambria's practice area in strategic executive coaching. She has more than 20 years of experience working with Fortune 500 companies and public sector organizations implementing a range of HR applications, including succession planning, performance management and assessment, recruitment and selection, and executive development. Ellen is currently coaching senior executives at a number of organizations, including Credit Suisse, Wachovia, and Deloitte. Other clients include AT&T, Fidelity, Assurant, Gap, Merrill Lynch, and MetLife. Ellen has a bachelor's degree in psychology from the University of Michigan, a JD from Wayne State University, and a master's degree in industrial relations and personnel management from the London School of Economics.

**Richard Mansfield** has more than 25 years of consulting and executive coaching experience. His current focus is on developing assessment tools and methods to support leadership development and organizational assessment. He has developed numerous 360-degree feedback instruments, feedback reports and resource guides to support development planning and executive coaching. He is a coauthor of *The Value-Added Employee,* a resource guide for professional development. Before starting his own consulting practice, Richard was a Vice President at the Altwell Group, Director of Research at McBer and Company, and an Associate Professor of Human Development at Temple University. He holds a BA in social relations and an EdD in human development, both from Harvard University.

**Judy Otto,** MEd, founding partner of Foundations for Change, has 30 years of experience in organization development, team building, and executive coaching with such companies as the American Management Association, Dana-Farber Cancer Institute, Entergy Nuclear Northeast, The Gap, General Electric, Hewlett Packard, The Nature Conservancy, and Northeast Utilities. She is a founding member of the Executive Coaching Forum and coauthor of *The Executive Coaching Handbook* and *Appreciative Leaders: In the Eye of the Beholder.* Judy has served as adjunct faculty with The Center for Creative Leadership, Columbia University's International Senior Executive Program, Boston University's Executive Challenge Program, Antioch University, and Northeastern University. She has also been an affiliate of Peter Block's Designed Learning and of Development Dimensions International.

**Herminia Shermont,** MS, CNA, RN, is Director, Surgical Nursing Program/Patient Services Department at Children's Hospital Boston. Herminia has been a Nurse Leader for over 20 years and has numerous presentations and nursing publications to her credit.

**Susan M. Shaw,** RN, MS, is Director of Clinical Operations at Children's Hospital Boston. She is a dynamic leader with 30 years of leadership in nursing and health care. Her current role involves leading the department in its effort to recruit and retain the next generation of nurses. She is actively involved in the senior leadership of the department of nursing and patient services. Susan co-led the implementation of the coaching leadership model at Children's Hospital Boston.

**Lew Stern** is President of Stern Consulting and Founder and Director of the Graduate Certificate Program in Executive Coaching at the Massachusetts School of Professional Psychology. He has an active international practice in executive coaching. Previously, Lew was Senior Vice President at Manchester Consulting and before that Vice President of ODI, an international consulting firm where he served such global companies as AT&T, Federal Express, American Express, Proctor and Gamble, and the Royal Bank of Canada. He is co-founder and past president of the New England Society for Applied Psychology and co-founder and past chairman of *The Executive Coaching Forum.* He is also a co-founder and board member of the Graduate School Alliance for Executive Coaching. He received his master's and PhD in personnel and counseling psychology from the University of Minnesota. He is coauthor of numerous articles and books including *The Executive Coaching Handbook, Straight Talk,* and *Trust-Based Leadership.*